Re-culturation
An Attempt to Reconstruct Northern Indian Christian *Saṁskāras* in the Light of Manusmṛti and Law of Moses

Re-culturation
An Attempt to Reconstruct Northern Indian Christian *Saṁskāras* in the Light of Manusmṛti and Law of Moses

A Postcolonial Subaltern Response

Tapas Ghosh

CWI

Christian World Imprints

First Published in 2020 by

Christian World Imprints
Christian Publishing & Books from India
C-3, Shop No. 14, Ground Floor
Wazirpur Industrial Area, **Delhi-110052**
cwidelhi2017@gmail.com
info@christianworldimprints.com
www.ChristianWorldImprints.com
Phone: +91 11 41526079

ISBN: 978-93-5148-348-9

Printed in India.

Contents

Foreword

The 'text without context is pre-text' as I always say. The universal message of the Gospel must have its inroad into the local context, be it philosophy, culture or custom. Theology and mission discourse in Asia has been debating on the issue of Western model in the context of the local aspiration, tradition, custom, and culture. The Asian population has various challenges from within, be it caste, pluralism in religion, culture and language or the long colonial legacy. The pertinent missiological question to define culture within culture is important. The hierarchy of culture in India that is imposed either by the caste Hindu, Muslim or by the European colonist has made the postcolonial studies contextually relevant. The domination of a culture within culture is the root cause of loosing cultural identity of many people. Quest for identity and self-determination in the context of faith needs to be addressed from the context of cultural colonization of Asian/India Christian. The mission and culture debate is going on and yet lot more to do, but the discourse in this research has enriched us and opened up various dimensions to accomplish our endeavor.

Dr. Tapas Ghosh is known to me when he joined at Allahabad Bible Seminary in 2009 as a faculty of religions. As a Hindu convert from an educated Bengali family, he holds a different kind of view that may not be so similar to the conventional ideas of the Gospel and Mission in India. His ability to think differently is a positive contribution for a constructive future for Indian mission. I was not aware of his academic ambition but later I found his ability, so supported his further studies at the University of Bonn, Germany. He completed his major academic work (Ph.D) under the Dept. of Philosophy, to the Institute of Asian and Oriental Studies, 2018. The title of his research, '**Re-culturation: An Attempt to Reconstruct Northern Indian Christian *Saṁskāras* in the Light of Manusmṛti and Law of Moses - A Postcolonial Subaltern Response**' has dealt with the basic issue of mission and culture from the Indian context and it is geographically located to North India.

The argument in his research demonstrates the fault lines of the colonial mission model which is contested from his interpretation of Indian plurality which is, sometimes, highly debatable, at least to me, yet his argument has a logical point to ponder upon. The advocacy to shift from the Western-centric to Indic-centric (Indian-ness that he used) is very postcolonial. Few of the findings that may be summed up are the followings:

1. In explaining the plurality of India, his argument neither subscribes to the traditional Christian view nor supports the right-wing narrative that has overshadowed the plurality of India. He advocates the diversity as a fundamental de-centralized system in which hegemony and freedom are existing simultaneously.
2. He separated very sharply Indian and Hindu culture to show the problems in the colonial perception of India. This perception, according to him, has posed a challenge before Indian Christian to construct their culture, i.e., a cultural dilemma.
3. His postcolonial methodology demonstrates the very quest for search 'self-identity and self-determined' aspiration of Indian Christian, then he argued that both the colonial mission and the right wing new narrative have created the subalternity and neither can define the future of North Indian Christian (also read Indian). It shows that even when Indian Christians were saved through Jesus but they have entered into another system that has also denied their quest for self-determination.
4. The use of Manusmṛti shows his risk-taking spirit. Interestingly, he does not support that this book could be used for the betterment of Indian Christians but proving how this book has constructed dominating Indian cultural traditions in the way Moses contributed to Hebrew people.
5. Two issues of his research work are Christian 'name' and 'baptism' and among these two, the 'name' as an academic subject is a new dimension for many of us.

I appreciate his hard work and his new academic perspective. It may contribute to the field of mission and culture in the 21st century when we are going through uncertainty in India. The theology and mission can not overlook the contextual reality and this work has re-affirmed once again and provoking us to for retrospection on the issue of mission and culture from an Indian perspective.

Rev. J. Sunradaraj
Principal
Allahabad Bible Seminary
General Secretary
Evangelical Church of India
Prayagraj, U. P., India

Acknowledgement

Mr. (L) Jagatbandhu Ghosh & Mrs. Manju Ghosh (parents)
Mr. L. Thanglhun Khongsai & Mrs. L. Nengnei Khongsai (parents in law)
Mrs. Hoikhonem Lunkim (wife), Naomi Neijakim Ghosh (daughter)
Mr. Manas Kumar Ghosh (brother), Mrs. Elfriede Malessa (Oma)
Vicar Dr. Simon Wiesgickl & Vicar Matthias Schwarzer
(Anchor of my Deutscheland life)
Ms. Esther Runkel (sister in Jesus), Mrs. Maria Wilms (friend)
Rev. J. Sundara Raj (Principal, ABS)
Prof. Dr. Dr. Manfred Hütter (Supervisor, Ph.D
&
Jesus Christ, my Peace.

Abbreviation

Manusmṛti	MS
Samaj Dharma	SD
Born Christian	BC
First Generation Christian	FGC
North Indian Christian	NIC
Euro-Western Christianity	EWC
Indian Christian	IC
Euro-Western Mission Model	EWMM
Pre-independent Indian Christian	PIC
Euro-Western Biblical	EWB
Euro-Western Biblical Name	EWBN
Luke	LK
Genesis	Gen
Daniel	Dan
Euro-western	EW
Schedule Caste	SC
Church of North India	CNI
Other Backward Caste	OBC
Evangelical Church of India	ECI
Northern Evangelical Lutheran Church	NELC
Assembly of Believer's Church	ABC

Chapter 1

Introduction

This research, titled '**Re-culturation: An Attempt to Re-construct Northern Indian Christian *Saṁskāras* in the Light of Manusmṛti and the Law of Moses: A Postcolonial Subaltern Response**' is an attempt to analyze the colonial Christian tradition among North India Christians in order to re-construct *saṁskāras* from within Indian culture, extracting its primary resource from the Manusmṛti (MS[1]) and the Law of Moses (Torah), as a postcolonial response. The saṃskāric re-construction of our hypothesis is to be actualized through a model namely '**Space and Place**' to accommodate the voice of the culturally subaltern Christians, their colonial agony, postcolonial aspiration (both BC & FGC[2]), overcoming the burden of colonial nomenclature, and heuristically researching for self-reliance and self-identity, and to transform the thus far isolated alien North Indian Christian (NIC[3]) culture as an integral *Samaj Dharma* (SD[4]) of India.

1.1. Statement of Research Problem

Our research problem is to investigate the alien colonial Church traditions, cultures and practices that are found among NICs, and to examine whether or not the Christian community in North has been experiencing the cultural subalternity due the strategically displaced from their own culture after conversion to Christianity by the colonial Church. It would further take an attempt to re-construct the colonial culture and the saṃskāric displacement

---

[1] MS, the abbreviation of Manusmṛti, hereafter will be used throughout the book.

[2] BC: Born Christian, one from Christian parents and FGC: First Generation Christian (new converts) and hereafter these abbreviations will be used in the entire book.

[3] NIC: North Indian Christian and hereafter NIC will be used in the entire book.

[4] SD: Samaj Dharma and hereafter SD will be used in the entire book.

from within Indian saṃskāric culture, incorporating the nuances of *saṁskāras* of MS and the Law of Moses as a postcolonial subaltern approach for epoch-making self-identity or Indianness of NIC through de-colonizing the colonized NIC tradition.

1.2. Elaboration of Research Problem

Our research will primarily concentrate on the *saṁskāras* (not necessarily sacraments) with an intention to deal with some basic issues for the constructive re-culturation and social integration from within Indian cultural paradigm. It is not assimilation, adaptation, acculturation, etc., per se, but a process of reviving 'lost' cultural aspects that were replaced from the socio-cultural life of NICs after conversion to the Christianity during the colonial mission. The colonial legacy mainly among BCs is a prevailing feature. Homi K. Bhabha has explained it as a psychological nature of the colonized people (mimicry) that exists among the subaltern groups. The colonial cultural features have been prevailing in different forms throughout the Indian society and few features have been absorbed positively by the general public, but others are conflicting to the SD, for example, the Christian doctrinal view on religious plurality or other faiths. The colonial Christianity portrayed the entire Indian religious traditions, religions and culture negatively and therefore, converts were strategically separated from the parental social system and culture to create a European oriented Christian community in India. Same is the truth in other colonized communities like Central, West and Southern Africa. It is a social phenomenon that stands opposite to the Indian plural culture. In India, the existing 'integrated people' [example of St. Thomas Christians in Kerala] were 'disintegrated' due to the faith-change; therefore, in this research, we are attempting to find a possible re-integrating model that would create a new 'Space' for NICs within the socio-cultural reality of India. This theoretical possibility will envisage its practical aspect incorporating the voice of the mass in postcolonial India.

The doctrinal position of the church and the theological possibility of interpreting the biblical text in accordance to the cultural aspiration of people are to be taken as a 'given context' to reinterpret the scripture and improvise the colonial *saṁskāras*. For the colonized converts, the doctrines and *saṁskāras* of Churches are reprehensive and repulsive, even though the Church in Europe had experienced schism due to doctrinal reinterpretations and practices. The colonized Christians, now, may ask for the contextual relevance of faith and practice, and it is a futuristic outlook to create a suitable '**space**' for them. It is simply a quest for the 'religious autonomy'. The '**Space and Place**' model is, therefore, a new hermeneutical tool which is employed to envisage the possibility of interpreting the present *saṁskāras* and to reconstruct the cultural aspiration of NICs. In India, the religious conflict and religious plurality are two opposite social reality but the colonial Christianity, in principle, refused to be the part of Indian plurality, then decided to push forward their mission through a conflicting path. Possibly, the doctrinal position has prevented to do so, in order to re-affirm the 'ONLY' true religion by negating the very existence of others. Such dichotomical paradox resulted havoc to the native Christians. It was the colonial mission policy that complemented to the colonial political policy. And therefore, the conflict was the natural counter product. Now attempt to bring a religious 'climate change' among NICs by creating a new '**Space**' is the biggest practrical challenge. This climate change has two-fold intentions: firstly, interreligious harmony and second cultural re-construction. Christianity, being too rigid in doctrine and practices, has become irrelevant to the 60% socially marginalized people (subaltern groups) as an alternative viable space for socio-religious lebration. The reasons are i. Promotion of a different culture among new converts; ii. Denying the co-existence of multi-faiths (socio-religious plurality) in a given society; and iii. Negation to the parental heritage/culture after conversion. This paradigm shift from one culture (native) to other culture (largely foreign) is an important aspect and the centrality of our research argument.

As far as MS and Law of Moses are concerned, it is empirically proved and accepted by people/scholars that these two sources are largely responsible as the formative cause behind their respective culture including some problems like rigid caste system or extreme monotheism. And the Torah, being part of the Bible, is logical and argumentatively competent to reuse for the cultural re-construction. It is true that MS is a controversial book (Ambedkar, the first half of 20th century and Dalit Movement hold MS responsible for caste discrimination), yet it is the undeniable truth that MS has contributed and influenced immensely to the Indian socio-religious culture including Dalit/ subaltern groups qualitatively and quantitatively, subtle and gross, profane and mundane. Factual truth remains that people' culture (social or religious) keeps evolving not in absentia of these two books.

The colonial rule, its mission and the cultural displacement of the colonized people is a global phenomenon, particularly in Asia and Africa. Christianity and the colonial political policy are identical that had a global plan to convert the entire world into the European/Christian prototype. Hegel's '*Weltgeist*' can establish this logic to a great extent. This policy has successfully implemented among the converts since they were under the direct control of the colonial Church. Thomas Babington Macaulay's educational reformation of India-1835 that replaced the Indian traditional educational system, including major Indian languages of eduations like Arabic, Sanskrit, etc., with the British-English system (instruction and curriculum) is the best example in favor of our argument being postcolonial.

So far as the cultural displacement is concerned, it is *saṁskāra* that will elaborate on the practical aspects of this issue. The Indian socio-religious cultural behavior within a family, region or in the society (intra and interpersonal customary gestures and manners) was replaced by the British or other European mission agencies as per their background or origin; eventually, they created many smaller isolated Indian Christian communities like British-Indian Christian, Portuguese-Indian Christian, German-Indian Christian, etc. There was no Indian-Christian out of the colonial mission. Their songs, rites, dresses, style of the social interaction, manners, food, etc were completely colonial. A separated alien community grew in India under the rule and rites of the colonial mission's jurisdiction that uprooted the native converts culturally. For example, the marriage dress in India is largely 'red' or 'bright' color but the colonial mission implemented the 'white' European dress for marriage. Respect for an elder to touch 'feet' and the colonial Church replaced it by 'hand-shake'; entering to religious place with barefoot and Church made it with shoe and there are many such. The convert's relationship with relatives (those who were still in parental faiths) was regulated by the Church, often prevented them to meet other family members including parents. The list is long. The whole socio-religious function of Indian people is either reflected or attached to *saṁskāras*, therefore it has taken as the central focus of this research.

The postcolonial in this research is not taken as the strict sense of the classical meaning, but it has two aspects of usage: firstly, it is used as a methodology that has applied for argument and secondly, it is a context that creates a favorable space to aspire for the autonomy (post-colonial i.e., independent India, since 1947, in the political sense) of NICs from the colonial Church traditions to determine the future of their socio-religious life. Therefore, the postcolonial has both subjective and objective usage here. 'Subaltern' denotes the state of the Christian community who were forced to accept whatever was imposed on them, therefore, they lost the autonomy and self-hood. Their life was nurtured, governed, restricted and ruled by the authority of the colonial Church. To state the factual truth of Indian converts, Sattam Pillai said that Indian Christian came out of caste/Brahmin and now again captived under the colonial Church; therefore, Indian Christians were never free from subjugation. In this sense, NICs in this thesis is called subaltern, contextually, subaltern.

1.3. Rationale of Research and Its Significance

i. Our research is precisely dealing with the Protestant traditions in the Northern region of India for a possible re-construction of the present *saṁskāras* for re-culturation.

ii. The Euro-Western Christianity (EWC) has transformed Indian Christian (IC) culturally into the European-Christian which eventually disassociated and disintegrated them from the native socio-cultural reality to foreignness, projecting Indian culture synonymous to the Hindu culture and also advocated Euro-Western culture as superior to the Indian culture and religion.
iii. It has separated native Christians from the rest of native Indians, and then they came under the subjugation of the Church authority, hence became subaltern in their homeland.
iv. Thus, NIC [and also IC] has been a minority faith group by losing the cultural heritage, for example, using white *shari* (woman's dress) in marriage in place of red/bright *shari*. White *shari* symbolically denotes 'widowhood' except some special occasions.
v. There is a psychological dilemma among NIC [also IC] to accept Indian culture since the colonial culture has succeeded to demarcate Indian culture as Hindu culture. Pyscho-religious hesitation is persistent to incorporate Indian culture as the homeland cultural identity. Therefore following the colonial cultural features are now known as the Indian Christian culture. The 'mimicry' among the colonized converts as Homi Bhabha explained is a continuity and present challenge for reconstruction, even though there is a need for a cultural re-integration.
vi. A sociological dialectic from within the plurality of India for NIC is a postcolonial quest and challenge.
vii. Research is investigating the matrix and roots, and at the end, some possible suggestions for NICs as an attempt for a cultural makeover, i.e., Indian-ness.

1.4. Defining key 'Terms'

1.4.1. Re-culturation

The term 're-culturation' denotes reviving Indian cultural aspects and incorporate them for NIC that was lost during the colonial period after conversion. It will explore Indian manners, customs, signs, symbols, i.e., *saṁskāras* to integrate North Indian Christians within SD. The 'Indian culture + Christian faith – colonial culture' is the heuristic possibility and the objective reality of 're-culturation' in this research. It also means the interior transformation of present colonial values through the integration of Gospel values to Indian culture as a process of creative relationship building between Gospel and Indian Culture. Opoku stated, 'The person who is dressed in other people's clothes is naked, and the person who is fed on other people's food is hungry.'[5] E Stanley Jones' *Jesus on Indian Road* (1925) or Dayanand Bharti's *Living water and Indian Bowl* (1997 & 2004) also expressed the same view.

1.4.2. *Saṁskāra*

Most of the ancient literatures including MS have elaborated *saṁskāra* as means to conduct life: social, cultural, religious, spiritual, family and individual. In the Indian context, it is not limited to any particular religion; even every religious tradition has differences in the numerical number of *saṁskāras* which, by the passage of time, have been evolving, and eventually, they were not only restrictly as the mere religious rite but also treated as the Dharma. Neumerically, the sixteen *saṁskāras* of MS, even though numbers are not fixed, are instrumental to the religious, family and social life. *Saṁskāra* is actually the fundamental of the culture of India. MS prescribes the practice of *saṁskāras* from the inception in womb to the death of a person and even after death. '*Saṁskāra*' is not 'sacrament' in the sense it is understood and interpretaed in the Christian tradition. The Oxford English Dictionary defined 'sacrament' as a religious ceremony or act regarded as an outward and visible sign of inward or spiritual grace.' Such definition cannot justify the complexity of *saṁskāra* which establishes a relation between castes, gender, social conduct, social-family and individual duty, stages of life, economy, etc. In the research, we have used the socio-cultural meaning of '*saṁskāra*', not strictly on religious sense.

1.4.3. Samaj Dharma

'Samaj Dharma' is the functional social system which is dharmic in nature and content. SD has evolved around two features: *Varna* (*Jati*, loosely known as caste) Dharma and *Ashram* (individual duties) Dharma. The term 'Dharma' denotes duty and Samaj means society. It connects individual with masses and vice versa and has constituited around certain norms. Indian plurality and diversities are nurtured and evolved around 'Dharma'. MS and Torah identically advocate the concept of SD to which individual, family, and society are interconnected, and individual and society are interdependent. In our research, the reconstruction of NIC's culture is actually an attempt to integrate NIC within SD because of their social segregation after conversion has taken them away from basic functional system of the Indian society. The colonial Christianity stands just opposite to the SD since converts were constructed and formed a separated faith-based community not so much as an integrated social unit. The reconstruction is envisaged in this research through SD.

---

[5] K.A. Opoku 'Skinny but Imperishable Truth: African Religious Heritage and the Regeneration of Africa' in *Studia Historiae Ecclesiaticae*, No. 38 (Spl. 2012): 151.

1.4.4. 'Space and Place' Model

The '**Space and Place**' model is the completely new model that THIS research has introduced to implement the reconstruction of *saṁskāras* for NIC. The term 'Space' advocates to bring the flexibility into prevailing colonial rigidity through a rick-taking amendment to the present culture that stands against the Indian tradition to accommodate the changes. The 'Space' includes the mental and psychological transformation from the 'past' for a self-searching future. It is to enlarge the horizon of the Church within the larger multi-dimensional Indian society that will transform not only the Church herself but also the Indian society. 'Space' will also help to face the challenges that pose a 'fear of being minority', living among 'Hindus'. It is an emancipatory step forward integration. The 'Place' in other hand is a platform for practicing the changes that are brought in to. It is important to implement the theoretical suggestions on the practical reality. If 'Space' is the hypothesis, the 'Place' is the thesis. 'Place' includes individual and Church as well as the process of doing theology under the ambit of public theology. This model will explore the theoretical possibility to the level of practical reality.

1.4.5. Subaltern

The term 'subaltern' as defined by Ranajit Guha is the 'group of people' from the below (law caste and tribes), non-privileged, marginalized and often oppressed by the elites.[6] This group intends to deconstruct the elite history in order to express their history as worth noticing.[7] It has a general category and also localized category. Our research argument modified the above definition, because in India, Christian subalternity is not nessecerily a subjugated community, but it is a community that was trained to be subjugated to the colonial supremacy (Western Christian faith & culture) through the process of redefining their 'new' faith within Indian multi-dimensional plurality. Therefore, subalternity here is to be understood in the context of the dilemma of cultural identity of NIC. Subalternity of NIC occurs when neither the Westeren culture what they were trained to adopt became impossible to take ownership and the Indian culture that they were trained to give up became impossible to get rid off completely. It has created a socio-cultural vacuum to define their identity. This cultural oppression of NIC is what we are considering as the centrality of argument. The identity of NIC is constructed on the colonial narrative as the only alternative means to reassert new 'faith', and this process has oppressed the 'right to decide' of NICs.[8] We are arguing for the 'self-

---

[6] Ranajit Guha, 'Preface' in *Subaltern Studies 1*, (1982): vii.

[7] Robert E. Erykenberg, *History & Belief: The Foundation of Historical Understanding* (1996), 294.

[8] Saral Chatterjee 'Editorial' in *Religion and Society*, June (1989): 1.

determining-right' of NIC as the beginning of reconstruction of the present through a systematic cultural revival, overcoming psychological and practical subalternity to the colonial legacy.

1.5. Research Method

The Postcolonial Subaltern methodology (elaborated in Chapter–III) is the method on which whole thesis is being argued, based on the Homi Bhabha's concept of Hybridity, Ambivalence and Mimicry, followed by Gayatri C. Spivak's '*Can the Subaltern Speak*?' within a 'Space and Place' model to introduce a reconstructed Samaj Dharma for NICs within Indian culture. For our empirical research interviewed 100 peoples from 15 states of Northern India among pastor, theological faculty and lay Christians along with 2 focus groups. The MS of Windy Doniger (2000 edition) and Asha Rani Tripathi (2015) and NRSV Bible are used for this research. The 'voice of people' (postcolonial subaltern voice) that reflected in empirical data is given priority over theoretical anecdote to envisage the importance of this research.

1.6. Scope and Limitation

This research will primarily focus on the Northern region of India among mainline Churches (Protestant) like CNI, Methodist, Lutheran and independent movements like Yeshu Darbar. To bring argument more Indian-specific and contextual, we shall incorporate other regional Christian cultures like of North-East Christianity (tribal) and St. Thomas Church tradition of Kerala to support the main argument. We are locating our debate within North India and postcolonial quest of NIC for identity reconstruction within a specific cultural framework (of s*aṁskāra*) drawing textual support from MS and Torah.

1.7. Previous Research

Academically speaking, there is no previous research that deals with this research problem directly, even though some researchers are separately explained MS and Moses within the Indian cultural context or selectively dealing with one *saṁskāra*. It is Sattam Pillai who first attempted to use the Old Testament tradition to re-construct Indian Christian life and practice, way back in the 1850s. He argued that European Christianity contradicts to Indian religious and social culture and found that *saṁskāras* in the Old Testament are similar to Indian society. The recent substantial work is found in T. M. Manicham's book, *Dharma According to Manu and Moses* (1977). His basic argument is based on philosophical speculation that has analyzed by the comparative methodology. More recent research is done by Thomas Cherukat in his Doctoral Dissertation on 'Christian Sacraments and Hindu Samskaras: A Theological Study on Baptism and Confirmation Compared to the Hindu Initiation Rite of Upanayana Samskara in the Context of Inculturation and

Inter-Religious Dialogue in India,' under the Faculty of Catholic Theology, University of Vienna (1991). Both have a Roman Catholic perspective aiming for Catholic Christians, whereas our research aiming for Protestant Christians. The ecclesiological difference plays a vital difference in both approaches. Apart from these two works, there is no such research or academic project is available as par my search goes. Edward Said, Homi Bhabha, Gayatri C. Spivak dealt with the postcolonial issues and Ranajit Guha explained the subalternity as acknowledged. This research has used those resources with a new pragmatic dimension for NIC and it is completely new research by its approach and argument.

1.8. Structure of the Book

The book is divided into seven chapters: firstly, it has provided an Introduction to Thesis, followed by the elaboration of context on which this research is being conducted in the second chapter, then in the third Chapter, it gives the methodological approach to the research and on the fourth chapter, we argue on why MS and Torah are considered as a primary source for the reconstruction of NIC and chapter five has taken the issue of 'Name' as a *saṁskāra*, especially Euro-Western names among NIC and relating to subalternity; followed by the purification *saṁskāra* to argue the alteration of existing 'baptism and conversion' of Church as the central reason of cultural displacement in chapter six. In Chapter seven, the social reconstruction and its various dimensions are explored for a new SD of NIC as a postcolonial quest for identity, being an Indian and Christian at the same time. In the end, we put a general conclusion.

Chapter 2

Formative Background and Context of Research

Introduction

The direction of re-culturation is to be set on the framework which will lead the research objective to bring into a logical and viable conclusion for NICs from within the Indian cultural matrix. The vision of re-culturation in India is a challenging task for two reasons: i. the colonial conceptualized of India culture synonymous to Hindu religious culture; ii. the conservative position of Church that still propagates the Gospel over other faiths, mainly Hinduism as the antagonist.

This chapter will be attempting to elucidate the entire context that would explain why re-culturation in 21st century for NIC is relevant and it will elaborate the central aspects like **Firstly**, the characteristics of Indianness: considering the physical cultural plurality and how such plurality will be able to provide a new hermeneutical possibility to reconstruct NIC's culture. It will also reflect on how far the 'mistaken' notion of India as a Hindu-nation both by Euro-Western mission and right-wing *Hindutva* groups is justifiable and **secondly**, it will analyze the Euro-Western Mission Model (EWMM) to envisage the gravity of cultural conflict that was experienced during the colonial period to argue and establish the 'cultural-loss' narrative which is the main hypothesis of this research and it would also underscore the cultural 'subalternity' of NIC.

The purpose is to envisage the underlying aspects of the Indian traditions or Indianness as a culmination of diversity and such argument will penetrate into the unwarranted reservation among NIC [also IC] that often connects the Indian traditions to Hinduism, and then it would be logical to enter into the re-culturation feasibility into a state of plausibility. The formative objective is to look into the possibility for a cultural re-orientation from Euro-centrism to Indo-centrism.

2.1. Locating Cultural Debate: European Homogeneity and Indian Heterogeneity

There is no doubt that India has immense cultural diversity and it is truly composite in nature. In the process of developing Indian composite cultural tradition, each cultural unit is independent and inter-dependent on each other. Indian cultural integrity is Indian potentiality. Apart from cultural diversity, India also has four major home-grown religions alongside Christianity, Islam, Zoroastrian as a foreign religion and many primal traditions. Historically, there is no sustaining hostility or has socially separated from each other. The native religions are dharmic in nature. This is the centrality of Indian religion and cultural character.[9]

Many European and Western missiologists and thinkers like H. Richard Niebuhr (*Christ and Culture*, 1951), Paul Tillich (*Theology of Culture*, 1959) during the colonial era and contemporary revival church movements took such Indian positioning as adverse to Gospel. This positioning of EWM has failed to capitalize on the positive aspects of culture to penetrate the Gospel of Jesus to the native people and replaced Indian culture from the native converts. Dharma (not religion) stands opposed to it. In the case of Gospel which is dynamic in nature, the Indian cultural symbolism is available to present Gospel to the Indian population. It would have apt for the Euro-Western Christianity (EWC) to be culturally baptized in Indian cultural water to become culturally Indian.[10] According to Dr. K. P. Aleaz, the Gospel can emerge with double dimensions in Indian context: i. one is the gospel of integral relation between religion and culture, resulting in cultural symbiosis and a composite culture through ongoing interaction between religions; ii. the gospel of God in Jesus emerging from the Indian culture or rather the Indian hermeneutical context which in reality goes beyond the scope of the previous Christian concepts like 'indigenization' or 'inculturation' that may ratify the harmony and integration that exist between religions in India as well as the resultant Indian composite culture.[11]

We wish to put forward this argument of integration through a 'Space and Place' model within *Samaj Dharma* (SD) in which the Gospel would naturally be a part of the social reality. In another way, Christianity must emerge as

---

[9] Eric J. Lott, "Religious Faith and the Diversity of Cultural Life in India", *Christian Faith and Multiform Culture in India* ed., Somen das, Bangalore, United Theological College (1987), 48-84.

[10] V. C. Samuel, "Christianity and Indigenization" in *Abba Salama,* Vol. VII (1976): 60-92.

[11] K. P. Aleaz, *The Gospel of Indian Culture* (Calcutta: Punthi Pustak, 1994), 2.

SD for common masses. In SD, isolation/separation between religion and culture does not exist. If the Gospel of Jesus and Indian culture complement to each other, it not only provides a self-identity of Christian but also enriches composite Indian culture.

Saṁskāras which are the reflective code of Indian culture i.e., Indianness is widely talked subject in the field of the mission of Church. Hermeneutically and missiologically, the words like contextual, adaptation, assimilation, etc. are taken our serious attention to refining the relationship between Gospel and culture both in West (Clifford Geertz, 1973, Jeffery C. Alexander & Steven Seidman, eds., 1990) as well as in India.

During the colonial period, the heterogeneity of Indian culture was conceptualized as homogeneity Europeans. We must explore homogeneity and heterogeneity to illuminate this issue. The Roman nation-culture that dominated Europe through Christianity has failed to conceptualize the heterogeneity of Indian cultural nationhood. An attempt to convert India especially Christian converts into a 'One Nation-One Culture' system was the prime objective of the colonial rulers and Christian mission.

The subject 'Mission/Gospel and Culture' had got attention almost from the inception of Christianity and debate on this issue have got central focus when the gentiles started coming within the ambit of newly formed Jewish-oriented Christian faith (Acts Ch. 15). Later, the Church under Roman homogenous nation-culture model has developed a Christianized homogeneous culture, a Roman prototype. And in the later stage, this model took control over the entire Christian population in Europe. In contrast, India or Chain and even smaller country like Thailand stands opposite to European homogeneous concept. According to Rajni Kothari, Indian heterogeneity has developed due to the absence of any centralized authority and therefore eventually localized groups with their distinct culture became a sub-part of the whole diverse cultural ambit of Indian concept.[12] Whereas Europe was heading towards a Christian-oriented homogeneity and India has been upholding the cultural nationhood under heterogeneity, so Indian heterogeneity includes diverse religions, castes, races and ethnicities, languages, etc.

The European concept of homogeneity (one nation-one culture-one religion) stands opposite to Asian social system, mainly India. The Christian mission has implemented the model of homogeneity on the Indian population at large and Indian Christian (IC) in particular. In the case of Indian converts, the homogeneity model was enforced on them, and therefore they were de-cultured. Indian being a cross-cultural heterogeneity does not assimilate

---

[12] Rajni Kothari, "Integration and Exclusion in Indian Politics" in *Economic and Political Weekly*, 22 October (1988): 2223.

into the EWM's homogeneity concept. The subalternity of NIC/IC is to be understood in this context when being in new faith has limited the freedom to define.

Under heterogeneity, Indian social groups are finding their social identity which comprises culture, food habit, language, religion, ethnicity, art, music, etc. Herriot & Scott-Jackson explained this issue saying that social identity is a social category to which an individual affiliate naturally to family, ethnicity, language, religion, geographical location, etc.[13] They also said that a historical construct has been developing among them that is composite and multi-dimensional with heterogeneity in nature. This historical construct is timeless[14] and logical growth under the influenced by many values and factors as explained by Gouveia and Albuquerque.[15] In India, a deep-rooted homogeneity exists within the ambit of heterogeneity. If we explain the society that is in the Manusmṛti, we noticed two paradoxical realities. In one hand, Manu was attempting to bring a kind of homogeneity when he not only prohibited Aryan people to marry outside their community but also restricted marriage outside caste system,[16] and on the other accepted mixed community[17] as a close part of Aryan society. This flexibility is the central cause of developing Indian heterogeneous culture.

According to Dien, the cultural identity of a group/nation has a historical development and process and it evolves in various levels of time.[18] In the Indian context, such historical process is still continuing. Each historical period, due to the political and religious influences, India has added new identity in her composite cultural identity. Looking at the development of culture in Europe, it seems to be what Bierbrauer and Roller argued upon. Former pointed out to the legal institutions of developing a cultural system,[19] later said that it is role and rule of the institution are responsible behind a cultural system.[20] EWM's

---

[13] P. Herriot & W. Scott-Jackson, "Globalization, Social Identities and Employment" in *British Journal of Management*, No. 13 (2002): 249-257.

[14] J. D. Vigil & G. Hanley, "Chicano Macrostructural Identities and Macrohistorical Cultural forces" in *Journal of Historical Sociology*, No. 15(3) (2002): 395-426.

[15] V.V. Gouveia & F.J.B. de Albuquerque, "Human Values and Social Identities: A Study in Two Collectivist Cultures" in *International Journal of Psychology*, No. 37(6), (2002): 333-342.

[16] MS Chapter III.

[17] MS 10.VI, MS 2.XXIII.

[18] D. S. Dien, "The Evolving Nature of Self-identity across Four Levels of History" in *Human Development*, No. 43 (2000): 1-18.

[19] G. Bierbrauer, "Toward an Understanding of Legal Culture: Variations in Individualism and Collectivism between Kurds, Lebanese, and Germans" in *Law and Society Review*, No. 28(2) (1994): 243-264.

[20] E. Roller, "Reforming the Spanish Senate: Mission Impossible?" in *West European Politics*, No. 25(4), (2002): 69-92.

concept of culture is similar to that kind of institutional culture. The Law of Moses, somehow, may fall into this category since his laws were implemented on whole Israel community and none was given freedom to bring any change or to violet. In the case of India, Manusmṛti was not the sole law book for Indians. As well as 18 to100 law books[21] were operating to monitor various people's groups locally. Therefore, Manu was not an institution in the Indian tradition but the modified suggestive norms of Vedic cultural history. Institutionalization of the Law of Manu was an attempt of the British administration to govern various Indian *Astika* Faith groups by one single religious law like the Christian Law.

Indian Heterogeneity

Social Identity	Historical Context	Economic Parameter	Institutional Factor	Geography
Mass public culture, Language, Religion, Social mobility for members, Ethnic groups	Mythology, Chronology of historical events, Historical icons, Colonization,	Traditional Economic, Economy and morals, Modernity and Traditional economic value	Role of customary laws, Religious Laws, Modern Democracy & Human rights, Traditional law, and modernity	Geological Setting, Its relation to culture, localized homeland concept

Above table depicts various factors attached to any culture and it is diverse and complex. From the above argument, if we try to analyze the mission of the colonial Church then we actually get a clear notion why the culture of NIC is a contentious social issue. The monoculturalism of the EWM and the most complex heterogeneity of India have no unifying platform during the colonial period. The construction of India as predominantly a Hindu cultural nation was a gross mistake of the EWM, rulers, and academicians.

Factually, within cultural India and nation-India, heterogeneity is the fundamental base of history, and any attempt to convert into a homogeneity nation-state would be against the *dharmic* tradition of this land. The mission of the colonial Church was one such attempt to create an artificial religious oriented homogeneous Indian Christian community. Later it is proved to be a mistaken move that has created the massive cultural crisis in the life of NIC. Therefore, we are locating the cultural debate within the Indian dharmic tradition.

---

[21] John Bowker, *The Message and the Book: Sacred Texts of the World's Religions* (New Haven: Yale Uni. Press, 2012), 179-180.

2.1.1. The Characteristics of Indianness: The Culture of Practical Plurality

A nation identity, physical or cultural, is directly connected to her ethnic, linguistic, custom, symbol, dress, food habit, architecture, music, literature along with its geography, climate, etc. For nation creation, historically, the ethnolinguistic factor is the centrality; religion is an additional unifying force, for example, the creation of Israel (since Moses) or Pakistan (M. A. Jinnah). In the case of India, it is a subject of debate to define the possible reason in developing a nation (not a nation-state). Political India as a nation was non-existence till 1947, but India as a cultural nation was a reality since the last 5000 years or so through a constant 'induction-deduction-expansion' process.

The projection of 'physical and cultural' India as 'a' nation was first framed by Middle-Eastern and Greek, later by European/Western travelers, missionaries, scholars and finally by the British ruler. Under European construction of India, the land and people regardless of the diversity was framed under the religious category; assumed it to be religiously Hindu-nation. From the Christian mission perspective, it was a 'Land of Other Faith', thus a missionary narrative was projected to 'civilize and save' native heathens. Such positioning is the beginning of de-culturation for native Indian Christians.

2.1.2. Cultural Arguments of India in the Context of Research

Culture denotes all the capabilities and habits acquired by a human person as a member of a particular society, such as knowledge, belief, art, law, customs, etc.[22] It is the whole way of life, material, intellectual and spiritual that describes the way human beings think, feel, believe and behave and therefore culture is a comprehensive term and includes patterns and modes of the external behavior and basic postures, values, beliefs, world views, etc.,[23] in other sense, way of life.[24] In the case of India, E.B Tylor's definition is true if each diverse community in India is taken as independent from each other. Then the question may pose what is Indian culture? The simple answer would be '*dharmic*' culture. Constructing or visualizing India as a single unity of homogenous origin is incorrect. For example, many Western tourists learn '*namaste*' before coming to India, assuming for its pan-Indian applicability, without knowing its geographical limitation because the South, North-Eastern

---

[22] E. B. Tylor, Primitive Culture: Researches into the Development of Mythology, Philosophy, Language, Art and Customs (London, 1874).

[23] T. V. Kunnunkal, "Our Glorious Heritage and Challenges of the Future", *Composite Culture of India and National Integration* (Allahabad: Indian Institute of Advance Study, 1987), 168.

[24] Akhil Gupta and James Ferguson, "Beyond 'Culture': Space, Identity and the Politics of Difference" in *Cultural Anthropology*, Vol. 7, No. 1 (Feb. 1992): 6.

including main Indian tribes don't use it. The culture of India functions on a localized geographical mapping. The composition of many such local traditions was connected by the prominent cultural traditions of the Vedic and Buddhist that can be called the 'multicultural plurality.'[25] The Cultural pluralism in India is not because of its capacity of adaptation, but for its characteristics being a non-centralized system which fundamentally accepts the human potency as plural and regulates under the cosmic order of *Ṛta*. Therefore, it is a synthesis. Indian cultural formation is continuity.

The first serious halt of this 'induct and deduction' process took place during the Muslim rule and the colonial period. The European scholars/ Missionaries attempted to construct India based on their own methodological applications and people who came to the direct control of the colonial rule and EWM (like native converts) suffered from an identity crisis and culturally de-constructed. Native converts are subjugated and forced to accept imported Christian culture, thus the subalternity has become a standard of living within the colonized NIC. From such context, a counter-narrative of 'native vs foreign' started getting the social importance, and as a result, the anti-Christian movement and the revival of the Vedic culture emerged. NIC [also IC] eventually accepted the colonized narrative of 'India as Hindu nation' what M. N. Thomas explained as the formation of the communal Christianity. Arjun Appadurai argues that a bridge among various social groups is possible through a 'contact-communication' across cultures and between societies.[26] This radical cultural paradigm shift has raised serious sociological issues which will be addressed to find answers and their historicity.

2.1.3. Analysis of Survey on Plural Culture of India

The response from the post-colonial new generation Christian leaders and laypeople reveal the interesting features in the General Survey Report.

Q. I – Does Indian have a single culture or multi-culture?

93% agreed that India is a multicultural country and only 3% opines to have single culture and 3% didn't define it either way. It clearly shows that in North Indian a paradigm shift has been taken place.

Q. II – Do you agree to say that Indian culture is Hindu culture?

[25] Akhil Gupta and James Ferguson, "Beyond 'Culture': Space, Identity and the Politics of Difference" in *Cultural Anthropology*, Vol. 7, No. 1 (Feb. 1992): 7. V

[26] Arjun Appadurai, 'Putting Hierarchy in its Place' in *Cultural Anthropology*, Vol. 3, No. 1 (1988): 36-49.

From 100 people, 32% believe that 'yes' and 68% think 'no'. Therefore, 1/3 of NIC is still continuing the colonial narrative even through majority has another view.

Q. III – Hindu culture is part of Indian culture. Do you agree?

The survey shows that 94% of NIC believes that it is a part of Indian culture and only 6% gives other view and 1% has no opinion on it. It can be true that NIC does not want that complete cultural credit will go to the Hindu, so a social-re-positioning is slowly influencing them.

Q. IV – Hinduism is not a religion but a culture. Do you agree?

The opinion is divided, 65% think that is it a culture rather than be called as a religion and 26% takes it as religion and 3% has no particular answer. This outcome may contradict the colonial narrative of Hindu culture is a religious culture, not just Indian culture. It is a fact that Indian culture (*saṁskāras*) exists even outside the Hindu religion.

2.2. Defining India

2.2.1. The Name 'India': What does it stand for?

Defining the name 'India' is a fascinating subject of research and important to understand the modern 'India'. The Constitution of India accepted two names: 'India' and '*Bharat*' as equivalent.[27] Apart from these two, other ancient terms emerged in the different historical period such as *Aryavart* (territory of Aryans used in *Rig Veda*), *Bharatvarsa* (extended territory of Aryans, in *Vishnu Purana*), and *Hindustan* (People of Indus valley by Persian by 5th century BCE, replacing [S] = Sindhu by [H] = Hindu) and later Greeks in 4th century BCE used '*Indikê*, then via Latin through the British came the word 'India' that actually locates a land within the North-Western region. European usage of the term 'India' by replacing the existing popular name '*Hindustan*' was the part of the colonial reconstruction. If 'Sindhu' is a river basin, and people lived there were Aryans, then, the Persian use of 'Hindu' surely refers to people, not the Hindu religion.[28] Except these two names given by the outsider, '*Aryavarta*', the place of Aryan is popular and mentioned in the Manusmṛti.[29] '*Bharat*', another popular name (belongs a noble king as well as mythical ideologue entity) mentioned in *Puranas*,[30] dated as early as

---

[27] The Constitution of India, opening statement in Article 1: India, that is Bharat, shall be a Union of States.

[28] T.M.P. Mahadevan, *Outlines of Hinduism* (Bombay: Chetana, 3rd ed. 1999, 1954), 12-13.

[29] *Manusmṛti* 2:21-24

[30] S. M. Ali, The Geography of the Puranas (New Delhi, 1966), 109.

1st CE.[31] In spite of its historical dispute, '*Bharat*' holds a symbolic identity and unity, and that meaning is transmitted even into the present interpretation. From the late 19th century, native scholars/leaders recapitalized the idea of '*Bharatvarsa*' (Land of Bharat, i.e. India) to achieve political freedom from the colonial rule. RSS (right-wing Hindu religious organization) is even fighting to change name 'India' with '*Bharat*' because the former has a foreign origin. None of above names does address the wholeness of present political India, because India geographically extended towards East till Myanmar, shrinking in North-Western part known today as Afghanistan and Pakistan, but it loosely identifies a vast land and people connected by a culture. Our survey says that 87% NIC will be happy to be called as Hindustani, but not as Hindu and 10% people have an objection to the word 'Hindustani' and 3% has no view on it.

According to Arvind Sharma, the meaning of 'Hindu' is ever changing reality, geographically and politically, even though it appears to have a fixed connotation.[32] Nirad C. Chaudhuri argues that Hindu (ism) stands different from other religions, that for its followers, it is not an alternative to the world, but primarily the means of supporting and improving their existence in it. Therefore in Hindu/Indian society, every worldly activity has connected the dharma and everything is religious in the world.[33] In another way, the demarcation between religion and culture is not very categorical.

Historically, Hindustani, Hindustan, Hindu, India, *Bharatvarsa* or *Aryavarta* neither qualify a religion or a complete geographical area or people or a particular culture or a political unit exclusively. After independence in 1947, nearly 562 independent princely states were integrated to form the nation-state and since 1949, there is no serious internal independent movement (except Nagaland) to break away from the republic. Two major factors that worked in favor: i. a prevailing ancient culture that had the capacity to integrate diversity; and ii. the new direct democracy that has created a space empowering everyone into participatory democracy. Our focus is on culture, not on modern politics, even though the religio-political ethos of King Ashoka is now the national symbol of identity and culture of unity.

Therefore, the name 'India' is more accurate to her cultural acumen, not political or religious. In re-culturation of NIC, our attempt is to present Indian culture in which the Vedic tradition is taken as a major contributor, not quantitatively but qualitatively. Such investigation leads to bring out the cultural nuances of India from the insights of dharma.

---

[31] *Vishnupurana* 2.3.1-2

[32] Arvind Sharma, *Hinduism for Our Times* (Delhi: OUP, 1997), 6.

[33] Nirad C. Chaudhuri, *Hinduism: A Religion to Live By* (N. Delhi: OUP, 8th Impr., 2003; 1979), 9-10.

2.2.2. Indianness: Analysis to Explain the Pluralistic Framework

The proceeding from above argument, a question may arise in the context of multiple meanings of the name 'India', then, how to define 'Indianness' that might provide the logical support to the re-culturation hypothesis? To address this central question, we need to analyze the possible insights of Indianness.

Plural society conceives a multi-ethnic, multi-religious, multi-lingual, multi-cultural identities within its population, and from that context, India might stand for the world's most complex pluralistic society. Within a plural society, one ideology cannot have superior status over others, if so; society can't be called plural; for it creates 'othering' as a category.[34] It is neither parallelism nor majoritarianism, but a gradual process to create an atmosphere that will naturally allow even the least to exist with dignity. There was no imposition of Aryan culture on the other existing Indian cultures, but only fusion through an acculturation process.[35]

Indian culture expresses a religious diversity and inter-religious interaction since the Indus Valley Civilization[36] as Indian cultural antiquity (non-Aryan), included in the Aryan fold[37] or in South Indian Aryan God is ethnically represented through Dravidian culture.[38] Later in the medieval period, the *Bhakti* tradition with Islam, especially with Sufism in a philosophical expression of union with the divinity (like Kabir) and at the same time Islamic brotherhood and Bhakti spirituality, helped to bring Sikhism, an outcome of Hindu-Muslim conflict. And also many renaissance (from early 19th century) leaders were deeply influenced by Jesus Christ like Keshab Chandra Sen, Vivekananda, Gandhi, etc.[39] In Indian culture, religious supremacy and heretic is a non-existential in the sense Christian faith advocates and it is a very important feature of Indianness.

Pluralism is a sensitive and subtle existence of non-similar and Harold G. Coward thinks that religious pluralism is a special challenge what world religions are facing today.[40] I defer because, except an exclusive position of

---

[34] M. M. Thomas, *Risking Christ for the Sake of Christ* (Delhi: ISPCK, 1999), 3.

[35] RomilaThapar, *Ancient Indian Social History: Some Interpretations* (Hyderabad: Orient Longman, 1984), 215.

[36] John Keay, *India: A History* (London: HarperCollins, 2000), Chapter 1. Cf. Paul M. Collins, Context, Culture and Worship: The Quest for Indianness (New Delhi: ISPCK, 2006), 170-171.

[37] A. L Basham, *The Wonder that Was India* (Calcutta: Rupa/Pontana Books, 1971), 21-24.

[38] Narayana Menon, "The Foundations of Composite Culture in India" in Composite Culture of India and National Integration (Allahabad: Indian Institute of Advance Study, 1987): 71.

[39] M. M. Thomas, *Acknowledged Christ in Indian Renaissance* (Madras/Bangalore: CLS/CISRC, 1970).

[40] Harold G. Coward, *Pluralism: Challenge to World Religions* (Delhi: Sri Satguru Publications, 1996), 94.

a particular religion, it poses no challenge. John Hick's argument sets on the conviction which holds that a particular religion supposed to have the valid response to the divinity and it alone knows the 'truth' concerning the nature of reality.[41] Paul F Knitter said that Christian theology (Church too) is confronting today to acknowledge the validity of other faiths.[42] Knitter's observation is a practical truth, especially in the Indian context, where majority rural Christian evangelists are living in a house owned by a Hindu (religiously) and propagate the Christianity, condemning (generally) the same Hinduism as nothing less than false. Indian *dharmic* (not exclusively religion) culture which has been practicing the plural expressions of the Single Truth, thus challenges Christianity to have an Indian orientation and to play a constructive role in upholding Indian plurality which is actually an opportunity.

The diversity of India is the major challenge to analyze rationally. Culture and cultural diversity are pan-Indian topography. Any scientific investigate (Applying a single methodology and category) will face an impossible task to actualize what Indianness is all about. Our research will, therefore, allow the notion of plurality as the framework to visualize Indianness, keeping aside the general presupposition of Indian culture synonymous to Hinduism, that to me, factually incorrect. We shall investigate to justify how far the underlying unifying notion is a socio-cultural truth. According to Amartya Sen, the mistaken Indian identity as explored by the Western scholars defines it as caste-based homogeneity derived from the so-called Hindu (Vedic religion), rather looking into the deep-rooted heterogeneity spread all over India.[43] Susan Bayly in her argument disagreed to accept the claim of orientalists on Indian culture (caste-based hierarchically monitored) which has nothing to do with the vast majority of people living in India.[44] Her observation is right in the sense that Hindu culture has no implication to many communities, mainly on tribes. The ground-breaking framework on which plurality of Indianness has been nurtured is the Vedas which denounced centralized and doctrinal codification of faith and advocated the plurality as the ultimate reality. Eugene M. Makar's the idea of India is also limited to majoritarian view related to Hindu social structure.[45] His assessment is proved to be limited in the light of social customs of tribes and many of scheduled caste communities that

---

[41] John Hick, *God Has Many Names* (Philadelphia: The Westminster Press, 1982), 88.

[42] Paul F. knitter, *No Other Name? A Critical Survey of Christian Attitudes towards the World Religions* (London: SCM Press Ltd., 1985), 17.

[43] Amartya Sen, *The Argumentative Indian: Writings on Indian History, Culture and Identity* (Penguin Books, 2005).

[44] Susan Bayly, *Caste, Society and Politics in India from the Eighteenth Century to the Modern Age* (Cambridge University Press, 1999).

[45] Eugene M. Makar, *An American's Guide to Doing Business in India* (2008).

are different from the Hindu caste system. Des Dearlove observes that Indian society offers its children to grow up in learning diversity.[46] Dearlove is able to get a larger reality of India, and even more practical in the context of modern time. Arjun Appadurai (eminent anthropologist on South Asia) thinks that the Indian culture is a living museum, not stagnant as it was viewed by the Europeans during the Christian era.[47] To my observation, the Indian society is more syncretic where heterogeneous heritages have been evolving since ages to present time.

2.2.3. What is Indianness?

Re-culturation in a particular context demands to define the context itself, and our research context is Indian culture. I begin with a question: what is the Indic characteristic or Indianness considering its complex diversities; be it language, customs, rituals, dress, food, color, ethnicity, religious traditions (*Sampradayas*), etc. To find a rational answer, I would like to depend on a traditional saying '**Unity in diversity**' or in my word '**practical plurality**'. Diversity or Plurality is not the existence of diverse social units within a boundary, but emergence a conscience among those diverse communities that keep people connected to each other, affirm others and look for a harmony being plural as a natural social system. My argument confers the logic of Lesslie Newbigin (the outcome of his experience in India) where he has distinguished the 'pluralism' as 'ideology' from 'plural society'. The plural society is the reality of life, cherished by common people; not just the society is plural.[48] It itself is an 'ideology' that could be called 'Indianness' or Indian culture. Therefore, the culture of monotheistic oriented tradition likes of Muslim or semi-monotheistic Christianity has become counterproductive in the Indian context. It is not true that in India Muslims or Christians cannot have their freedom of exclusive culture, but it must be within the framework of social plurality, avoiding in creating a monocultural community under religious nuances as we noticed during the colonial mission. In another way, Indianness as a culture has a capacity to reconstruct itself with a new entity's entry.[49]

---

[46] Des Dearlove, "On the Verge of Something Extraordinary" in *Business Strategy Review*, London Business School (Spring, 2009): 17-20.

[47] Ajun Appadurai, 'Putting Hierarchy in Its Place" in *Cultural Anthropology*, Vol. 3, No. 1, (February, 1988): 36-49.

[48] Lesslie Newbigin, *The Gospel in a Pluralist Society* (Eerdmans: Grand Rapids, 1989), 1.

[49] New Entities in Indian Society: Major groups are: Greek after Alexander (326 BCE), Gandhar Art; Arabs, Turkish, Iranian, Mughals etc. Muslim cultures (632 CE till date) in Art, architecture, dance and music, judiciary, food, clothing and many more; Europeans (Mainly Portuguese and British after 16th CE) as Western culture like Christianity, education, dress, democracy, etc. Sufi since 10th CE; Parsee more in business culture, and all contributed in languages and religion too. All are part of present Indian culture in some form or other.

Let me bring one political scenario to explain this plurality. During 2004 -2014, India had: the President of Indian National Congress (the largest political party), the most powerful political persona, an Italian Roman Catholic woman (Mrs. Sonia Gandhi, Indian citizen by marriage); the President of nation, a Muslim (A. P. J. Abdul Kalam); the Prime Minister, a Sikh (Dr. Mammohan Singh); Defense Minister, a Syro-Catholic but atheist (A. K. Antony); Foreign Minister, a Brahmin Hindu (Pranab Mukherjee). This is what the logic of Newbegin's Indian plurality or Indianness that I am arguing upon.

Despite problems in ancient or in modern time, a vision of Indianness was in public discourse from the beginning of the Vedic era that professed the idea of the plural expression of One Ultimate God (*ekam sad viprabahudavadanti.*).[50] When the Vedic tradition allowed questioning on the very existence of God as the subject to prove (except Uttar Mimamsa/Vedantic theistic expression: 'There is God'), it actually appeals to resolve the question through a plurality and negate the 'monopoly over Truth'. This plurality is the foundation of Indianness as a general notion. Encounter to Islam and Christianity's idea of the unparalleled Truth and second to none, and since the early 20th century, the right-wing Hindu groups (RSS+) have been attempting to unify diverse Hindus (*Hindutva* ideology) like of Christian or Muslim, and after 90 years such ambition remains untenable. The Indian secularism as reflected in the Constitution of India, largely the vision of Gandhi, is the reflection of traditional plurality in modern democratic form.

To give a sustaining reality to Indianness/plural culture, it is not only the vision of leaders (religious or political) but also the participation of common people who play a vital role resisting the counter-ideology to preserve the plural social fabric. It is practically a participatory plurality, a thinking process and a psychological aspect based on Vedic theistic plurality.

2.2.4. Indianness and Hinduness: Are They Same?

Does the Indianness is similar to Hinduness? Etymologically or religiously, Hindu does not confer Hinduism as we discussed earlier. It needs to resolve at this point if not, the re-culturation for NICs in this research will be a dispute. The historical facts suggest that India has been shaping herself, culturally and religiously by the two mainstream paradoxical ancient ideologies that set Indian imperatives, namely *Astika* (Aryan-Vedic, theistic in nature) and *Nastika* (non-Vedic, non-theistic in nature). Both ideologies are the main contributors to construct Indianness, and interplay of these two further enriched the Indian plurality, since there was no absolute hegemony of either. The main reason, I argue, there was no supreme centralized authority to monitor religious affairs

[50] Rig Veda 1:164.46.

and even though both traditions ruled ancient India separately hundreds of years. The failure of nearly 700 hundred years Muslim rule or 190 years European (British) rule to convert India into a Muslim or Christian nation (as happened in Arabs world and Latin America) is precious because of this plural culture. Later after the final decline of Buddhist tradition (6th century onwards) and raise of the Vedic tradition gave the Vedic followers an upper hand to create a social perception that India is Hindu (religion) nation. The arrival of Islam and serious social conflict which was a completely new kind of religio-political imperative to Indians had improvised the notion of Hindu faith as the sole religio-culture defender. This historic fact reshaped the clinical differences between the Hindu tradition and the Hindu religion. The European scholars and missionaries are largely responsible to frame 'Hindu tradition' as Hinduism. Truth is that the Hindu religious culture is not the Indian culture in totality, and at the same time, Indian culture can't be understood without Hindu religious traditions. This is one dimension to define.

Other aspects are related to enormous ethnic groups like Tribes, OBC/SC (Dalit) who are also the part of this Indianness narrative, but they are not necessarily Vedic-Hindu. This aspect is very delicate and also has an alternative socio-political narrative. If Hindu tradition is taken as a cultural hegemony that delimited minor cultural groups, then, India, by now, might have developed a unified monoculturalism but that didn't happen. No two states or communities are practicing the same culture, even though they are religiously Hindu. Culture in India has been changing within every 50 km, even shorter. I don't ignore the impact of the majority on a minority that leads a cultural conflict time and again. For example, there is a linguistic conflict between South and North on the Hindi language. In 2014, this tension once again fuelled when the present Central Govt. planned to project 'Hindi' as the national language, and many linguistics groups opposed and it was taken back. Nationally, the minority culture was not replaced by Hindu culture by a policy, but they are either able to keep their identity or had fusion (Samaritan Culture). Therefore, at present, India has nearly 500 hundreds of tribal groups (8.6% of the total population), religiously belong to indigenous faith, Hindu, Christian, and Buddhist etc.; 2500 OBC (Other Backward Class, 41%) groups and SC (Schedule Caste, 16.6%) belong to Hindu, Muslim, Buddhist, Sikh and Christianity or other. Many tribal groups (Naga, Mizo, Khasi, Kuki, etc. almost Christianized, 98%) in the North-Eastern region are completely out of Aryan/Hindu originated culture. Even though Aryan, Dravidian, Dalit, Tribes are different religiously, ethnically, linguistically or culturally, a sense of belongingness to live together has not ruled out. India has a 'lesser-known' (not popular) culture which is too diverse, and there is a 'known' culture, confused with the Hindu (religious) culture.

2.2.5. Indianness from the Multi-dimensional Ethnography

Let me present ethnographical explanation, now, to analyze the complex and diverse cultural narrative that has a particular vision of Indianness, and also try to bring the cultural interdependent identity as a viable social phenomenon.

Since 1870s, emergence of a new kind of Indianness by reviving the 'Pure-Hinduism (Vedic Hinduism) as the symbol of *swaraj* (self-rule) by the Arya Samaj[51] culturally and politically[52] or Swami Vivekananda (1863-1902, founded the *Ramakrishna Mission and Math*), slogan 'Practical Vedanta'[53] or Vinayak Damodar Savarkar (1883-1966, President of Hindu Mahasabha), slogan '*Akhand Bharat* (undivided India)'[54] or 'Hindutva' of RSS (1925) has gained substantial popularity to define a new kind of Indianness, yet Indian culture has not got any major change, except the politicization of Hinduism (since 1985s) that has possed a threat to the stability of plurality at present. Let us explain the plural composition of Indian culture.

2.2.5.1. Aryan or Vedic Culture

Aryan invasion and conquering other ancient Indian tribes do not qualify the British (European) theory of 'superior' versus 'aboriginals', since the historical fact of occupation both by Aryans and Tribes in Indian continent does not differentiate from each other. According to S.M. Channa, Aryan superiority status was a British political-religious agenda to divide Indians from Indians, by stating relatively tall fair skinned Aryans as a superior race over dark-skinned, flat-nose tribes (*Sudras*). Early European orientalists like Sir William Johns (founder of the Asiatic Society) and later Max Muller, have developed this religio-political theory with the help of some Hindu *Pandits* like Mrityunjaya Vidyalankar, who provided the scriptural documents to European scholars. This 'elitist theory' was racial by nature. In the late 19th century and early 20th century, the racial Aryan-German affinity got a complete political nature. Even Max Muller retracted from his earlier position by stating: Indo-Aryan just a linguistic group not racial.[55]

This propaganda, as Mr. Channa said, is well reflected in the mind of the high caste Hindu in the renaissance (Raja Ram Mohan Roy) and nationalistic

---

[51] Arya Samaj was founded in 1875 in Bombay - to spread the doctrines of the Vedic theism.

[52] J. Sharma, *Hindutva: Exploring the Idea of Hindu Nationalism* (New Delhi: Viking / Penguin, 2003), 8.

[53] Swami Vivekananda, *Complete Works* Vol. III (Calcutta: Advaita Ashram, 1951 & 1999).

[54] Jyotirmaya Sharma, *Hindutva: Exploring the Idea of Hindu Nationalism* (New Delhi: Viking/Penguin, 2003), 127. See also, Savarkar, *Hindutva*, 7th Edition (Mumbai: Swatantryaveer Savakar Rahtriya Smarak, 1999), 28.

[55] S. M Channa, ed., *Encyclopeadia of Indian Tribes and Castes*, Vol. I (New Delhi: Cosmo Publications, 2004), xi.

movement (Dayanand Saraswati). Thus upper caste psychology as superior racial progeny from Aryans over rest of the Indian people has made a permanent inroad by reconstructing relatively egalitarian society into a divided hierarchical society based on *Jati* and Dharma.[56]

2.2.5.2. Dravidian Culture

Another argument placed by D. Devakala and M. Deivanayagam[57] that claims the Indus Valley Civilization belongs to Dravidian (dark-skinned Southern people) referring to the ancient *Sangam* literature[58] (3rd century BCE to 3rd century CE) in Tamil that provides the evidence of their argument. More study is required to establish and acceptance of this claim. Setting apart the scholar's merit on this argument, Southern Indian communities (Kerala, Tamilnadu, Karnataka, Andhra Pradesh, Telangana) are different physically, culturally, architecturally from North Indian people, and there is a lot similarity with Indus Valley iconography. The social perception confirms the Dravidian antiquity is older to the Aryan, which is an outcome of the European theory of the Aryan invasion to Indus valley area.[59] This claim contradicts to the North Indian narrative that projects the Aryan civilization is the oldest and ultimate pride of India. The Indo-Aryan is lived in the vicinity of the Dravidians and there was an ongoing process of cultural fusion in food habits, iron technology, the development of the caste structure, religious beliefs and practices as well as genealogies and myths.[60]

After all, there is no agreement even in scholarly research or in a society that counts both traditions as one. In that respect, the plurality narrative is further used to solve this debate and tension. Our intention is to look into this diversity when re-culturation feasibility is debated against the two opposite views; one from right-wing Vedic hegemony and other is colonial construction of Hindu monolithic India.

---

[56] S. M Channa, ed., *Encyclopeadia of Indian Tribes and Castes*, Vol. I (New Delhi: Cosmo Publications, 2004), xi.

[57] M. Deivanayagam and D. Devakala, see: http://www.geocities.com/Athens/Ithaca/1412.

[58] 'Sangham literature': The earliest extent literature of the Tamils is called Sangham literature and it is dated between 500 BC and 200 AD. Though a considerable part of the early poetry has been lost, some of the parts and patrons decided to preserve a part of it in certain ontologies (about 4th century AD). This are the Ten Idyllas (*Pattuppattu*) and the Eight Astrologers (*Ettutthai*) Four hundred and seventy three poets, of whom 30 are women, have been identified. This are mainly classified into two. *Akam* or Esoteric dealing with love and *Puram* or Exoteric dealing with war.

[59] Gregory L. Possehl, *The Indus Civilization: A Contemporary Perspective* (Rowman Altamira, 2002), 238.

[60] Romila Thapar, *Ancient Indian Social History: Some Interpretations* (Hyderabad: Orient Longman, 1984), 216-238.

2.2.5.3. Dalit Culture

The Dalit narrative (early 20th century) has a strong alternative view of Indianness based on the historical evolution of the caste system legitimized in *Dharmasastras* (mainly Manusmṛti) as *Mlachha*[61] to denote a group of people outside of Aryan *Varna* system,[62] inferior to Aryan and untouchable. Jyotiba Phule, the first Dalit leader to coin this word Dalit (in Sanskrit) means broken, crushed, downtrodden, etc., and later B. R Ambedkar converted it to a movement against Hinduism, because, to him, Hinduism is directly responsible for people's suffering. Therefore, he along with 600,000 Dalits left Hinduism on 14th October 1956 and converted to Buddhism and that was known as the Neo-Buddhism in India.[63] Interestingly when Christian mission uses Ambedkar's view on Dalit to criticize Hinduism, it is the same Ambedkar who criticized Christianity for the practice of caste. Gandhi named Dalit as '*Harijan* (People of God) but Ambedkar refused to accept it, to him, this term does not represent their actual social status, rather covers up. Recently, this movement is closely identified with the Dravidian movement, because both movements view the Brahmanical Hinduism as the antagonist. Dalit culture is based on *Katha* (oral folklores) which was overshadowed by the dominating high caste Hindus. Within the context of Dalit emancipation, the re-construction of culture, economy, human dignity, etc., has a strong reputation on the traditional view that equates India culture as Hindu culture. Many of characters/stories in epics like Shambuka, a *Sudra*; Shabari, a hunter's daughter in Ramayana or Eklavya, a *Sudra* in Mahabharata are interpreted and re-introduced to communicate the untold Dalit history. Dalit movements are highly politicized and gained huge social momentum in the socio-cultural arena. India has 16.6% Dalit and 33.8% Christians are from the Dalit community.[64] Our attempt to re-construct of culture needs serious consideration of their basic cultural features, re-introducing their history and culture, oral traditions, rituals, rites, festivals, and such reconstruction can further enrich the process the composite culture in India.[65]

---

[61] *Mlechha* in Manusmṛti 2:23 is used to identify all non-Aryan, either just an outsider or as inferior to Aryan or untouchable.

[62] Manusmṛti chapter 5.

[63] S.M. Michael (ed.), *Dalits in Modern India: Vision and Values* (New Delhi: Vistaar Publications, 1999), 14.

[64] Sachar Committee: A Govt. of India Committee to assess condition of Muslim and presented in Parliament in 2006.

[65] Nirmal Minz, "Religion, Culture and Education in the context of the Tribal Aspirations in India" in *Journal of Dharma*, Vol. XII, No. 2 (April-June, 1987): 153.

2.2.5.4. Tribal (*Adivasi*) Culture

Tribes (8.6% and 645 ethnolinguistic groups[66]) live all over India mainly in their own territory. They are completely outside the caste system, even though tribes like '*Bhils* and *Gonds*' in Rajasthan and Gujarat region upgraded to *Kshatriya* after gaining political power[67] and absorbed within the '*varna*' system.

The origin of Indian tribes is debatable, taking physical feature; one group (dark-black skin) belongs to the Negroid origin, lives in most part of India since the time of Indus Valley Civilization or before; and another group belongs to Mongoloid (white skin, short height, and flat nose) origin, lives Himalayan region and thickly in North-Eastern India. They preferably live in forest and hill regions, reflect very different culture from mainstream India and can be identified with the 'Animist' as E.B Tylor has defined in the category[68] because the present life condition of many Indian tribes (mainly Christian tribes) are highly westernized after conversion.[69]

Communitarian customs and endogamous practices have kept their uniqueness intact in great extent. Socially, they were never religiously Hindu or part of the caste system, enjoyed their own social administrative system to rule them and such is true even today. According to Sheetal Thakur, Indian tribal is more functional in nature. Culturally, tribes are going through many changes because of conversion and modernization. The Negroid tribes are in constant fusion with regional dominating culture (largely Hindu) and the Mongoloid tribes are largely westernized due to a mass conversion to Christianity. According to D.N. Majumdar, Hinduism and tribal religion have a lot of social exchange and interaction, for example, *Riangs* of Tripura and the *Garos* in Meghalaya.[70] Many tribal gods like *Kali* and *Chandi* in Eastern Indian are fully part of Hindu fold.[71] Constant orthogenetic and heterogeneity changes are taking place.[72]

---

[66] A. K. Das, 'Scheduled Tribe-A Socio-Economic and Cultural Profile in West Bengal' in *Bulletin of C.R.I.*, Kolkata (1991): 2-4.

[67] S. M Channa, ed., *Encyclopeadia of Indian Tribes and Castes*, Vol. I (New Delhi: Cosmo Publications, 2004), viii.

[68] S. M Channa, ed., *Encyclopeadia of Indian Tribes and Castes*, Vol. I (New Delhi: Cosmo Publications, 2004), viii.

[69] S. M Channa, ed., *Encyclopeadia of Indian Tribes and Castes*, Vol. I (New Delhi: Cosmo Publications, 2004), x.

[70] D. N. Majumdar, 'A Study of Religious Practices among the Son Koch of Garo Hills" in *Bulletin of the Dept. of Anthropology*, Govt. of India, Calcutta, Vol. XVII, No. 3 (1970): 325-55.

[71] R. C. Majundar, *Indian Religion* (Calcutta: Calcutta University Press, 1969), 55.

[72] Yodendra Singh, *Modernization of Indian Tradition* (Faridabad: Thomson India Press Ltd., 1977).

The Indian tribal vision of life has emphasized a new narrative for social harmony, equality, collectiveness and it provides another kind of plurality. Therefore re-culturation for Indian Christian must emerge from within each such cultural setting.

2.2.5.5. Anglo-Indian Culture

The origin of this community goes back to early European trading and the ruling period since the beginning of the 17th century. The name 'Anglo-India' is the Indi-European mixed progeny, mainly from the unmarried partnership (European/British man and native woman). They were almost separated from the rest of society till Indian's independent, 1947. The constitution defines them:

> An Anglo Indian means a person whose father or any of whose other male progenitors in the male line is or was of European descent but who is domiciled within the territory of India and is or was born within such territory of parents habitually resident therein and not established there for temporary purposes only, Article 366 (2).

The constitution also has empowered them to elect their own members for the Parliament (two members) and State Legislative Body (Seven states). In 1947, their population 800000 came down to 350000 in 2010 due to mass migration to the West to find the much familiar cultural life and employment.[73] In compare to the Indian population, they might be very tiny but have a special socio-political status and significance. The general social perception of this community is negative due to long separation and many practices that faced moral questions. To a great extent, Anglo-Indian culture is also responsible to project a negative picture of Christianity, equated alongside to westernized affair.

2.2.5.6. Contemporary Indian Culture

The portrait of the Indian culture seems drawing a sketch of the ancient history predominantly influenced by the Vedic Hindu (Religious) tradition, but there is another India which aspires for development, social freedom, justice, health and education, personal religion, progressive and global and even material aspiration. India has the largest middle-class in the world nearly 700 million and global involvement in the technological field.

What is modern India? Stephen Cohen might have put rightly, "India is an ancient state but a modern civilization."[74] It surely addresses a duality in

[73] Blair Williams, *Anglo Indians* (CTR Inc. Pub, 2002), 189.

[74] Stephen Cohen, *India Emerging Power* (Washington D.C.: Brookings Institution Press, 2001), 36.

Indian society in contrast to the Western Model of Civilization where an effort is made to ensure maximum life support to the last person (not all nations are fully successful) and modernity is repealing the old. If Cohen is right, Martin Heidegger's vision of the future world may not be seen a feasible immediate reality, when he stated, "The fundamental event of the modern age is the conquest of the world as picture."[75] Globalization is not to be limited to the people's movement or wider cross broader commercial trade, as it is defined by Brain Longhurst saying that it is a situation where socio-cultural life would no longer be firmly limited to a particular place with strict geopolitical boundary.[76] It is empirically evident that the globalization has impacted and changed Indian cultures at a great extent, but, it is also true what Stephen Cohen observed. In this changing scenario, India is still very close to ancient ethos, *saṁskāras*, *sanskriti,* and religion. Postcolonial India is a secular democratic republic, having 80% religious Hindu yet not a constitutionally Hindu and put on Gandhi's vision of secular India.[77] This Indian version was supported by Harvey Cox who opines that a state, being secular, can create a peaceful co-existence of religions, instead of separating from them.[78] There was no Hindu revolt or movements to oppose such a constitution except right-wing Hindu groups (RSS+). The colonial Church failed to actualize this cultural vision of India and still wish to hold India as a Hindu nation and Christians are a minority. This traditional Christian perception is a hindrance for a postcolonial construction. Secularism in India does not separate itself from religion,[79] in contrast, accepts all; but many mission slogans (Win India for Christ, Save Lost Souls, etc.) still largely wish to visualize 'Hindu or other religion free India' as the end result of the mission. For such dogmatic position, Christianity has been struggling to integrate within Indian plural social system.

In our research re-culturation, this modern aspect will play a vital role, not in the area of outward re-culturation, but psychological re-culturation of Indian Christian.

---

[75] Martin Heidegger, "The Age of the World Picture", *The Question Concerning Technology and Other Essays*, trans. & introduced by William Lovitt (New York: Harper and Row Publishing Inc., 1977), 134.

[76] Brain Longhurst, et. al. *Introducing Cultural Studies* (London: Pearson Longman, 2008), 59.

[77] Brojendra Nath Banerjee, *Religious Conversion in India* (New Delhi: Harnam Publications, 1982), 125. & B.L. Fadia, *Indian Government and Politics* (Agra: Sahitya Bhawan Publications, 2008), 104.

[78] M. T. Cherian, *Hindutva Agenda and Minority Rights; A Christian Response* (Bangalore: Centre for Contemporary Christianity, 2007), 36.

[79] N. K. Chowdhry, *Indian Constitution and Education* (Delhi: Shipra Publications, 2009), 3.

2.3. Euro-Western Mission Model (EWMM) and Subalternity of NIC

To deal with a pertinent question on 're-culturation of NIC and its contemporary important', a vivid analysis of three segments of Indian Church history: i. the characteristic of St. Thomas Christianity; ii. Portuguese Roman Catholic Missionary, especially referring to the Synod of Diamper and Protestant Mission, iii. Contemporary Indian Church and her cultural identity are essential. The aim of analysis the above three areas will help us to define the argument of the subaltern status of NINC [also IC] during the colonial Church and at the same time to capture the ground reality that will justify the necessity of re-culturation for the contemporary Indian Christianity.

This analysis is to incorporate a number of issues as listed below:

i. Issue related to the culture of St. Thomas and Syrian Christian and their relation to Indian culture.
ii. Issue related to religio-political doctrinal exclusivism of European Christianity: Roman Catholic and Protestant Mission and their subsequent consequences.
iii. Issue related to the contemporary Indian Church movements and identity.
iv. Issue related to the challenges and possibilities of re-culturation.

The formative objective is to look into the possibility for a cultural re-orientation from Euro-centrism to Indo-centrism (Indic) as a postcolonial quest.

2.3.1. Analysis of History of the Indian Church: Cultural Conflict Assessment

The origin of Christianity in India is believed to be as old as Christianity itself, since the arrival of St. Thomas (Syrian tradition) in 52 CE is accepted. Then after a millennium and a half, in the 16th century, the Roman Catholic Church and at the beginning of 18th century the Protestant Church arrived in India from Europe. From the late 19th century and early 20th century, various independent Protestant denominations, mainly from the USA have been entering on Indian soil.

We shall try to be analyzed about the history of Church and her mission related to the above list issues to depict a broader framework to establish why the culture of North Indian Christians needs an Indic relook.

2.3.1.1. St. Thomas Tradition

The apostolic antiquity is evidential,[80] though debates are on. The presence of St. Thomas in Kerala,[81] India by a regular West-Asia merchandise route in 42/52CE,[82] and later it was affiliated the East Syrian Order. Accepting the antiquity, L.W. Brown and the First Prime Minister Jawaharlal Nehru both opined that Christianity could not be considered as a foreign religion and it was a part of Malabar society as like others.[83] This tradition had the capacity to be with other Indian traditions in harmony for 1500 years till European Christianity arrived.

2.3.1.1.1. Cultural Assessment of St. Thomas Tradition

One can question whether Thomas Christianity was Indian or indigenous? Dr. Roger E. Hedlund observed that from the 3rd and 4th century onward, this tradition was 'Syrianized', which prevented it to be a 'pan-Indian Church,'[84] though it took upon substantial local customs and lived in the least social conflict. Being within the 'museum of races and cultures in the Keralite region,'[85] it harmonized doctrines within ritualistic and customary makeover[86] and remains under the Syrian for another 1500 years.

L.W. Brown expressed the strongest favor saying that being the foreign origin, the Thomas Christian emerged as a truly indigenous church (within *saṁskāras*: childbirth & Childhood, marriage customs, inheritance, fasting, burial practices, dress, food, naming, education, social festivals, relation to other faith, temple, etc.).[87] As the re-culturation of European Christianity was through Greco-Roman culture and later it appeared to be the basic Christian

---

[80] Julius Richter, *A History of Missions in India* (Edinburgh: Oliphant Anderson & Ferrier, 1908): 30.

[81] A.M. Mundadan, *History of Christianity in India*, Vol. 1 (Bangalore: Theological Publications in India, 1982), 21.

[82] E. Tisserant, *Eastern Christianity in India* (London: Orient Longman, 1957), 10.

[83] L.W. Brown, *The Indian Christians of St. Thomas* (Cambridge: Cambridge University Press, 1956), 16.

[84] A. Mathias Mundadan, *From the Beginning up to the Middle of the Sixteenth Century (up to 1542), History of Christianity in India*, Vol. I (Bangalore, Church History Association of India, 1989), 115.

[85] K.P.P. Menon, *History of Kerala Written in the Form of Notes*, Vol. 1 (New Delhi: Asian Educational Services, 1982), 73-76. Ethnic Kerala was mixed with Dravidian and North Indian Aryan (Brahmin) alongside with Buddhist and later Muslim with a small influential Jewish.

[86] K.P.P. Menon, *History of Kerala*, Vol. 2 (New Delhi: Asian Educational Services, 1983), 445. The early Christian were believed from four Brahmin families called *Pakalomattam, Sankarapuri, Kalli* and *Kaliankal*.

[87] L.W. Brown, *The Indian Christians of St.Thomas* (Cambridge: Cambridge University Press, 1956), 167.

culture for the whole Europe and Western world; in the same way, Indian/ Hindu culture was used in the life of Thomas Christian. A. M. Mundadan gives credit to the uniqueness of the Nestorian Church for it,[88] whereas Stephen Neil and others think that the arrival of the Portuguese (by the Decree of the Synod of Diamper of in 1599) had eliminated the earlier indigenous traditions leaving just the *Syriac* forms,[89] and that has caused the communal disharmony between Christians and Hindus/Indian.[90] P.J. Podippara thinks that it is the inclusive, pluralistic and liberal theological vision to develop this identity as he put in another way, "Hindu in culture, Christian in Religion and oriental in worship."[91] C.V. Cherian observes the life of Thomas Christian is similar to the land they lived, hence became an essentially Indian religion.[92]

The logical conclusion from above opinions can be drawn that Thomas tradition could be taken as a viable re-culturation model as a framework to search for a new Indian identity for contemporary North Indian Christians, and the code of Manusmṛti and Torah will elaborate the cultural aspects of this model.

2.3.1.2. Roman Catholic Mission

2.3.1.2.1. Features of Mission and Colonialism

The European invasion in India was primarily for commerce either by Marco Polo (last quarter of 13th century) or by Vasco de Gama in 1498 CE. The Portuguese Mission as a state-sponsored religio-political enterprise[93] was to fulfill the state obligation.[94] The conflict-assessment analysis will be limited to the issues involved in cultural deconstruction.

---

[88] A. M. Mundadan, *Indian Christians Search for Identity and Struggle for Autonomy* (Bangalore: Theological Publishing in India, 1982), 27.

[89] Jesudas M. Athyal and John J. Thatamanil (eds.) *Metropolitan Chrysostom on Mission in the Market Place* (Tiruvalla: Christava Sahitya Samithy, 2002), 55.

[90] Stephen Neill, *A History of Christianity in India* (Cambridge: Cambridge University Press, 1985), 47. Before the arrival of Portuguese there was communal harmony and cordial relation between Christians and Hindus. It was presumed that Christian population increase not by proselytizing but by power of their life style.

[91] Placid J. Podippara, *The Thomas Christians* (London: Longman and Todd, 1970), 27.

[92] C.V. Cheriyan, *A History of Christianity in Kerala* (Kottayam: Kerala Historical Society, 1973), 153.

[93] K. M. Panikkar, *Asia and Western Dominance* (London: George Allen & Unwin Ltd., 1953, Rept. 1993), 280.

[94] Julius Richter, *A History of Missions in India* (Edinburgh: Oliphant Anderson & Ferrier, 1908), 44.

The process of politicization of Christianity from a persecuted religion to a persecuting religion started after 313 CE by the *Edict of Milan*,[95] jointly by Constantine the Great of Western Roman Emperor and Licinius of Eastern Emperor, following the *Edict of Toleration by Galerius* in 311 CE, and that was completed in 380 CE by Theodosius-I, by announcing Christianity as state religion. The major shift in State-Church era is to institutionalize the whole doctrines and practices, and different to that state position is none less than 'heresy' (the Council of Nicaea 325 CE and Arianism heresy debate). Monoculturalism was in practice as a symbol of Roman Catholic Jurisdiction which eventually extricated paganism from the entire Roman world.[96] In the present world, the Muslim-Christian or Christian-Hindu conflict can also be analyzed from the perspective of this monoculturalism tradition. The monoculturalism of the Portuguese Jesuit Mission[97] is well reflected in the decree of the *Synod of Diamper*,[98] which, to me, can be treated as '*Tyranny of Religion*' in India. The mission of Fr. Francis Xavier (1506-1552) was to re-claim 'heathen' for Christ'[99] and to achieve a pre-determined goal, he used the state power over Indian-pagan.[100] Later when Robert de Nobili (1577-1656) adopted Hindu (Brahmin) culture as a method to win High caste, it was viciously opposed by the Arch Bishop of Goa, forbidding him to baptize, accused him polluting Christianity by pagan elements. To Julius Richter, Nobili's model reflects the simple monastic order of India,[101] but to Sita Ram Goel, (Indian right-wing nationalist writer) both Francis Xavier and Nobili are 'Pirates in Priests' Clothing'. This is a very strong comment, and I use it here to assess the gravity of cultural conflict. Long before Goel, Mughal Emperor

---

[95] Constantine and Licinius, "*The Edict of Milan*', in documents of the Christian Church, trans. & ed. Henry Bettenson (London: Oxford University, 1963), 22. Initial intension of it was to give religious freedom in welfare state.

[96] Jeffrey Richards, *The Popes and the Papacy in the Early Ages 476-752* (London: Routledge & Kegan Paul, 1979), 16.

[97] Xavier Koodapuzha, *Faith and Communion of the Indian Church of the Saint Thomas* (Vadavathur: Institute of Religious Studies, 1982), 144.

[98] The Synod of Diamper took place in Kerala from 20th to 26th June, 1599, mainly to bring all Indian Syrian Church under the control of Roman Catholic.

[99] K.M. Panikkar, *India Through Ages* (New Delhi: Discovery Publishing House, 1988), 225-226.

[100] K. M. Panikkar, *Asia and Western Dominance* (London: George Allen & Unwin Ltd., 1974), 281.

[101] Julius Richter, *A History of Mission in India* (Edinburgh: Oliphant Anderson & Ferrier, 1908), 63.

of Akbar (1542-1605), in his royal court, observed the Jesuit mission as a mark of intolerance and lack of respect to other faiths.[102]

Therefore, the Portuguese invasion in India and to Thomas Christian, not only alienated Christian tradition in India but also separated native Christians permanently from their own cultural heritage that led to the present identity crisis.

2.3.1.2.2. De-Indianization of Indian Christian

The Synod of Diamper declaration is the epitome of Christian cultural crisis and it is to be taken in the context of the earlier relation between Nestorian and the Roman Catholic Church. This denominational rivalry erupted even in India too. Jesuit objected in two points: Indian elements in life, liturgy, and worship must be scraped and their Nestorian affiliation must be ceased. It has not only destroyed the identity of Thomas Christian but also pushed one Apostolic Church into several divisions.[103]

The objectives of the Synod are as follows:

1. To the Glory and Praise of the Trinitarian Affirmation of Faith
2. To perpetuate Christian belief and living in the diocese
3. To ensure the growth and spread of the Catholic belief and reckoning
4. To declare allegiance and obedience to the Roman Pontiff
5. To eradicate heresies and pagan practices
6. To abrogate heretic verses from religious books and liturgy
7. To destroy books containing perverse and pernicious errors
8. To abjure the faith and allegiance to the patriarch of Babylon
9. To perpetuate correct observance of the Holy Sacraments and
10. To set up an orderly functioning of pastoral guidance and control

2.3.1.2.3. Decrees that played a Significant Role in De-culturation

Decree 1: Believing *Onam*[104] for good crops and prosperity and *Onam* related social events, regular purifying bathing (the only baptism is the final soul cleansing) are declared as superstition.

---

[102] K.M. Panikkar, *Asia and Western Dominance* (London: George Allen & Unwin Ltd., 1974), 281.

[103] Total eight denominational Churches were formed after the Synod of Diamper between 1599-1975.

[104] *Onam* is a harvest festival in Kerala falls during Aug-Sep, and later it was linked with Hindu God Vishnu. Actually it is the visit of the king Mahabali to whom God Vishnu was afraid of. The Era of Mahabali is considered as the golden age in Kerala. Interestingly, it has non-Aryan link and worship. Presently is observed by almost all Keralite around the world. It is now a four days state holiday. *Onam* is the cultural identity of Keralite.

Decree 5: Pagan practices: believing star, rebirth, various sacrifices, etc. are seen as a pagan practice, so sin, and therefore, observing them one will have to face at least one-year excommunication.

Decree 6: *Raksha* (*Manthrams*/protection): some signs are used at home or thread, oil used for body, etc., as for considering as anti-Christian and satanic. Excommunication was must till repentance.

Decree 7: Church controlled money lending system (Usury) with 12% interest per annum. If not obeyed for thrice, he will be excommunicated from Church and society.

Decree 9: Christian and other faith people lived together in society and such social setting was not good for Christian faith because other faith influence used to come to them.

Decree 14: Men wearing Ear-rings: it was for both men and women, was stopped for men and children.

2.3.1.2.4. An Assessment of Portuguese Mission

i. St. Thomas Christianity as one among many religions was almost isolated.
ii. Church and people were latinized.
iii. Socially marginalized.
iv. The Synod of Diamper remained a great dispute.
v. Church parochialism put into practice.[105]
vi. The church is seen as an extension of political power, not only spiritual/ religious.
vii. Since force conversion was among lower caste, it became a religion for lower caste.

This Synod is the extension of the policy in which the use of violence was legitimized to search 'colonies' and 'souls', and even Indian Apostolic Church was not left out. To Jesuit, Thomas culture was not only pagans but also dangerous for smooth commerce.[106] Was Thomas Church against of Jesuit? According to H. C. Perumalil & E. R. Hambye, Thomas Christian was simply not agreed to give the apostolic lineage, local customs, and practices. The words of Jawaharlal Nehru are illustrative: "The Gospel of Jesus, the gentle but relentless rebel against untruth and injustice, could so easily be made a tool of imperialism, capitalism and political domination."[107] This was

[105] Paulos Mar Gregorious, *The Indian Orthodox Church–An Overview* (Kottayam: Sophia Publications, 1982), 53.

[106] C.P. Mathew & M. M. Thomas, *The Indian Churches of Saint Thomas* (New Delhi: ISPCK, 1967), 27.

[107] Dick Kooiman, *Conversion and Social Equality in India* (New Delhi: Manohar, 1989), 26.

the beginning of **subalternity** of native Christian. It not only took away the basic right to live and practice religion but also separated them from their own culture, society and social life. Christianity has lost its legitimacy to be a constructive unit within plural India and her *dharmic* tradition.

EWM, mainly Roman Catholic Church gave more emphasis on caste which divided the Church vertically in two groups: Brahmin Church and Dalit Church. The European missionary and colonial ruler were more comfortable high caste for political reason and so Hindu high and Christian high caste enjoyed higher post in Govt. administration as well as in Church.[108] Therefore those lower caste who accepted Christianity to avoid various social discrimination, are now facing the same kind discrimination within Christianity. It was against the high rhetoric of equality what was preached by EW missionaries.[109] Low caste Christians forced to accept: separate inferior seating place-lower chair or on the ground, separate baptism, separate Holy Communion, no common together, no marriage with high caste, often separate cemetery. 'Unwittingly they are considered as a Dalit even after accepting Christianity and thus has proved that the claim of equality in Christianity is untruth and fraud.'[110] In South Indian caste and color of skin plays a role i.e. fairer skin color is high caste and dark skin is Dalit.[111]

2.3.1.3. Protestant Missions

Beginning of 18th century was marked by the presence of Protestant mission,[112] (Bartholomäus Ziegenbalg and Heinrich Plütschau of Halle German Mission came to India in 1706) which was not much different than Jesuits in attitude and persuasive mind over pagan native.[113] Much later William Carey, a Baptist missionary from England arrived at the Eastern part of Indian (Bengal) in British territory in 1793. He, being restricted by the East India Company fear of losing commerce due to evangelism, was devoted to bringing social welfare through printing press, education, translation of Bible (nearly 40 Indian languages) and also published Hindu scriptures[114] and standardized many local

---

[108] Robinson, 2003, 48.

[109] Amaladass, 1997, 23.

[110] Indian Bibliographic Centre, 1999, 84.

[111] Hardgrave, 1969, 91.

[112] Julius Richter, *A History of Missions in India* (Edinburgh: Oliphant Anderson & Ferrier, 1908), 103.

[113] Hugald Grafé, *The History of Christianity in Tamilnadu, History of Christianity in India*, Vol. 4, Part. 2 (Bangalore: Church History Association of India, 1982), 188.

[114] J.T.K. Daniel and R.E. Hedlund, *Carey's Obligation and India's Renaissance* (Serampore: Council of Serampore College, 1993).

languages. He is known as the Father of Modern Mission, not only in India but also in the whole of Asia.

The colonial Church stood as a symbol of superiority and segregated new converts from India culturally and spiritually. It was a European import to India; for example, in Tamilnadu as German Lutheran, in Bengal as English Baptist and Church of England, in Punjab as American Presbyterian, in Meghalaya and Mizoram as Wesleyan Presbyterian, In Northern India as American Methodist, in North-East India as American Baptist, in Andhra as Salvation Army, Quaker etc. Each one created a new island in own image. European enforced their attire over native Christians and this change was a mark for victory and civilization. To Raja Rammohan Roy (1772/74-1833), such an act was a mark of encroachment over the rights of poor...and cannot to be viewed in the eye of God or justifiable to the public[115] and to V. Chakkarai (1880-1958), it was foreign intrusion over native religion and culture.[116]

At the end of the 19th century, a binary distinction of European-Christianity verses Indian-Hindus has become a social reality. Therefore new converts were naturally moved away from Indian culture as the product of bipartisan policy.[117] The British educational policy, unfortunately, was the part of religious imperialism as Claudius Buchanan, a missionary in India and spokesperson said:

> The missionaries asserted that since God laid upon Britain the solemn duty of evangelizing India, the Government should not hesitate to throw its weight into the struggle. They demanded above all open Government patronage of Christian education and vigorous warfare upon the abuses associated with the Hindu religion.[118]

Even highly regarded Alexander Duff, Scottish missionary stated that Hinduism spread like a dark universe where all life dies and death lives.[119]

---

[115] T.V. Philip, "Christianity in India during Western Colonisation: Conflict, Reconciliation or Adjustment" in *ICHR*, Vol. XXI, No. 1 June (1987): 16.

[116] Jacob S. Dharmaraj, *Colonialism and Christian Mission: Post Colonial Reflection* (New Delhi: ISPCK, 1993), 13.

[117] Arthur Mayhew, *Christianity and the Government of India* (Delhi: Gyan Publishing House, 1988), 27.

[118] T. C. Joseph "The Myth of the Colonial Connection" in *The Sunday Statesman*, September 20 (1987): 4.

[119] T. V. Philip, "Christianity in India during Western Colonisation: Conflict, Reconciliation or Adjustment" in *ICHR*, Vol. XXI, No. 1 June (1987): 20.

Largely, it was a sense of superiority[120] and hopes to bring all Indian people under Christianity and to be loyal to the British.[121]

2.3.2. Cultural Narrative and Christian Mission in India: Problems & Prospects

Let me bring out the landscape of the church's relationship with Indian culture to analyze the imperatives for re-culturation. The EWMM and socio-cultural paradigm of India are contradictory. The European cultural norms as superior in comparison to Indian is a presupposition which is still a reality in the West and many mission agencies that are remotely controlled from the West (through financial aids and ideological liability) to implement Western (cultural) Christianity through rigorous proselytization. This undoubtedly has accelerated conflict in a religio-political scenario in India from the last quarter of the 19th century (*Arya Samaj*) until today. Many Hindu organizations like *Hindu Maha Sabha*, RSS, VHP, and political party like *BJP*, *Siva Sena* have taken a serious note of westernization through Christianization as a cultural threat. As a result, Hindu-Christian relation has experienced a new low since 2014. As many as eight states have already passed the Anti-conversion Bill to combat the conversion oriented mission activities. More recently in 2014-2016 under BJP rule, the campaign of *Ghar Wapsi* (Home Coming) is on rising to bring back Christians and Muslims into Hindu fold. The Gandhian secularism and Nehruvian socialism ideology are, socio-politically, encountering the cultural nationalist groups even though many from the liberal group also believe that Christian mission has an anti-Hindu-Indian religio-cultural agenda. Christian community, practically, is losing the ground support, because of the 'perception' war.

The church is also facing a legal battle when the Supreme Court asked to clarify the stand of Church on caste system within Christians. It is the same caste system against which Church pulled up Hindu religion as discriminatory and advocated Christianity to offer social justice and equality. Church, in post-independent India, argued retracting from the old colonial position and stated it as a social problem, going beyond Hinduism.[122] The argument confuses the stand of Fr. Francis Xavier for low caste and Robert de Nobili for high caste. Indian Church uses caste as Hindu religious system of injustice to present the gospel and argue in civil court as a social issue.

---

[120] Poikail John George, "Racist Assumptions of 19th Century Missionary Movement" in *IRM*, Vol. LIX, No. 235, July (1970): 271-283.

[121] Jacob S. Dharmaraj, "A Brief Review of Alexander Duff, English Education and Colonial Connections in 19th Century India" in *ICHR*, Vol. XXV. No. 2 December (1991): 82-83.

[122] 'Do Christians also practice caste system? Asked by the Supreme Court', Chief Justice of the Supreme Court, K.G. Balakrishnan, *Times of India* (Delhi Edition) 20th July, 2007.

The contemporary mission (be discussed later) has divided into two groups: the mainline Churches like CSI, CNI, Methodist, Baptist, Lutheran or Mar Thoma, etc., have minimized evangelical work (preaching Gospel to other faiths); and Pentecostal, Charismatic, Presbyterian etc., along with many Para-Church organizations like GFA, FMPB, EFI, ECI etc., set priority to preach Gospel mainly among Hindus and tribes. Mainline Churches are in the direction to reduce socio-religious conflict; whereas the second group is a kind of Zionist not only to preach Gospel, but also condemn Hinduism with colonial language.

The larger issue raised here indicates an ongoing interplay between religious truth claims and its cultural expressions. Recently USA, South Korea, and many others are sponsoring the charismatic groups who are trying to re-establish Western hegemony through faith, stating Indian culture is nothing less than Hindu culture. This is why; B.R. Ambedkar pointed out (from freedom struggle context) that follower of foreign religions as semi-national. It is an extreme comment but justified in some way when Church prevented native Christians to join freedom movement as anti-Church/British.

A search through a radical introspective analysis for a cultural interpretation is the primary retrospective task of re-culturation which may offer to gain a cultural identity for North India Christians as a postcolonial quest and self-determination.

2.3.2.1. EWMM and Some Indian Christian Thoughts

Indian Christian leaders like A. J. Appasamy, M. M. Thomas, Subba Rao, Sadhu Sundar Singh of the 20th century, opposed to the Western mission policy as monoculturalism, intolerance to plurality, unqualified judgmental to other faiths and culture. This was the time when Christianity as foreign (Western) religion was an established social reality.[123]

It is the fact that Indian Christian hermeneutics/theology was pioneered by a Hindu reformist (Raja Rammohan Roy) and they are very much part of Indian theological education, church, and life. The Dalit Christian leaders named it as the Brahmanical theology and anti-Dalit. Roy proved a point that native Christian did not enjoy religious freedom during the colonial period. The question being asked, how the Gospel-culture relation may help to emerge an Indian hermeneutics from within.[124] Some pertinent theological views of Raimundo Panikkar, Christopher Duraisingh, A. P. Nirmal, P. Chenchiah, H.A. Krishna Pillai, Aloysius Pieris (Sri Lanka), K. P. Aleaz and others have contributed to resolving this issue. Christopher Duraisingh has demonstrated

---

[123] C.B. Firth, *An Introduction to India Church History* (New Delhi: ISCPK, 1998), 111.

[124] J. R. Chandran, "Christianity and World Religions-The Ecumenical Discussion" in *The Indian Journal of Theology*, Vol. 30, No. 3&4, (July-Dec. 1981): 186-203.

that 'terms like localization, indigenization or contextualization imply the following misconceptions: the gospel is external and alien to us...there is a dichotomy between message and context, but we should note that Indian Christian consciousness is co-constituted by the Judaeo-Christian tradition and elements of our pan-Indian heritage through their continuous confluence; we are Indian hyphenated Christians.'[125] According to A. P. Nirmal, 'indigenization' is a contradiction in terms because it is an artificial attempt to make indigenous that which is not indigenous...Theologically, it is also branding God as a foreigner to our country and culture. What we need is to interpret the indigenous God in our indigenous history in its religious, cultural, philosophical and socio political aspects in order to arrive at an indigenous theology...[126]

P. Chenchiah demonstrated the possibility of the new emerging in the meanings of the gospel, for what the living forces of Hinduism and other religions are able to provide a positive key that can explore a new dimension of Jesus with a richness which would pan Indian. He also said that it is not necessary to give up one's own religion, culture, and country to accept Jesus.[127] The thought of H. A. Krishna Pillai was to bring a new functional meaning of Jesus going beyond the atonement theories, and the meaning of Gospel truth should not play the role of juridical justification, but to release a fresh life for the humanity.[128]

Christian leaders like Kaj Baago to whom, indigenization is nothing but going away from Western Christianity to another religion and culture with Christ alone.[129] Paul Gregorios, quite contrary, stated that 'indigenization' means putting a local culture on Christian faith, and question to the supporters of Indianness that if one can understand Western medicine, philosophy, technology then why not Christian faith too.[130] He may be right as an academic

---

[125] Christopher Duraisingh, "Indian Hyphenated Christians and Theological Reflection" in Part I A New Expression of Identity" in *Religion and Society*, Vol. XXVII, No. 2 (June, 1980): 80-101.

[126] Arvind P. Nirmal, Some Theological Issues connected with Inter-Faith Dialogue and their Implications for Theological Education in India" in *Bangalore Theological Forum*, Vol. XII, No. 2 (June-Dec, 1980): 107-129.

[127] P. Chenchiah, "The Church and Indian Christian", *Rethinking Christianity in India*, ed., V.G. Job (Madras: A. N. Sundarisanam, 1938), 81-100.

[128] D.D. Hudson, "Hindu and Christian Theological Parallels in the Conversion of H.A. Krishna Pillai 1857-1859" in *The Journal of American Academy of Religion*, Vol. 40 (June, 1972): 196-205.

[129] Kaj Baago, *Pioneers of Indigenous Christianity* (Madres/Bangalore: CIS/CISRS, 1969).

[130] Paul Gregorios, "Not Gospel and Culture" in *The Star of the East*, Vol. XI, No. 1-2 (March-June:1989): 24-26.

possibility, but he, surely, didn't count the behavioral aspects of mass people, the culture of the land.

M.M Thomas focused on a Christ-centered syncretism which means, Christians are open to interpretation at cultural and religious levels with Jesus Christ as the principle.[131] It is, to him, an open idea of Indian secularism within a Christ-centered non-communal fellowship. M.M. Thomas said that Church-centered Christian community behaves like communal since it is isolated from society. Aloysius Pieris, a Roman Catholic theologian from Sri Lanka, has pointed out that 'Christian religion minus European culture' into an 'Asian culture minus non-Christian religion' that is an impossibility. In Asia what is needed, is not just re-culturation but 'enreligionization' of the Church.[132] Raimundo Panikkar also has seen that cultural incursions have religious consequences... the need of today is for inculturation, not inter-culturation.[133]

A theologian like K.P. Aleaz advocated that the Advaita Vedanta which has the enduring influence on the cultural life of India that enables to bring diverse units like races, religions, and cultures together socially and politically, stands for unity and universality in the midst of diversities and it can function as a symbol of Indian composite culture.[134] Indian religious culture is not external to the secular; it is the inherent potency of the secular, therefore, there is a secular-sacred continuum which reveals the relationship between the gods and the humans from the inception of Indian civilization.[135]

Acculturation cannot be the enforcement but it required to bring an atmosphere where two cultures will interact within a system of natural synthesis, not the way EWMM wanted to do so in India and elsewhere. It is a fact that EWMM for great extendable to infuse that westernized Christianity as pure Christianity, and Indianness is seen as something unwanted. Therefore, the official standpoint of the Churches is not encouraging the natural manifestation of the gospel from within Indian culture which is composite and comprehensive.

---

[131] M. M. Thomas, "Christ-Centred Syncretism" in *Religion and Society*, Vol. XXVI, No. 1 (March: 1979): 26-35.

[132] Aloysius Pieris, "Non-Christian Religions and Cultures in Third World Theology" in *Vidyajyoti*, Vol. 46 (1982): 158-170.

[133] Kuncheria Pathil, ed., *Religious Pluralism: An Indian Christian Perspective* (New Delhi: ISPCK, 1991), 120.

[134] S.J. Samartha, *One Christ-Many Religions: Toward a Revised Christology* (Bangalore: SATHRI, 1992), 124.

[135] B. K. Rayburman, "Structure of the Sacred Ritual Terracottas" in *Man in India*, Vol. 54, No. 1, (1974): 85-89.

2.3.2.2. EWMM and Indigenous Movements

The issue of Indigenous Christian movement in India is perceptively a struggle for searching identity. The consciousness or regency of such quest has few dimensions: bipartisan of West and native believers and low status of the native in Church during colonial era; forceful cultural replacement policy; the rise of national spirit after enlightenment and the Sepoy Mutiny (1857); Western control of many present Churches, continuous religio-cultural conflict, etc. Indigenous movements are divided into many categories like adopting Hindu culture; redefining own traditional cultures within broader Hinduism like OBCs and Dalits; tribal culture etc. There are many types of research to redefine communitarian cultural traditions, many of them, thus far, are loosely identified as Hindu culture and others are not. For example, Dr. James Massey argued that '*Chaura*' as a Dalit Hindu community in Punjab has its distinctive culture outside Hinduism.[136] These are a huge uphill task for re-culturation since many social and political movements are fighting for own identity and many of them are accepted by the Civil Govt. With the rapid change of social demography, Christian mission and identity quest face new challenges which are complex in nature and content.

The first portrayal of Euro-Western centric mission may appear a bit too much critical, even though, this is what has caused the identity crisis. Counter-movements to EWMM mission, there emerged some indigenous movements, individually or organized manner including few Western missionaries took part in it. First of this kind was initiated by Keshab Chandra Sen (1838-1884, leader of Brahma Samaj[137]) in Bengal, presented Jesus as the socio-cultural symbol, not as the Lord of Christianity, emerging from Hindu spirituality.[138] In West India, a poet, Brahmin, new convert, Narayan Vaman Tilak (1862?-1919) objected baptism ritual and doctrine as anti-social which disconnects one from his/her parental heritage and introduced local form spirituality to communicate Jesus. To him, cultural heritage is the best preparation of Christian conversion. In South India, Sattam Pillai (1823-1918) is known as the founder of first Indigenous (Tamilnadu) Church namely *Hindu Church of Lord Jesus* (1858), completely rejecting Western domination (administratively and culturally, first ever in Indian subcontinent), used a new contextual, cultural, social and

---

[136] James Massey, "Christianity and Culture: Their Relationship in 19th and 20th Centuries in Punjab" in *Religion and Society*, (December 1989): 18-32.

[137] Bramha Samaj: It is the first registered society in 1828, initiated by Raja Rammohan Roy. It had the separate law differed to Hindu law, and by that logic, critically it can be said not to be a Hindu society. But how to say Rabindranath Tagore, who was a samajist, was not Hindu. It was a rationalist religious movement based on AdvaitaVedantic monotheism, against of puranic popular Hinduism. BS is considered as the pioneer of Indian renaissance. Sen was most influenced leader next to Roy.

[138] David C. Scott, ed., *Keshub Chunder Sen* (Madres: CLS, 1979), 63.

religious hermeneutics to interpret Bible and adopted new rituals, customs for believers as well as in Church which had as many as 6000 members. After his death, Western Church domination again overpowered this movement. Today, re-culturation in CSI and other Tamil Churches are following the Pillai's footsteps in some form or other.

In North India, Sadhu Sundar Singh (1889-1929) is known as the indigenous epitome of Indian Christian. He did not adopt Indian culture like of Bede Griffiths or Swami Abhishiktananda, but continued Indian cultural way to follow Jesus. He might be the most influential and accepted Christian cutting across denominational limitation. In South India, his model is now an emerging reality,[139] namely Laymen's Evangelical Fellowship. His famous saying is, 'The water of life in an Indian cup.' He also left the institutional Church. In Eastern India, Brahmabandhav Upadhyaya (1861-1907) initiated the ashram movement, and later Rajendra Chandra Das (1887-1976) established an ashram in Varanasi and worked there for 47 years as viable as an antidote to westernized Church which, to him, distorted Gospels.[140] This movement got momentum in the middle of the 20th century, and now there are as many as 120 Christian ashrams across India. I would like to use a prayer written Rabindranath Tagore on Christmas Day, and it is used by E. Stanley Jones (one of the pioneers of Indianization and Ashram movements, Sattal Christian Ashram) in his book '*The Christ in Indian Road*,

> "Great-souled Christ, on this the blessed day of your birth, we who are not Christians bow before you. We love and worship you, we non-Christians, for with Asia you are bound with the ties of blood... There is no room for thee there in Europe. Come, Lord Christ, come away! Take your stand in Asia-the land of Buddha, Kabir and Nanak. At the sight of you, our sorrow-laden hearts will be lightened. O Teacher of love, come down into our hearts and teach us to feel the sufferings of others, to serve the leper and the pariah with an all-embracing love."[141]

Very unfortunately, institutionalized Church defied the voice of India, by separating the 'that time FGCs' from mainline societal ambit and kept like a convict within a strict rule. Church has produced a lot of Christian in the cost

---

[139] Werner Hoerschelmann, *Christliche Gurus: Darstellung von Selbstverständnis und Funktionindigenen Christseinsdurch unabhängige, charismatischge führte Gruppen in Südindien* (Frankfurt: Peter Lang, 1977), 124.

[140] H. L. Richard & R. C. Das, *Evangelical Prophet for Contextual Christianity* (Delhi: ISPCK, 1995), 100.

[141] E. Stanley Jones, *The Christ of the Indian Road* (New York: The Abingdon Press, 1925), 115-116.

of erasing Indianness from them. Keeping such history in mind re-hearing 'people's voice' is a contextual necessity for re-culturation of native Christian.

2.3.2.3. Insider Movement

People who live in their own religio-cultural tradition but accept Jesus and his Gospels as the spiritual guide often do not take baptism or neither join institutional Church are known as Insider Movement in India. This movement, even though, is highly criticized by mainstream Churches for its syncretic form, is gaining missiological attention in India. Herbert E. Hoefer,[142] in his book "*Churchless Christianity* (1991)" named them as '*Jesu Bhakta* – a devotee of Jesus' estimated to have 160000 followers within Hindu fold. It can be understood as the adoption of the pluralistic *dharmic* model which, in some way, has a provision of taking Jesus as deity yet remain as Hindu socially.[143] It is also known as Crypto Christian. History of this movement goes back to 1930s and it is another way of dealing with the cultural issue and also a counter product of the westernized Church.

It is interesting to notice that most of the indigenous movements are initiated by the new converts. This movement has been addressing issues like family counseling, social relationship, marriage, childbirth, burial, etc. in order to find a solution faced by FGC. Inspired by the indigenous movements and its practical success, many organizations, very recently, are attempting to carry out much localized movements, like **Maharashtra Village Ministries** (1981), is a product of the student body of Union Biblical Seminary, Pune, is now having 85 missionaries and 24 congregations and their main motto to plant Church on localized pattern, even if they are associated with CNI, Lutheran and other denominations.

2.3.2.4. Ashram Movement

The Ashram is another viable model taken for indigenization in India from the late 19th century. Even though Ashrams are mainly run by Catholics, but largely it keeps the Indian religio-cultural framework both practically and denominationally. Some famous Ashrams are *Christukula Ashram* in 1921, *Sattal Christian Ashram* in 1930, *Saccidananda/Shantivanam Ashram* in 1938, *Kurisumala Ashram* in 1958. They are inspired by Brahmabandhav Upadhyaya's ashram movement in the late 19th century. The ashram is not a monastery, it is a simple spiritual center, preferably vegetarian, run by a spiritual guru, not a pastor. This movement got prominence among Christian

---

[142] Herbert E. Hoefer is known as the founder of 'Insider Movement' in India.

[143] Kelvin Higgins, "The Key to Insider Movements: The Devotee's of Acts" in *International Journal of Foreign Mission,* 21:4 (Winter 2004): 156.

not as an alternative, but just another expression. It is yet to explore its full potentiality.[144]

2.3.2.5. Tribes and Indigenization

Tribes with their 8.6% population with 461(other statistics show 645 groups) distinct groups living in India[145] have been playing a significant role in Indian history. They are categorized into various regions and ethnic root and some groups are nomads in the Ladakh region and central India.[146] There is a radical change in tribal life and culture due to British rule, conversion to Christianity and Hinduism, social-modernization and democracy. Presently we notice a triangular complexity: i. Hindu-influenced tribes, Christian influenced tribes and primal practiced tribes. Many tribes are looking to overcome Christian and Hindu influences on them by reviving like folk dance, cultural festivals, songs, music, dress code, customary laws, etc. In North-Eastern India, Baptist Church in Nagaland, Presbyterian and Baptist Church in Mizoram and Meghalaya and in Central India, Lutheran, Methodist, Catholic, and also Pentecostal Church are advocating and theologizing cultural re-construction among tribal Christians. The Sachar Committee (Govt. of India) report reveals that one-third (1/3) of the Christians in India belonged to the notified Scheduled Caste or Tribes of the Constitution.[147] Largely search for tribal identity within a broader political landscape or in Church is on the process. New generation Christians are accommodating modern life within the ambit of cultural revival, be it religious, cultural, commerce, etc. Tribal re-culturation is comparably easier since they do not face a religious opponent like Hindu tradition within Church.

2.3.2.6. Challenges of Indigenization

i. Euro-Western tradition on which Indian Christianity is functioning for centuries; today to bring changes is a challenge, even though many Indian Churches use a good number of indigenous songs and musical instruments.
ii. **Posturing**: The posture in worship is another challenge to overcome. Church, basically, follows sitting arrangement on chairs, prayer on the knee, shaking hands or kissing as greetings, use shoes inside the church, pulpit, her preaching style, etc. The colonized Churches are reluctant to bring any radical change, but the post-colonial Churches and new

---

144 Eddy Asirvatham, *Christianity in the Indian Crucible* (Calcutta: YMCA Publishing House, 1955), 64-92.

145 S.J. John Mundu, 'Tribals in Transition: Upward or Downward Movement?' in *Sevartham*, Vol. 36 (2011): 7.

146 Cyril Hans, 'The Adivasis of Jharkhand: Contemporary Issues and Responses' in *Sevartham*, Vol. 36 (2011): 35.

147 http://en.wikipedia.org/wiki/Scheduled_Castes_and_Scheduled_Tribes (10.05.2016).

movements are introducing an indigenous form of Christian worship and life. Their posturing is culturally Indian, not exclusively Hindu.

iii. **Language and Preaching**: Language used is either outdated or unfamiliar to people. Colonial translation of literature, liturgy, preaching, songs, etc., was dictionary based transliteration, not a proper expression of language. Example, the local word used for 'Breaking the Word' is the same as breaking a hard object by a hammer. Contemporary indigenous thinkers like Dayanand Bharti said that hardly any common Indian can understand what the meaning of Church language is.[148] In North Indian use of Urdu (not Hindi) is still understood as a good expression which sends a negative notion to common people or FGC is taught to learn Urdu as Christian language in North India. Church has hesitation to promote the Hindi language to express the Gospel to people.

iv. **Other Challenges**: To overcome the interconnectedness of Indian cultural diversity to Christianity, a careful study is needed. Struggle to find the better alternative indigenous model to change the deep-rooted westernized traditions, to study the complex linguistic and cultural diversities, aspiration of each ethnolinguistic community require systematic planning, friendly atmosphere, denominational collaboration, etc. More authentic publications are needed to communicate the rationale for the change to common people. And another area to be dealt with is Global Christian electronic Media which is propagating westernized Christianity around the world and it has also revived some old colonial history and creating a negative perception about Christianity.

2.4. First Generation Christian (FGC): Some Case Studies to Analyze Contemporary Context

2.4.1. Case Study No. I

Subrata Chakrabarty:[149] A Jajaman-Brahmin (Hereditary profession priest) he is FGC, converted in 1992 and became an evangelist. He was deeply convinced by the teachings of a para-church which taught him: the Bible is the only divine scripture and all Hindu scriptures are false, gods-goddesses are human-made and the devil, so they must be thrown out of the home and he must separate himself from all festivals. He did the same with his parental Hindu family. Reacting to his new religious stand on his parental faith, he was separated from family and society. Only people he used to meet are few Christians for two hours on Sunday, nearly 125 km away from home. Later

---

[148] Dayanand Bharti, *Living Water and Indian Bowl* (Delhi: ISPCK, 2004), 70-71.

[149] He is new Brahmin converts. Family profession was to conduct regular house worship (puja). He is from Midnapur, West Bengal, researcher worked with him for one year (1994-95) at Raina village of Burdwan Dist., West Bengal, India, as an evangelist.

he was shifted in distance land for missionary work. When I met him in 1994 (after 10 years of his conversion), he used to cry utterly and wished to meet his parents, brothers/sisters, friends and wanted to go his village where he grew up. The situation appeared to be difficult for him to reconcile. My advice was to tell sorry to parents and seek forgiveness from them. Such advice has raised suspicions in the mind mission leaders and suspected to my faith commitment and conversion. His mind was oozing beyond faith: longing to meet own people, his mother, father and many others who were once close to him. A cry 'unheard' shows the deep-rooted crisis in colonial Christian mind which seriously lacks human value and compassion of Jesus.

2.4.2. Case Study No. II

Researcher's Own Life:[150] From the beginning of my conversion, I hardly accepted anything without questioning and did not allow Church leaders to interference into my personal or family matter beyond a limit. First conflict (1990, before baptism) occurred when I opposed going only one Church and rejected to accept denominational Christianity. To me, all churches are spiritually and religiously mine, even though doctrinally and administratively different. I inherited it from my parental faith which, to my best sense, offers me a better socio-spiritual space and teaching.

As a result, I was out of Church (not taking membership) for 17 years. Second conflict (1994): on my father's sudden death, on that very day, no Church leader visited my house, fear of facing religious argument on funeral rite, but on my return to mission office (I was an official evangelist), I was asked to clarify whether I took part in my father's funeral rites or not. This inquiry appeared as the prime for Christian leaders over the death of my father. The question here is; how the compassion and love of Jesus for people can be replaced by religious brutality (Numbers15.32-36). Interestingly, it was my mother stood with me and being the first son still alive, my younger brother did the necessary religious funeral duty.

Third Conflict (1994) in relation to my father's funeral, knowing that I didn't take part in Hindu funeral rituals; they started using me as 'Faith Mascot' to raise fund in South India. I was forced to share this particular testimony of how God helped me to stand by the biblical faith in the time of my father's Hindu funeral. On refusal to sell my departed father's funeral rite to raise fund, I was officially punished, rebuked, shamed in public, and marked as non-committed Christian. Since I kept a cordial relationship with my family and previous faith community, in Christian circle I am known a half-Christian,

---

[150] Research is the first son of liberal educated Hindu family (West Bengal, India) and is only and first convert. He worked as an evangelist 1990-2012 and as a faculty in Seminary since 2002.

and projected me as a negative image. Being an FGC, I live in a paradoxical world: i. my ancestral society knows I have left their faith and culture and, ii. for many Christians, I am still half-Hindu. Sadly, the Church has no solution to this crisis.

2.4.3. Case Study No. III

A Lady of 70 years:[151] Bengali women including many Muslim and some Christians use a white bangle and *sindur* as a sign of marriage. These are a very emotional, religious and cultural symbol for a married woman. This lady at the age of 70 accepted Jesus and baptized in Kolkata in 1993. After baptism service, at the office room, a few leaders taught to hold her and broke her white bangle by force. That was an utter shock to her, unbelievable happening, psychological trauma, she cried out loud and pleaded them to stop, but her plea failed to reach to a spiritually deaf ear. She collapsed unconscious and later decided not to follow Christianity anymore. The breaking of the white bangle is the sign husband's death. This symbol is her pride, identity of being married, emotional aspect of life, social credibility and wishes for her husband's long life.

Of course, it looks like a very emotive one-sided non-academic presentation. In great extent, it may be true, but at the same time, it tells a story that gives us profound logic why re-culturation is so urgent for Indian Christianity and it also indicates how wrongly colonial mission understood Indian culture, even in the 21st century and the picture does not change much. This kind of conversion is actually proselytization. Since re-culturation cannot be limited to mere academic, this research will incorporate a few other 'fact-finding' case studies to bring its empirical weight. There are many untold stories that will rationalize the need for re-culturation. Accepting Jesus in India (also elsewhere) impacts every aspect of life: individual, family, social, political, cultural and what not, and through such Church-mission surveillance on FGC; reconstruct a new culture is a challenge.

The cultural questions in the mind of FGC that are rising from above Case Studies:

i. Why do I need to leave my society?
ii. Why do I need to eat beef/pork to prove new faith?
iii. Why am I separated or advised to separate from my parental society?
iv. Why do I visit only one Church, not other Churches? Do they not worship Jesus?
v. Why shall I be buried instead of cremation?
vi. Why do I not to join in social festivals, feasts, ceremonies, etc?

---

[151] A lady of 70 yrs., near Diamond Harbors, South 24 Parganas, West Bengal, never went to school, lives in a remote village, accepted Jesus along with her husband in 1993.

2.5. Re-culturation and the Church in India: The Challenges and Possibilities

The basic Christian tenet of God becoming Human in a particular time and culture, and that very God through Christianity, therefore, eventually appeared to be the praxis of developing a universal faith-based culture during the colonial period. This very notion needs to be revisited. Culture is a humanizing process[152] and human nature is evolved around a particular culture or cultures. The revelation of the Bible cannot be taken without a particular cultural framework. The Gospel of Christ constantly renews the life and the culture, so the culture-specific autonomy must be considered as a format of Gospel for a believer.[153] The history of EMM in India, for some reasons, ignored this logic.

The Greco-Roman history, the elitist philosophical dimension used to divide the world into the civilized and the barbarian and later westernized Church did the same as a policy by implementing the concept of Christendom' as monoculturalism. The romanized monoculturalism prevailed in the European Church that has planted the seed of cultural conflict in India. Such ideology was the obstacle in engaging cultural dialogue in India. Therefore, re-culturation is not an external adjustment of what Robert de Nobili did, but a continuous process of evolution.

We need to allow a particular culture to enrich the Gospel, may it be a family value, literature, art, architecture, philosophy, *saṁskāras* or plurality. The colonial Church observed Indian plurality as a matter of utter confusion and chaos because Europe after Christianization did not experience religious plurality. Only recently, Europe has been experiencing a limited plurality. Indian reality is viable enough to contribute the hermeneutical aspects to interpret and construct a Christian culture for native followers. The denial of religious *swaraj* (freedom) is another challenge before North Indian Christian to overcome their subalternity.

Jesus, in Indian cultural expression, can be the icon of 'Dharma', if it is not confused with 'religion', and therefore, Indian re-culturation from within Indian hermeneutical context would be feasible. This is what *Swaraj* is expected to, but, it is yet to happen as the main characteristic of North Indian Christian.[154] Other factors that hinder the re-culturation process are traditions of nearly 450 years of EWC which is reluctant or hesitant to inherit Indian cultural aspects within Church. There is a prevailing perception that Indian culture is same as Hindu culture. This perception is one of the challenges. Another hurdle comes from Hindu cultural nationalist groups that are to

---

[152] A. Thazhath, *The Quest for Identity* (Trichur: TIT Publications, 1992), 38-43.

[153] Paul M. Collins & Paul Pulikkan, *The Church and Culture in India, Re-culturation: Theory and Praxis* (Delhi: Cambridge Press, 2010), 2.

[154] Badrinath Chaturvedi, *Finding Jesus in Dharma* (Delhi: ISPCK, 2004), 1.

generalize the whole Christian Mission as something anti-India/Hindu. A negative perception has further strengthened in the mind of the majority that leads to suspect every act of Church/Christian. Hindu-specific mission activity has galvanized this idea at great extent.

Therefore, sustainable re-culturation is a long process and various internal and external forums are to be explored to implement new cultural aspects.

When we speak of liturgical re-culturation or liturgical adoption, we have to remember two different realities such as 'faith and culture' or 'religion and culture'. Even though we may differentiate its meaning but in its essence, it is very difficult to separate them. As an expression of faith, one celebrates the liturgy and participates into it, but indeed that celebration has to take place in a particular cultural context. Therefore, we can say that both are interconnected with each other. Re-culturation or liturgical adoption does not mean introducing the Hindu religious practices in our Christian liturgies rather we need to have a clear idea regarding it and that are related to it. Primarily we need to understand Culture, which is the essence of a human community, based on habits, characters, custom, behaviors, and way of life of the people and when we speak of liturgical re-culturation or adoption in this regard certain important and different terms should be clarified to understand it.

2.6. Issue of Subalternity

There are many reasons to state the subalternity of North Indian Christians. In this thesis, subalternity is not used in the literal sense, but word is to communicate the status of North Indian Christian as subordinate to the colonial people. Within Church, Christian was divided into the category of ruled and ruling. Native Christian was treated as the property of the colonial church. The following are the areas that will explain the subaltern status of colonized Christian in North India.

i. *Subalternity and Church Seating Arrangement*: Most of the colonial Church's seating arrangement was divided on the basis of European and native. Prime seat, front, balcony, etc were reserved for European and that too was divided according to the rank and files of officials. Indians supposed to seat far end on a long bench or in many cases on the floor. End of service most of Indians had no right to hand-shake with Europeans.

ii. *Subalternity of Salary System*: One issue that shows subalternity is the salary of the priest. K. M. Banerjee, first Indian clergy in Anglican Church in Kolkata faced discrimination. The question of low salary of native clergy in comparison to British/European. Within a year, he resigned as a priest on this issue. Natives were not counted equal to European even they were Christian by faith.

iii. *Subalternity and Structure of Resident*: If we see the construction of residential quarters for native and European, we notice the subalternity. In Church campus where quarters for the colonial priest was 7000-10000 sq. ft, for an Indian not more than 1000-1500 sq. ft. It shows that native Indian Christians after being Christian forced to live a life subordinate to colonial people.
iv. Native Christian leaders are taught to wear neck-tie, covered shoes to show the civilized manner of Europe. They had no choice to used Indian religious dress, color, adopt native symbols on the dress. By using such un-match dress code they actually distanced themselves from others. The dress is cultural and on many occasions of life those cultural symbols are must but native converts were forced to use what was against their own tradition.
v. Most of the converts during the colonial period were taken out of home for two reasons: i. after conversion family separated them and ii. Mission policy was to bring them in one particular place (colony) away from home. This system has completely separated their local root, relatives, etc. They were trained into a new culture under the European priest. Till today such campus Christian is witnessing in India.
vi. Natives were not permitted to talk and mingle other faith people. They supposed not to joint marriage, festival or any social occasion. Imposing such laws on them, after a few decades they are actually entered into a new cultural system which neither European nor India.
vii. Food is another colonial imposition on native converts. It is a policy to fed cow meat for a single reason: a convert would not be able to go back to his/her parental family/faith since cow meat is strictly prohibited to Hindu community.

Seeing these facts, we are arguing North Indian subalternity from such life situation. Subalternity is a state of subjugation into which an individual has no right to decide for his/her. During the colonial period, North Indian Christian (even others) had no choice of their own. They were made Christian in the cost leaving behind their own heritage and culture.

Conclusion

I conclude with a statement of Dietrich Bonhoeffer, "There is a one great country that I should like to visit, to see whether it may be from there that the great solution is to come, and that is India; for otherwise all seems to be over, and the great dying of Christianity to be at hand...Who is there who still believes them? The invisibility kills us. If we cannot find the presence of Christ in our personal lives, then perhaps we may find it in India."[155] This statement has no axiomatic applicability, yet can provide a possibility that his observation can be taken as a seriously introspective. Above argument helps us to know that a cultural conflict between strict dogmatic institutionalized Christianity and *dharmic* de-centralized tradition of India is on. When India does have antagonized position to Jesus and his Gospels, then socio-cultural conflict rests on a singular difference that is what might be the observation of Bonhoeffer. D. Bharti also said, 'Contextualization is not compromised, nor conforming to the image of the world, but rather allowing the gospel to become incarnate in the existing culture in faithfulness to the Bible.'[156] Re-culturation is not to be seen as a revolt against the Western Church, some fundamental things will remain with Indian Church, but to give an Indian look is the part of religious freedom and expression.

The Indian ethnocultural heterogeneity was interpreted by the EWM as a homogeneous culture which was identified only with **Hinduism**, negating the multi-dimensional plurality of religion, ethnolinguistic traditions, regional rigidity and mobility and also the invisible social structure of Dharma which is responsible to integrate diversity without diluting the difference. Thus, NICs [also IC] was separated from the Hindu culture and eventually disintegrated from Indian culture and came under direct control of the colonial culture and the authority of Church and the 'freedom of choice' of religious life being Indian Christian was determined by the EWM; hence, they became culturally subaltern to the colonial culture.

Open Question for Further Debate

i. How the Thomas Christian, being rooted in Jerusalem, was able to internalize the Indian plural context?
ii. Why the EWM failed to acknowledge the Thomas tradition or Indian culture?
iii. How to defend the inter-connectedness of the colonial-commercial-religious model could be the viable religious model for Indian people?
iv. To what extent the plural Indian culture may help the process of re-culturation in India today?

[155] K.V. Paul Pillai, *India's Search for the Unknown Christ* (New Delhi: Fraz Publishers, 1978), 17.

[156] Dayananda Bharti, *Living Water and Indian Bowl* (Delhi: ISCPK, 2004), 76.

Chapter 3

The Methodological Consideration

Introduction

A methodological approach to this research would consider the 'Post-Colonial Subaltern' method to investigate and analyze the issues related to the title. There are two terms, 'Post-colonial' and 'Subaltern' which would provide the fundamentals methodological insights to enter into the research argument. The 'Post-colonial' theory is generally a quest for self-identity, primarily has been seen as a socio-political-cultural movement in entire colonized countries after WW-I. Within colonized India, the Christian community was also colonized by EW Church: religiously and culturally.[157] The political and religious nexus in colonial setting was a policy-matter therefore; Indian Christians were also colonized to achieve a common goal which often used Christianity as a tool to strengthen the colonial rule. Hence, it is to investigate the status of Indian Christians and their 'subalternity' in North Indian context.

Post-colonialism is one of the major methodological trends in the present context of India. There are historians like Rajiv Malhotra (*Breaking India*-2011) or Arvind Sharma or RSS ideologues are involved in re-writing the whole Indian history and arguing that whole Indian history was colonized and writing to fulfill the purpose of the colonial rulers. Such re-reading has sharply divided into two major groups: pro-Indian and pro-colonial (liberal). Therefore, in the present context to study historiography of the history of Christianity in India from a post-colonial perspective is a major academic challenge. Though the history of Christianity in India can be traced back to the 1st century, yet any serious study on historiography and its methodology have neglected the past in

[157] Wati Longchar, *Returning to Mother Earth: An Indigenous Perspective* (Kway Jen: PTCA, 2012), 148.

the sense of its application and utility on present Christian life for Indianness of Indian Christian Church. Early colonial writers ignored the Kerala Christian tradition and glorified European Christianity over others and it causes the subalternity of Indian Christians and the social life of native Christian was subjugated and their religious right was taken away after conversion. They were overpowered and governed the community. Questioning to the colonial authority for self-reliance was a pending North Indian Christian quest, mainly socio-cultural life. Since the early 20th-century anti-colonial historical research was initiated and in recent years (since the 1980s) native historians and scholars have begun to get momentum and social acceptance. It has studied critically the past histories, methodologies, and historiography as a whole and noticed that a re-examination is very much needed in order to understand the native history. It is true that factual history under this methodology may not always be error-free, so merits and debates within Indian scholars are an inevitable and continuous process.[158]

Enforced culture upon North Indian Christian during the colonial rule encounters a serious credibility crisis and faces a huge challenge to hold its infallibility-claim. The Post-colonialism in our research will be applied to re-read the cultural history of North Indian Christians (NIC) and their subalternity. It would consider *Samaj Dharma* (social life and responsibility) as an end goal of NIC of this research and this theory would not only identify the issue related to NIC but also attempt to reconstruct life and culture of NIC as a subaltern quest and it achieve it, 'Space and Place' model would enhance the feasibility of such reconstruction. To argue the practical aspects of this academic work, empirical data are to be used as supplementary to theory.

There has been a growing interest in the area of study on Christian identity-quest in post-colonial era in India to re-construct the cultural nuances (of *saṁskāras*) from within Indian insights.

3.1. Context and Reasoning for Postcolonial Subaltern Methodological

The Indian Church and mission movements in North India (also pan-Indian) are a symbol of colonial occupation alongside to the European rulers. Indian Christians in the pre-independent era (before 1947) was the object of Church and Mission, not allowed to be the subject of Church. Becoming a subject is essential for the self-identity and being an 'object' is opposite to it. According to Roger E. Hedlund (Indian Missiologist), it is a period of distortions of indigenous Indian Christianity.[159] An imported religion, customs, rituals,

[158] Woba James, "Methodological Issues and Historiography of Christianity in the 19th and 20th Centuries with Special Reference to Postcolonial Perspective" in *Journal of Tribal Studies*, Vol. XX, No.1&2, Jan-June & July-Dec (2015): 135.

[159] Roger E. Hedlund, *Quest for Identity: Indian Churches of Indigenous Origin: The "Little Tradition" in Indian Christianity* (Chennai/N. Delhi: MIIS/ISPCK, 2000), 47-63.

conduct of life, etc., are planted with the help of political power and under European Church authority on Indian soil and made people follow without questioning it. And here after the history of post-independent Indian Church is a continuity of EW legacy and history of the West, not of Indian. Hence, the status of subalternity emerged within this given context. A Postcolonial analysis shall be adopted to actualize the purpose and importance of this context to take the further issue of re-culturation and it will try to answer the questions of the validity of such an attempt.

Religion always attempted to play as a pivotal catalyst to re-construct the culture of the people. Both are interrelated and complementary in nature and function. Conflict arises when religion depends on political power to re-construct the culture of people. Expansion of Arab-Islam and European Christianity are proven the historical shreds of evidence. The social subalternity of NIC is to be understood in such a context when their voice was suppressed and minimized into a level to nothing. Post-colonial is, therefore, an attempt/revolt/rejection of their unwanted history and struggle for a new identity. The word 'proselytization', 'subjugation', 'inferior' (for native Christian) will be analyzed from a post-colonial methodology to investigate the motif colonial naming system, conversion, subaltern struggle, and cultural emancipation. We shall try to look into the issues why re-construction (of *saṁskāras*) of Christian is preeminent today.

3.2. Background Studies of Contextual Reasoning and Subalternity

Let us take a cue from two incidents in recent events: visit of Pope John Paul II to India in 1999 and the Centenary of Edinburgh-1910 in 2010. Pope John Paul II wrote on memorial book on his visit to India, 'a culture cannot survive if it attempts to be exclusive' on his visit to Gandhi's samadhisthal (burial site). If such an idea used to be a standing policy of EWM, the world would have a lesser cultural conflict during expansion of European Christianity. Most of the Indian people are in the opinion that his visit will increase the conversion related issue and may revive the historical tension between colonial rule and Christian conversion. Arun Shourie, in his book, "Harvesting Our Souls" (2000), criticized such visit on the ground of religious horse-trading. It is a social perception against Christian mission and even Gandhi also had the same opinion. China opposed the Pope's visit more on the political level, even though the subject is essentially the same.

Mission in Asia is a mark of a crusade against Asian people, and a complete 'one-way-traffic' from a Christian West to non-Christian East.[160] This has created a sociological rift between native and foreign, and native eventually came under the control of foreign: politically and religious in case

[160] http://www.edinburgh2010/org/en/resources/html (23.09.2015).

of converts. Since it paid no attention to Indian new converts, their aspiration, social values, morals, spiritual tradition, customs, etc.; native Christians appeared to be a symbol of complete subalternity: voiceless, under controlled, Church going and European rites following mass. In the post-colonial era, the Christian mission has to take the pain to begin a new cultural dialogue within India, leaving behind the colonial past.[161]

Subalternity is not a natural phenomenon, but a human creation. It was created within the very ideology of EWM that divides the world as civilized vs uncivilized, redeemed vs unredeemed, True God vs heathen or the words like Christian army, pagan (negatively), non-believers, unoccupied land, etc.; then it left no room for justice. Occupying politically or religiously is an unethical term which inflicts distresses and marginalizes occupied land and her people. In occupying policy, native virtually kept under strict political control and fates remain in the hand of the occupant. The report of John R. Mott (the Chairman of Commissions-WMC 1910) has a clear connotation of 'discovered and occupied' thesis. It is true that Indian civilization along with other ancient civilizations is much older than 'the then expansionist discoverers.'[162] Then, the question could be asked, what to discover and for whom? Such an exclusive ideology and nature of the mission is the fundamentals reason of subalternity of Indian converts. It is true that EWM was an essential part of the colonial project.[163] In 1910, Bishop V. S. Azariah (first Indian Anglican Bishop) raised the issue of how to go beyond ruler vs ruled dialectic and heading towards a friendship. He acclaimed, 'Give as Friends'. He objected the narrow view of EWM on Indian cultural and spiritual traditions that hindered the relation own natives because the colonial attitude stands on this binary policy.[164]

The whole Oikoumene and Missio Dei were doctrinalized and perceived within a colonial structure. In the mission, 'other' the Indian converts remain 'other' because 'others' is the object, never became part of God's mission, so, native Indians were subaltern politically and NIC, religiously. A comparison between Edinburgh-1910 and 2010 would help to take our argument further to analyze the colonial and postcolonial mission of the Church.

---

[161] Jacques Gernet, *China and the Christian Impact* (Cambridge: Cambridge University Press, 1987). Cf. Flex Wilfred, *Asian Dreams and Christian Hope: At the Dawn of the Millennium* (Delhi: ISPCK, 2000), 230.

[162] K. M. George, "Mission and Its Discontents: Towards a New Humanity, a paper presented during BTESSC Seminar on 3rd Feb., 2010 at United Theological College, Bangaluru, 4.

[163] M.P. Joseph, "Rethinking the Edinburgh Conference in the Context of Globalization" in *Witness in Context: Essays in Honor of Eardley Mendis*, ed., Monica J. Melanchthon and George Zachariah (Tiruvalla: Christave Shitya Samith, 2007): 154.

[164] Kenneth R. Ross, *Edinburgh 2010: New Directors for Church in Mission* (Pasadena: William Carey University Press, 2010), 55.

Edinburgh 1910	Edinburgh 2010
i. Emphasis on the mission of Church ii. West to Non-West, for conversion and Church planting iii. Other faiths as invalid, similar to the Old Testament, Christ is only way iv. Assimilation of native within Western culture as superior v. Praxis on 'foreign and home' mission, old and new church, western controlled.	i. Emphasis on the mission of God ii. Accepting plurality, complexity and contextual, inter-faith dialogue part of mission iii. The uniqueness of all faiths iv. Accepting the diversity of culture as a gift of God v. Multi-culturalism, globalization, church-center to people-center,

Between twos, Edinburgh 1910 approves the colonial nature of Church and her mission and in contrast Edinburgh 2010 is post-colonial in nature and global in character. Dr. Timothy Hembrom holds the colonial Church reason of tribal disintegration that acted not as a unifying force but played a role of decisiveness. And it alienated one from other within the community, and it further alienated one Christian from others due to the sectarian denominational settings which tribes (or Indians) ever experienced.[165] 'Can the Subaltern Speak?' is a postcolonial question and quest for new identity. Indian Christians were culturally bankrupt when EWM took away their musical instruments, songs, dances, rituals, dress code, ornaments, customs, values system, morals and what not. Native converts forced to live a state of utopia: assurance of heaven and denied of natural heritage.[166] They had no 'say', dignity and identity and the very life was also defined by the authority of Church. Subaltern people's material and spiritual life was a subject of Church. That was the actual life of NIC during long 350 years of colonial Church.

3.3. Postcolonial Theory and the Subaltern Methodology

In this research, we adopted and employed this particular methodological to deal with the question of subalternity of Indian Christians with special reference to North Indian Christians in the realm of culture. We have adopted the Postcolonial subaltern methodology to investigate the situation and condition of Indian Christians mainly living in Northern region and EWM policy which was used as the prime tool to introduce Christianity, to expand

[165] Timothy Hembrom, "Ministry and Mission from a Primal Perspective" in *Gurukul Journal of Theological Studies*, Vol. V, No. 172, January-July (1994): 41.

[166] Timothy Hembrom, "Ministry and Mission from a Primal Perspective" in *Gurukul Journal of Theological Studies*, Vol. V, No. 172, January-July (1994): 20.

it and to practice and systematize among Indian converts. Consequences of colonial mission policy, native Indian Christians were triple trapped: firstly, they were forced to denounce their spiritual heritage; secondly, separated from own people/family on the basis of faith and thirdly, separating from other Christian on the denominational rivalry.[167] Eventually, these led Indian Christians into a state of semi-refugee status in their homeland.

Antonio Gramsci, (an Italian Marxist ideologue, 1891-1937), was the first to identify a non-elite/subordinate social groups, called subaltern,[168] and according to him, the subaltern group often intellectually surrender to the dominant group.[169] In India, Ranajit Guha (the pioneer in 1980s) defines it as "the general attribute of subordination in South Asian society whether this is expressed in terms of class, caste, age, gender, and office or in any other way."[170] Homi K. Bhabha interestingly placed the term 'post' in Post-colonialism as a cultural space between the colonists and the colonized.[171] As one of the most contemporary approaches, it is potential and credibility method to address the question and issues of subaltern groups to re-construct (*saṁskāric*) identity-quest in the post-colonial period.[172]

The use of Subaltern in postcolonial methodology is an attempt to analyze the pertinent issue of the centrality of subaltern quest and their subjectivity[173] of cultural re-construction (of *saṁskāras*) within a given context of NIC.[174] The subaltern or subordinate situation of the vast majority of the Indian Christian population of India is primarily due to the EWM policy (See Ch. II).[175] The

[167] Timothy Hembrom, "Ministry and Mission from a Primal Perspective" in *Gurukul Journal of Theological Studies*, Vol. v, No. 172, January-July (1994): 41.

[168] Donna Landry and Gerald Maclean, eds., *The Spivak Reader* (London: Routledge, 1996), 23.

[169] Antonio Gramsci, *Selections from the Prison Notebooks*, trs. by Quintin Hoare and Geoffrey Nowell Smith (New York, Lawrence and Wishart, 1971), 227.

[170] Ranajit Guha, "Preface" in *Subaltern Studies I: Writings on South Asian History and Society*, edited by Ranajit Guha (N. Delhi: Oxford University Press, [1982], 4th impression 1999): vii.

[171] Homi K. Bhabha, *The Location of Culture*, Op. Cit., pp. 9, 10; Bart Moore-Gilbert, *Postcolonial Theory: Contexts, Practices, Politics* (London: Verso, 1997), 12.

[172] R.S. Sugirtharajah, *Postcolonial Criticism and Biblical Interpretation* (Oxford: Oxford University Press, 2002), 11-12.

[173] Darshan Perusek, "Subaltern Consciousness and Historiography of Indian Rebellion 1857" in *Economic and Political Weekly* 28 (1993): 1931.

[174] M.N. Srinivas, *Village, Caste, Gender and Method*, 192, 209-210, 216.

[175] Thomas Kadankavil, "Preface" in *Religion and Politics from Subaltern Perspective*, edited by Thomas Kadankavil (Bangalore: Dharmaram Publication, 1999): v.

subalterns are the voiceless people[176] who lost their self-hood: religiously and culturally and for our research NIC specific subaltern is undertaken.

3.3.1. Definition and Interpretation of Term 'Subaltern'

The term Subaltern was interpreted in different ways in various contexts. Largely, it denotes to Ranajit Guha, 'inferior status of people,'[177] be it the issue of caste, gender, class, mainly living in South-Asia.[178] He also stated that this social group reflects 'demographic difference between the total Indian population and all those whom we have described as the 'elite;'[179] whereas as Antonio Gramsci classified them as 'non-elite.'[180] Most of the scholars identify Indian subalternity within a 'caste' context[181] over the 'class' context,[182] whereas our focus is on NIC in the cultural and *saṁskāric* context.

In our research, we are defining NIC subalternity within the colonial context. The subalternity due to caste was partially true. Caste has two aspects: firstly, it represents the social injustice among Hindu social groups (within *varnas*) and secondly, it represents a social order which is beyond Hindu religious group (Every religious group in India practices caste system in some form or other). For our research, the argument would be restricted within Christian subalternity that is double fold: since majority Christians are from lower-caste, they have a low social status and being Christian they are lost their social mobility and came under Church. As early as the 1850s, Sattam Pailli points the Church controlled subalternity of native converts. Christian subalternity is a much deeper social issue than Hindu subaltern groups. Hindu

---

[176] V.V. Thomas, *Understanding Subaltern History: Theoretical Tools* (Bangalore: BTESSC/SATHRI, 2006), xiii-xiv.

[177] Ranajit Guha, "Preface" in *Subaltern Studies I: Writings on South Asian History and Society*, edited by Ranajit Guha (N. Delhi: Oxford University Press, [1982] 4th Impression 1999): vii.

[178] Ranajit Guha, "Preface" in *Subaltern Studies I: Writings on South Asian History and Society*, edited by Ranajit Guha (N. Delhi: Oxford University Press, [1982] 4th Impression 1999): vii.

[179] Ranajit Guha, "On Some Aspects of the Historiography of Colonial India" in *Subaltern Studies I: Writings on South Asian History and Society*, edited by Ranajit Guha (N. Delhi: Oxford University Press, [1982] 4th impression 1999): 8.

[180] Donna Landry and Gerald Maclean, eds., *The Spivak Reader* (London: Routledge, 1996), 23.

[181] Partha Chatterjee, "Caste and Subaltern Consciousness" in *Subaltern Studies VI: Writings on South Asian History and Society*, edited by Ranajit Guha (N. Delhi: Oxford University Press, 1989): 169.

[182] Gail Omvedt, *Seeking Begumpura: The Social Vision of Anticaste Intellectuals* (N. Delhi: Navayana Publication, 2008), 23; Sathianathan Clarke, *Dalits and Christianity: Subaltern Religion and Liberation Theology in India* (N. Delhi: Oxford University Press, [1998] 2nd Impression 2002), 7.

oppressed groups are safeguarded by the constitution and political class. The government has a justice system and development plans, but Christians are trapped twice: they are under Church traditions and customs are large western. Therefore, they are socially perceived as foreign followers and also practice caste system unofficially. They are not united due to denominational parochialism. Ironically, Christians are now curing behind Ambedkar as their liberative icon who spoke against Christian faith, their caste practice and foreignness. Socially, even though, Church since the 16th century has been fighting against Hindu social order and used it as trump-card to present the gospel as the ultimate liberation end goal, but practically failed to implement a stable and sustainable social alternative justice system for the nation or for Christians without a caste system. The psychological subalternity, apart from social subalternity, is another issue to be addressed and needs serious academic debate. The subaltern postcolonial methodology will be able to provide a new cultural paradigm to re-construct *saṁskāras* as an internal quest, not only as an external agent. It refers to the ability to act or perform an action. In contemporary theory, it hinges on the question of whether individuals can freely and autonomously initiate action, or whether the things they do are in some sense determined by the ways in which their identity has been constructed. Agency is important in postcolonial studies/theory because it refers to the ability of postcolonial subjects to initiate action in engaging or resisting imperial power.[183]

The aspect of subaltern aspiration is interlinked to their liberating consciousness. PIC[184] context is subjective to their internal duality which is contradictory by itself. Gramsci rightly explained that in one hand, they have their perception of culture, spirituality, culture-world view and on the other, their reasoning is submissive[185] to the dominant class (for research it is colonial Church). PIC had a consciousness of their social subaltern status, yet surrendered (somehow) to the colonial (Western) authority. In this dual nature,[186] once dominated PIC has slowly and definitely looked for a new identity. Psychological pride being aligned with the dominant reasoning (Western) and the realization of being uprooted (by westerners) have

[183] Bill Ashcroft, Gareth Griffiths and Helen Tiffin, eds., *Post-Colonial Studies: The Key Concepts* (London/New York: Routledge, [2000] 2nd ed. 2007, reprint 2009), 6.

[184] PIC – Pre-independent Indian Christian.

[185] Antonio Gramsci, *Selections from the Prison Notebooks*, trs. by Quintin Hoare and Geoffrey Nowell Smith (New York: Lawrence and Wishart, 1971), 227, quoted by Partha Chatterjee, "Caste and Subaltern Consciousness," 170.

[186] Gautam Bhadra, "The Mentality of Subalternity: Kantanama or Rajdharma" in *Subaltern Studies VI: Writings on South Asian History and Society*, edited by Ranajit Guha (N. Delhi: Oxford University Press, [1989] 4th Impression 1999): 54.

created a persistent dilemma.[187] Gautam Bhadra stated it as 'contradictory consciousness.'[188] According to Felix Wilfred, this process of a new identity as a socio-religious group accepts the insights of the dominant group as their own emancipation praxis.[189]

Considering the context of PIC, this duality is the main challenge to dress the issue and very discourse is the process of re-construction the socio-cultural identity (*saṁskāra*) coming out of subalternity of faith and culture of Euro-centric colonial Christianity.[190]

3.4. Postcolonial Theory and Its Interpretations in the Context to NIC

The school of thoughts of this theory is largely depending on the writings of Edward Said (*Orientalism*-1978), Homi Bhabha (*The Location of Culture*-1994) and Gayatri Chakravorty Spivak (*Can the Subaltern Speak?*-2010).[191] This theory is heterogeneous that incorporates issues related to historical, cultural, geographical, gender, religious, political and material aspects of a living community, expressed in various modes like literature, dance, music, art, oral traditions, etc.[192] The conceptualization of a particular condition during the colonial period is the central issue of this theory,[193] and it has a liberating de-constructive approach to the issue.[194] One trans-cultural

---

[187] Gautam Bhadra, "The Mentality of Subalternity: Kantanama or Rajdharma" in *Subaltern Studies VI: Writings on South Asian History and Society*, edited by Ranajit Guha (N. Delhi: Oxford University Press, [1989] 4th Impression 1999): 90.

[188] Gautam Bhadra, "The Mentality of Subalternity: Kantanama or Rajdharma" in *Subaltern Studies VI: Writings on South Asian History and Society*, edited by Ranajit Guha (N. Delhi. Oxford University Press, [1989] 4th Impression 1999): 64.

[189] Felix Wilfred, "Subaltern Religious Experience" in *Journal of Dharma*, 23/1 (January-March, 1998): 67.

[190] IC- Indian Christian.

[191] Gayatri Chakravorty Spivak, *A Critique of Postcolonial Reason: Towards a History of the Vanishing Present* (Harvard: Harvard University Press, 1999), "Can the Subaltern Speak" in *The Post-colonial Studies Reader*, edited by Bill Ashcroft, Gareth Griffiths and Helen Tiffin (London: Routledge, 1995): 24-28; *In Other Worlds: Essays in Cultural Politics* (New York/ London: Routledge, 1988); *The Post-Colonial Critic: Interviews, Strategies, Dialogues*, edited by Sarah Harasym (London: Routledge, 1990).

[192] R.S. Sugirtharajah, *Asian Biblical Hermeneutics and Post-colonialism: Contesting the Interpretations* (Sheffield: Sheffield Academic Press, 1998), 15.

[193] Leela Gandhi, *Postcolonial Theory: A Critical Introduction* (Delhi: Oxford University Press, 1999), 4.

[194] R. S. Sugirtharajah, *The Bible and the Third World: Pre-colonial, Colonial and Postcolonial Encounters* (Cambridge: Cambridge University Press, 2001), 244.

hybridism[195] is a phenomenon (Concept of Homi Bhabha) to be addressed here in the context of PIC. The question of rejection and acceptation of colonial culture as an absolute objective aspiration of PIC or colonial culture would also be a part of the new quest, what is called the hybridist of this discourse.[196] Post-colonialism deals with the effects of colonization on cultures and therefore, pre-colonial and post-colonial cultural history of post-independent Indian Christians are the central critical area undertaken by this theory.[197] Thus, R. Sharada Sugirtharajah points out that Post-colonialism "...is a discursive practice that takes a critical look at histories, textual productions, and visual and aural representations."[198]

The aim is to inspect the religious-cultural historiography of PIC as constructed during the colonizing process[199] and how to re-construct (of *saṁskāras*) a new identity for NIC. Spivak's pertinent question on the issue of 'Can the Subaltern Speak?'[200] can be taken as a praxis making tool for NIC in contemporary India. The quest for new identity which is Indian, then the international pressure from various Christian agencies because of Indian Church's much dependency on West for fund, doctrines and theological framework; NIC takes as a reference or psychological leniency to the West. Such condition is hindrance before NIC even now. Sugirtharajah rightly said,

> Post-colonialism is not simply a physical expulsion of imperial powers. Nor is it simply recounting the evils of the empire, and drawing a contrast with the nobility and virtues of natives and their cultures. Rather, it is an active confrontation with the dominant system of thought, its lopsidedness, and inadequacies and underlies its unsuitability for us. Hence, it is a process of cultural and discursive emancipation from all dominant structures whether they are political, linguistic or ideological.[201]

This state of mind is the challenge for research's objective conclusion.

---

[195] Cf., M.L. Pratt, *Imperial Eyes: Travel Writing and Trans-culturation* (London: Routledge, 1992).

[196] Simon Samuel, *A Postcolonial Reading of Mark's Story of Jesus* (London: T&T Clark, 2007), ix.

[197] Simon Samuel, "Review of Postcolonial Biblical Criticism: Interdisciplinary Intersections" in *Doon Theological Journal* 3/2 (July, 2006): 197.

[198] Sharada Sugirtharajah, *Imagining Hinduism: A Postcolonial Perspective* (London: Routledge, 2003), xii.

[199] Sharada Sugirtharajah, *Imagining Hinduism*, Op. Cit., xiii.

[200] Gayatri Spivak, "Can the Subaltern Speak? Speculations on Widow Sacrifice" in *Wedge* 7/8 (1985): 120-130; Gayatri Spivak, "Can the Subaltern Speak," in *The Post-colonial Studies Reader*, Op. Cit.: 24-28.

[201] R.S. Sugirtharajah, *Postcolonial Reconfigurations: An Alternative Way of Reading the Bible and Doing Theology* (London: SCM Press; St. Louis, Chalice Press, 2003), 15.

3.5. History of Postcolonialism as a Methodological Approach

Most scholars agree that it is a theory that deals the imperial colonial history, related to politics and culture,[202] therefore, it re-looks closely at the whole history of this period.[203] For example, Indian Church history is a colonial history which is colonial in nature and character, even though the mission was for Indians. During the dusk of the 20th century in India and lately in 19th century Europe, this approach started getting its usage as a theory.[204] But, it was the academic publication of Edward Said's book, *Orientalism*[205] that had drawn attention in the Western world. In his book *Culture and Imperialism*, Said argued that due to the powerful presence and influence of the empire, the native culture and religion became hybrid.[206] Homi Bhabha and Gayatri C. Spivak are the other two critics, besides Said, to occupy an important place in the forming of postcolonial theory. But as Sugirtharajah points out, these writers were hailed to be the instigators of the theory only after postcolonial study reached a certain degree of momentum.[207] Followings are the major contributors in defining various identities: subalternity (Spivak),[208] hybridity (Bhabha),[209] alternative historiography (Chakrabarty and Guha)[210] and resistance (Fanon).[211] The main premise was located within political, economic and cultural. Sugirtharajah points out that one of the major concentrations of Post-colonialism in the future would be to theorize about

---

[202] Stephen Slemon, "The Scramble for Post-Colonialism," *The Post-Colonial Studies Reader*, edited by Bill Ashcroft, Gareth Griffiths and Helen Tiffin (London: Routledge, 1995), 45.

[203] V.V. Thomas, *Understanding Subaltern History: Theoretical Tools* (Bangalore: BTESSC/SATHRI, 2006), xviii.

[204] V.V. Thomas, *Understanding Subaltern History: Theoretical Tools* (Bangalore: BTESSC/SATHRI, 2006), xix.

[205] Edward W. Said, *Orientalism* (London: Penguin Books, [1978] 2003).

[206] Edward W. Said, *Culture and Imperialism* (London: Vintage, 1994).

[207] R.S. Sugirtharajah, *Postcolonial Criticism and Biblical Interpretation* (Oxford: University Press, 2002), 16.

[208] Gayatri Chakravorty Spivak, *A Critique of Postcolonial Reason: Towards a History of the Vanishing Present* (Harvard: University Press, 1999), cf; "Can the Subaltern Speak" in *The Post-Colonial Studies Reader*, edited by Bill Ashcroft, Gareth Griffiths and Helen Tiffin (London: Routledge, 1995): 24-28; cf; *The Post-Colonial Critic: Interviews, Strategies, Dialogue*, edited by Sarah Harasym (London: Routledge, 1990).

[209] Homi K. Bhabha, *The Location of Culture* (London/New York: Routledge, [1994] reprinted 2010).

[210] D. Chakrabarty and Homi K. Bhabha, *Habitations of Modernity: Essays in the Wake of Subaltern Studies* (Chicago; Illinois: University of Chicago Press, 2002); Ranajit Guha, ed., *A Subaltern Studies Reader, 1986-1995* (Minneapolis: University of Minnesota Press, 1997).

[211] Frantz Fanon, *The Wretched of the Earth* (Harmondsworth: Penguin Book, [1961] 1990).

religion and address the question of how religion operates in a postmodern world.[212]

3.6. 'Space & Place' Model and Postcolonial Reconstruction

The 'Space & Place' (SP) is a new model which is research's brain-child. The argument has been seriously considering the applicability of academic exercise which will is real fruit-bearer. The postcolonial cultural reconstruction (*saṁskāras*) in this research will explore this new dimension called 'Space & Place'. SP[213] model is to address how the theoretical aspect of Postcolonial Subaltern re-construction (of *saṁskāras*) would possibly be implemented in the life of NIC. The SP model will acknowledge how to create a new 'space' for NIC in post-colonial Indian Church for their cultural reconstruction within the pluralistic tradition. NIC deserves a new 'space' within Church and in the larger society, keeping away the traditional cultural alienation and colonial Church tradition. The colonial subaltern community now needs to fulfill their suppressed aspiration to be a natural shareholder. In the process of reconstruction of *saṁskāras*, a 'space' must be created in the society to 'place' them within plurality and assimilated with their faith identity. Even if it is hybrid as Homi Bhabha said. 'Placing' is important because if placing is not proper or only faith-driven or politically motivated, placement will not serve the purpose of reconstruction and NIC will remain isolated within society. It will only raise tension. For example, foreignness tag on NIC can be reversed only when 'placement' of *saṁskāras* is spontaneous. 'Place' will create new neighborhood settings: culturally and religiously. The fear part of this process is what Antonio Gramsci and Spivak advocated that the subaltern community may fall again under so-called dominating or superior cultural, i.e., second colonized state. NIC must be free to adopt cultural aspects in their struggle to re-culture them, considering plural dharmic tradition in India. So 'Space and Place' model is an attempt to have a cultural rehabilitation for Christians.

The doctrines of the church and the theological possibility of interpreting the biblical text in accordance with the need for a particular life reality are to be explored within a 'given context'. It is often noticed the doctrine of the church, her rites, and theological possibility are reprehensive, even though the Schism of church preferably due to a theological reinterpretation of doctrine. Taking this history into consideration, it can neither be incorrect to re-interpret the text; nor objectionable to re-model rites to accommodate people by creating a suitable 'space'. Therefore, the 'SP' is a new hermeneutical tool to explore the theological possibility for thus far subaltern NIC.

---

[212] Sharada Sugirtharajah, *Imagining Hinduism*, Op. Cit., 142-143.

[213] SP – Space and Place.

In religious compatibility within pluralistic reality, like of India, where inter-religious socio-political conflict is not completely avoidable, therefore, an attempt to bring a religious 'climate change' by creating a new 'space' is the biggest challenge. If a religion used to be so rigid to create a new 'space', then, naturally it would fail to create any 'place' for people. Christianity as a religion is already irreverent to the mass, except it is educational institutions and monumental colonial gothic Church. It is a deeply sad situation. When a country of 1.25 billion people perceives a negative view on Christianity and mission of Church failed to meet the aspiration of the general public, so essentiality of a new model like 'SP' is appeared to more relevant.

3.6.1. Samaj Dharma (SD) and Its Relation to 'Space and Place' Model

Next serious challenge and question may subsequently be asked what would be the new state of life for NIC that will have the capacity to implement re-culturation of *saṁskāras* through 'SP' model. Keeping in mind the larger Indian social system and its basic functional mechanism, I wish to take up one major social aspect of Indian tradition: *Samaj Dharma* (SD-Social responsibility/duty/life) to explore a path-breaking possibility to actualize feasibility of 'SP' model for NIC. The concept of SD is not new to any Indian Christian, Indian theologians and missiologist like Brahmabandhab Upadhyay, R.C. Das and later by Christian Ashram attempted to explore this tradition tool. Upadhyaya's conversion experience and observation of Western Church; he took a final call to differentiate personal spiritual dimension and social commitment and explained that *Samaj Dharma* is a duty to society or nation building which must be strengthened through spiritual development (*Sadhana Dharma*). He remained socially (*Samaj*) Indian/Hindu and at the same time Christian (*Sadhana*) by faith. Upadhyay's model can be further explored to deepen our argument of re-culturation of *saṁskāras*. Looking at the history of the Indian Church, a radical paradigm shift is noticed including ashram movement and Churchless Christianity and Hindu (Indian) way of following Christ. Eventually, Tambaram Conference-1938 (Protestant) and Roman Catholic (2nd Vatican Council 1962-65) reflect such possible changes in colonized countries. This trend is still continuing in India with diverse forms and practices. In many cases, they are in deep conflict with tradition Churches who hold the Western position. *Yashu Darbar* in Allahabad is one such example where a new interpretation is being practiced that allows a follower of Christ within his/her own culture as it is, yet fully believer, taking part in Holy Communion including children without baptism. Many Muslim, Hindu, Sikhs are worshipping 'Jesus' together without being formal Christian. Upadhyaya visualized this form of 'unlocking Jesus' in India. R. C. Das (of Baranasi) was another pioneer for Churchless Christianity.

The research is attempting to bring a change in the former tradition of '*Samaj* and *Sadhana'* Dharma. Formerly, most of the attempts were during the colonial period and those people virtually separated from the mainstream of Church movement and that has made them insignificant to penetrate NIC. This isolation weakened the re-construction process and the same was true for Robert de Nobili. What we are suggesting here as postcolonial Church, is to implement SD in the life of common Christians, not with monastic fashion but in daily life. Such exploration is kind of conflict management within Churches that have no fear of losing a unique Christian identity in India.

The 'SP' model as a postcolonial aspiration for subaltern Indian Christians is to investigate the attempts to frame and shape a new identity, taking its resources from various *Dharmasastras* with special reference to the Manusmṛti and the Torah which fully visualized and advocated a *Samaj Dharma,* broadening religious life in social land space. A context of 'SD' is what Indian society is all about and sociologically speaking SD is practiced, governed and monitored within a law of Dharma of Manusmṛti.

3.6.2. Ambivalence Aspects of Samaj Dharma as Christian Life Reality

There are some pertinent features that to be looked upon to address the challenges for the Christian community in North India in order to argue the feasibility of Post-colonial Subaltern method within the SP model, the re-constructing culture of NIC.

3.6.2.1. Social Settlement Issue

Social settlement pattern is an important demographical issue to be discussed here. In North India, new converts during the colonial period were resettled as a new colony taken from different places. There are two logics: a. new converts (single or family) were no more accepted by parental family or society and they were forced to leave home; b. They were taken away by the Western missionary to form a new bloc within a society. They are known as 'campus Christian'. Historical consequences are enormous since people were isolated from parental society and family, and came under direct control of the Church. This re-orientation camp is the main cause of socio-cultural uprootment and implementation of EW Church culture. Due to such a long isolated life, the mental capability to re-induction of *saṁskāras* into the plural open society is a challenge. For Allahabad, twenty thousand odd Christians are living in a few colonies like Johnstoneganj, Muirabad, etc. During Muslim rule, India also witnessed such policy and they also had a system much similar to Christian even though Christians have better social acceptability.

3.6.2.2. Psychological Isolation Issue

It also has two features: at one hand, IC was made to believe that Christian faith is only true faith and superior to others. In the Hindu majority of India, they always look down Hindu as a false faith. To take Indian culture as their own, even being an Indian is psychological warfare within their very mind. It appears to be a kind of compromise. On the other, NIC believes (generally) to be living in a Hindu country, not in own country. A deep duality and dilemma have confused them to define their identity and future. This religiously controlled behavior works over rationality. Ambedkar points out that this dilemma of a foreign faith community poses a question of commitment to the nation. It hinders the process of re-culturation.

3.6.2.3. Common Inheritance Issue

EWM categorized Indian heritage on religious bias. EWM and European scholars failed to differentiate Indian plurality and Hindu tradition. Hindu as a define religion is also a European construct. Not able to actualize plurality and heterogeneity of India, EWM attempted to separate all Indian history, religion, and culture from new converts that created a huge vacuum in the life. This has deprived them to inherit Indian history as their history. It weakened the very existence of NIC. European Christianity took Greek philosophical system and Roman organizational structure to reconstruct Christianity, diluting the historical value of Jerusalem, and later such euro-centrism displaced NIC from India. For long sustaining colonial policy to create a new community within Indian society (read Thomas John Macaulay's educational policy argument), the de-inheritance system was put in place mainly on converts. The consequence is that Indian Christians hesitate or refuse to own Indian past, culture as their own. It is a serious crisis for re-culturation of *saṁskāras*.

3.6.2.4. Religious Consciousness Issue

It is another issue to deal with. An open and plural society in India, super sensitivity of religious consciousness in public discourse is serious social discomfort for Christian. Such consciousness, to me, is a phobia. NIC is consciously aware of their religious identity which determines their social communication to other faith people. In Indian plurality, such mental consciousness separates one from other or selectively define neighborhood. The relationship for NIC is religiously driven. In such context, implement of *saṁskāras* from Manusmṛti and Torah is a challenge.

3.6.2.5. Mission and Conversion Issue

The prevailing public discourse of Christian is religiously driven, even in many cases very subtle. A Christian likes to believe or taught to practice to share Gospel with other faith people as an essential religious duty and no chance should be lost. It is silly to notice that if a Christian brings a Hindu/Muslim or another faith person in Church; it is marked as a good character. This mission mind in plural society does hinder the further re-culturation process. These are few challenges before NIC to re-construct *saṁskāras* culturally within Indian cultural plurality. SP model as SD from a Postcolonial Subaltern methodology must take these challenges in the research.

Conclusion

This research has adopted 'Postcolonial Subaltern' method, emphasizing on 'post-colonial' which is a quest for self-identity against the colonial culture that is existing in the life of North Indian Christians (NIC) and 'subaltern' that defines the cultural state of NICs within larger Indian society. It has applied to analyze subalternity of Indian Christian with special reference to North Indian Christians during the colonial period and at present. Subalternity of NIC has a double meaning: firstly, new converts were separated from family, society, culture, custom, keeping in campus under the strict Church control and secondly, they were culturally de-constructed to form a new Europeanized Christian community through converts in India. From such oppressed context, this research has used the Postcolonial Subaltern method to reconstruct cultural subalternity of NICs from Eurocentricism to Indocentricism as to make existing NIC culture more Indian that it would assimilate NICs within Indian social system (as Samaj Dharma) by adopting a model namely 'Space and Place'. Empirical data through a questionnaire, interview, group discussion, testimony, a case study is being analyzed and used to argue the practical aspect of this research. Contemporary Indian Christianity (social perception) is a prototype of Euro-Western Mission (EWM), in which native Indians are treated as an object not as a subject. Being object, NIC had lost own identity and social relevance (Spivak-*Can the Subaltern Speak?*) during the colonial period.

Postcolonial Subalternity as a method was first initiated by Antonio Gramsci (1891-1937) and later Edward Said, Homi K. Bhabha, Gayatri C. Spivak, Ranajit Guha, etc. have enhanced this method. The whole dimension of the postcolonial method is to look the society from a binary division between ruler and ruled; elite and non-elite; poor and rich; oppressor and oppressed. This division has economic, cultural, political, religious, class, caste index. It is a struggle of the people living in the bottom line, looking for self-identity, dignity, equality, and justice, etc. This method has focused on two characteristics among subaltern community: i. struggle to reconstruct self-identity eventually ends as a hybrid culture (Homi K. Bhabha); ii. Possibly fails to overcome (psychologically) the inferior status even after being free from the operation.

The colonial perception of India as a Hindu country has developed a deep-rooted dilemma among NICs to incorporate cultural elements and therefore, continuing the colonial legacy. This is a re-construction challenge. In one hand NIC upholds the colonial Christianity and on the other NIC faces a cultural crisis. As a response, this research has made use 'Space & Place' model which advocates for a possibility to create a new space within Church tradition and place Indian culture minus Hindu culture for re-culturation. This hypothesis has dealt with the practical aspects of our research outcome.

Chapter 4

An Introduction of the Law (Dharma) of Manu and the Law (Dharma) of Moses and the Selective Saṃskāric (Sacramental) Praxis for Re-culturation

Introduction

The aim of this chapter is to analyze *saṁskāras* (sacraments) in Manusmṛti and Torahal tradition to objectify the possibility new model to reconstruct present Christian *saṁskāras* of NIC in the light of Postcolonial quest. It will also deal with the question that in what extent the Manusmṛti and Torah may provide a new praxis making a saṁskāric model re-construct NIC. Further, it may argue upon the reasons of selection of these ancient books for present research and to what extent, they are the axis-making important to a respective community.

The ancient law or dharma (traditional jurisprudence and customs) is often responsible for developing a formative identity for a particular community living in particular land. In our global world and within our nation-state setting, ancient laws have been playing an important role. Keeping such continuity in consideration, we would investigate and analyze the Laws of Manu and Moses and question whether any insights, values, and practices may improvise and provide an alternative cultural model to reconstruct the present cultural identity (*saṁskāras*) for NIC that would make culturally relevant. Thc word 'Dharma' would be used to communicate the veracity of the word 'Law' for the purpose of the thesis.

It will concentrate to provide an introductory note on the Manusmṛti and the Torah to settle a question by what we would be defining the specific areas of these two Laws that are to be compared and would further be elaborated to bring out a suggestive prescription for the re-culturation of contemporary NIC objectively.

The sacrament by its definition might sum up as a 'rite whose words and actions are bound up with God's saving activity in and through the church.'[214] Such an explanation must be properly expounded to express the doctrinal meaning since the various denominations and traditions have been in history redefined its possible inner essence. Since the number and meaning of sacraments differ, we will generally focus on larger protestant traditions as per the demand of this present research.

The objective of our argument is to find out whether in present NIC context, some sacramental rites are to be taken for major change towards a possible 're-culturation' and to see how far the history of Church has been dealing with this issue to avoid the criticism that rites are unchangeable and re-cultural might be called as unbiblical.

4.1. Defining Law and Dharma: Analyzing Category

The modern world believes in specialization, and therefore, the 'law' in social conceptual level communicates a limited civil meaning, varied in context and found in the respective constitution. In ancient period, all laws are actually customary and some laws eventually became statutory. *Saṁskāras* for Indians and *Halacha* for Hebrew are a primordial form of law. After the French Revolution, an attempt was taken to separate customary (religious) laws to form modern 'secular' laws for the new 'nation-state'. Traditionally, religious laws (dharma in limited meaning) cannot separate from civil law; therefore, those customs (written and orals) still have a larger role in life and society in India or Israel in comparison to modern law.

Traditionally, dharma has multi-dimensional usage that includes conduct, duty, ordinance, law, custom, customary observances of castes, religion, piety, justice, equity, virtue, morality, nature, character and characteristic quality, etc.[215] It is government and governance, it is a duty and obligatory, it is the axis of material and mental function. It includes all that is seen and unseen. This is dharma. In the Laws of Manu, it is the code of sacred and civil conduct (Dharma). The word 'Dharma' has different meanings in different contexts.[216] In the European context, 'law' has very specific meaning such as '*recht*' in German or '*droit*' in French or '*diritto*' in Italian, but unfortunately, none can be fully explained in English. It can be 'right/s', 'justice' or simply 'law'. In

---

[214] Jeffrey A. Truscott, *The Sacraments: A Practical Guide* (New Delhi: Christian World Imprints, 2016), 2.

[215] *Dharmiohi Tesamadhiko Viseso*. Chanakya Nitisastra 8.17.

[216] Nikunja Vihari Banerjee, *Studies in the Dharmasastra of Manu* (Delhi: Munshiram Manoharlal Publishers Pvt. Ltd. 1980), 1.

the same way, Dharma includes 'right conduct, obligatory duties, justice' etc. In *Dharmasastras* like Manu, Yajnavalka, Brihaspati, Arthasastra, etc., mean a complete set of system that unifies diverse people together within Varna.

According to Swami Sivananda, dharma in India is classified as: *Sanatana* Dharma (Eternal Law), *Samanya* Dharma (general duty), *Visesha* Dharma (special duty), *Varnasrama* Dharma (duties of Caste and Order), *Svadharma* (one's own duty), *Yuga Dharma* (duty of the Era), *Kula* Dharma (duty of family), *Manava* Dharma (duty of Human beings), *Purusha* Dharma (duty of male), *Stri* Dharma (duty of female), *Raja* Dharma (duty of king), *Praja* Dharma (duty of people), *Pravritti* Dharma (duty in worldly life) and *Nivritti* Dharma (duty in spiritual life). It simply shows its broader boundary, the same is true for Jewish that are codified in six hundred thirteen laws.

Sociologically speaking, the basic concepts of a theory of dharma are two folds: order and change. The order is conceptualized through the principles of hierarchy (*Varna, jati, purusarthas,* etc), holism (evolution from rudimentary to divine) and continuity between material and spiritual (through *karma*). Change is to be cyclical.[217] Some scholars like R. P. Kangle, dharma is 'law,'[218] others scholars like Prof K. J. Shah understands dharma in terms of the relationship of *Samanya dharma* (common law)[219] and *Visesa dharma* (special law).[220]

It is somehow clear that dharma or law in Indian and Hebrew context is a complete multi-functional system of people and comprehensive norms. Therefore the use of word 'law' is to be taken in that broader sense.

4.1.1. Defining Modern Law

There are many arguments to define the origin and purpose of 'law'. Taking the modern social function of the law, the ancient law may stand contradictory to a great extent. According to Friedrich Carl von Savigny (1779-1861), the nature of any particular system of law must be the reflection of the 'spirit of the people' (*Volksgeist*) and it cannot be consciously created phenomenon but a gradual distillation of the *volksgeist*. Law was found, not made, thus, his advocacy in some extent poses challenges to the modern legislation[221] because, modern law comes from the state, not necessarily from the people.[222] Taking

---

[217] Yogendra Singh, *Modernization of Indian Tradition* (Faridabad: Thomson India Press Ltd, 1977), 31-36.

[218] R. P. Kangle, Trs., *The Kautilya Arthasastra* (Bombay: University of Bombay, 1972).

[219] Dharma is applied to all *varnas*.

[220] Dharma is also specific to particular *varnas* and *ashrama*.

[221] Markandey Katju, Judge the Supreme Court of India, speech deliver on "Ancient Indian Jurisprudence" at Banaras Hindu University on 27th Nov, 2010, 14.

[222] Markandey Katju Ibid., 15-16.

Savigny's argument further, European Church enjoyed a kind of absolute authority to repeal the people's law and placed the Church law in the form of doctrine, customs, practices, rituals with divine overtone. The spiritual aspiration can't be seen as the threat to the people's customary existing law. The enforcement of Roman Catholic Laws to St. Thomas Christians in India and on native converts (see Ch II) can justify the need of reconstruction of present North Indian Christian laws as the Postcolonial quest ('*volksgeist*'). The post-France Revolution concept of law has a polarized ideological standpoint where dharma can bring both secular and sacred together.

The separation religion from state diametrically divided two different sets of law, and in West, a new social order started emerging outside of Church laws and it was glorified as the beginning of 'Enlightenment Era'; yet, traditional culture-specific (partly religiously oriented) nature of law can't be absolutely rejected, for example, the image of French Civil Code by a candlelight surely has a religio-cultural symbolism.[223] Therefore, even though, modern and religious laws are now separated, yet they supplement each other in many cases. So, the law is not always an emergency out of emergency and it is not to be seen purely within a political term, but it also needs to carry people's history and heritage, keeping space to accommodate ever-changing nature of human society.

4.1.2. Defining 'Law' and 'Dharma'

4.1.2.1. Dharma in *Astika* Tradition

Astika tradition, commonly known as *Vedic* tradition, does not elaborate and systematically formulate in the Vedas. Laws/dharmic laws as we find in *Dharmasastras* are not the same as they are in Vedas, even though, they have a certain *Vedic* origin. For example, a marriage that has been changing over the period.[224] In fact, *Dharmasūtras* of Gautama, *Apastamba* or *Vasistha* and *Smṛti* of *Manu* or *Yajnavalkya* have acknowledged and accepted the *Vedas* are the original sources of dharma. Thus, according to Gautama, the *Vedas*, together with other tradition and practice, is the source of dharma. Manu also regarded the *Vedas* as a source of dharma.[225] Yajnavalkya too accepted the *Vedas* as the genesis of Indian dharma.[226] It is clear that the *Dharmasastras* and the *Smṛtis* are grounded on the *Vedic* teachings as an auxiliary.

---

[223] Pierre Legrand, "How to Compare New" in *Legal Studies*, Vol. 16, No. 2 (1996): 232-235.

[224] Vide P.V. Kane's Article in the *Journal of the Bombay Branch*, Asiatic Society, XXVI, 1922: 57-82.

[225] Manu., 11.16.

[226] Yajnavalkya, I. 7.

The whole religio-philosophical and didactic piece of literature of India emphasizes the objective of dharma for spiritual realization, i.e., sacred law.[227] The *Atharva Veda* describes dharma as the axis (*dhṛ*) of the world. Upanishad schools affirm Brahman as S*atyam* (Truth), hence ultimate dharma (*Satyam Vada, Dharmam Cara*).[228] The philosophical Schools like the *Purvamimamsa* (Jaimini, 2nd-3rd BCE) define dharma as '*codanalaksano'or 'rthodharmam'* means the conduct in conformity with a *Vedic* injunction.[229] To Sabara Swami (3rd CE), dharma is the 'virtuous act.' In *Manusmṛti*, it is '*Vedokhilam Dharma-mulam*,'[230] means that the Veda in its entirety is the root of dharma.[231] In *Rig Veda*, dharma is '*rta*', the first cosmic order; secondly sacrifice (*Yajna*) and finally human conduct.[232] In the *Gita*, we find two aspects: one is particular (individual)[233] and social (universal)[234] within the moral status quo.[235] In epics (*Ramayana* and *Mahabharata*) the concept of dharma reflects the view of *Dharmasastras*.[236] Madhavacharya (founder of *Dvaita* School, 13th-14th CE) explained dharma as a sustaining and ensuring progress and welfare of all, for the world and beyond. Dharma is the commandments: positive (*vidhi*) and negative (*nishedha*). To Tulsidas (composer of *Ramacharitmanas*), dharma is compassion.

A close observation of various dimensions may appeal to draw a similarity with the Law of Moses or Jewish Law of the 613 commandments which provides a rule of governance similar to the dharmic laws in the Indian tradition. In compare Indian dharmic laws, the Protestant Christianity in its present form in India does not have such wide and holistic range of laws. The Law in *Manusmṛti* (Indian tradition) or the Mosaic Law (Jewish tradition), even though treated as religious texts; eventually they went beyond the religion and form a culture of people. Indian Christians need their Gospel to be culturally restructured in the Indian context and dharmic framework as a viable model.

---

[227] Jacob Kattackal, "Dharma the Great Goal of Life" in *Jeevadhara*, Vol. XII, No 67, (1982): 29.

[228] *Taiteriya Upanishad* 1.11.

[229] *Purva Mimamsa-sutra* 1.2.

[230] *Manusmrti* 2.6.

[231] Manu also deals with the views of others such as Kumarila Bhatta, the *Mimamsaka* exponent, and Kanada, the founder of *Vaisesika* System. *Manusmrti* 2.12 & 8.15.

[232] *Rig Veda* 1.24.8.

[233] *Gita* 2.7.

[234] *Gita* 4.8.

[235] *Gita* 4.7-8.

[236] *Mahabharata, Shanti Parva* 109. 9.11.

4.1.2.2. Dharma (*Dhamma*) in *Nastika* Tradition

Another dominating tradition is *Nastika* (preferably non-Vedic) as found in Caravaca, Jainism, and Buddhism. *Dhamma* (Pali) in Buddhism (same as Dharma in *Astika*) refers to the basic principle of world order, the law of karma and re-birth within the trilogy, 'Buddha, Dharma, and Sangha'. In *Mahayana* tradition, it is the 'manifestation of reality' with an end of result of positive void-ness (*sunaya*), the state of nirvana. It is transitory conditions that cause phenomena to come into being, ethical rules in thinking and governance of life. In Tibetan tradition, a trilogy of *dhamma* represents three metaphoric transitory states of evolving life. Walpola Rahula defines *dhamma* as the state of conditioned things and states, but also the non-conditioned, the Absolute Nirvana.[237] *Theravada* scholar Thanissaro Bhikkhu explains dharma in external level as the system of practice the teachings of Buddha and Buddhadasa Bhikku states the phenomenal level from nature order to individual duties. In the meaning of *Dhammakaya*, a possibility of 'Dharma-Body', the enlightened one (not physical-*rupakaya*) is actualized.

Even though two traditions are different, yet they contributed to developing a primary notion of 'Law or Dharma' in India, not only metaphysically but also practice that has shaped the thinking of Indian mind and lays basics of the conduct of life, i.e., culture.

4.1.2.3. Defining Law (Dharma) in Manusmṛti

Through the eyes of a modern world, if term 'law' synonymously exchanges with 'dharma', many may struggle to read perceptually. Etymologically the word '*dharma*' comes from the Sanskrit root '*dhṛ*', which means 'to support', 'to carry', 'to sustain' and 'to protect'. In Vedic usage, dharma is primarily cosmic order '*Ṛta,*'[238] even though, sometimes, *Ṛta* and *Dharma* are inter-exchange. Later in *Upanishads*, it became synonymous to 'Truth' which is the cosmic axis-making reality. In *Dharmasastras*, as Manusmṛti has implied as the cosmic order[239] which eventuality brought down to the social level as the 'correct conduct' (*sadācāra*) of the *varnas* in context of ethical meaning to explain the human relationship in a society in its theoretical idealism.[240] In Torah, it is rules and regulations of life and world, even cosmic. Those laws are perfect in nature since they are God's given. Infallibility is attached.

Its meaning depends on the purpose of application and context. *A Concise Sanskrit-English Dictionary* of Monier-Williams has used different words to

---

[237] Walpola Rahula, *What the Buddha Taught* (Grove Press, 1974), 58.

[238] Rig Veda 1:187.1 & 5:2, 15.

[239] Manusmṛti 12:50.

[240] Manusmṛti 1:81-82.

define its nuances like morality, duty, religion, work, justice, right, etc.[241] The colonial Indologists used three-term 'religion, ideology and law'. Among the three, 'religion' got most widely used with purely colonial construction to present Indian dharmic tradition compared to defend 'Christianity.'[242] Two popular European translators of Manusmṛti, William Jones (1794) and G. Buhler (1886) or recently by Wendy Doniger (1991) used 'law' in place of 'dharma'. European use of 'dharma' mainly in case of Manusmṛti translation was purely motivated to re-construct British ruled India. The colonial expression and idea of 'Religious Law' created an immense tension to the actual Indian concept of dharma.[243] The Supreme Court of India has defined, "Dharma is that which upholds, nourishes or supports the stability of the society, maintains the social order and secures the general well-being and progress of mankind."[244]

Therefore it is evident that the use of the word 'dharma' for Manu and Moses goes beyond the meaning of modern 'law' because the applicability and jurisdiction of these ancient laws are to be meant for each and every aspect of the private and public life of people and also to define the cosmic function. In compare to dharmic law, modern law has limited use. The social order of Manusmṛti and Torah as law under which the people are being governed i.e., the conduct of life, is actually the identity of people, whereas modern law, per se, is not identified with the culture of people. The holistic approach to life, nature, and cosmos in both laws, in the end, profess a spiritual objective i.e., *moksha* or salvation, the dharmic goal.

Dharma is an Indian term, not exclusively a Hindu religious term and within dharmic system four religious traditions (Vedic, Jain, Buddhist, and Sikhism) are functioning, governing and evolving. Since it includes both secular and religious aspects, it can't be concisely limited into a 'religion' category.

To define the difference between modern and ancient laws, H. S. V. Maine said that ancient laws like of Manusmṛti which not only governs social life but also individual and family life, hence opposite to modern sense. Maine's view on ancient laws can be contested, that is to say, the France Revolution context and the emergence of European modern law are largely against the establishment of Church (anti-Christian). William Jones compared Manusmṛti

---

[241] Rajiv Malhotra, *Being Different: An Indian Challenge to Western Universalism* (Noida: Harper Collins, 2013), 259.

[242] Nikunja Vihari Banerjee, *Studies in the Dharmasastra of Manu* (Delhi: Munshiram Manoharlal Publishers Pvt. Ltd. 1980), 2.

[243] Ibid., Nikunja Vihari Banerjee, *Studies in the Dharmasastra of Manu* (Delhi: Munshiram Manoharlal Publishers Pvt. Ltd. 1980), 2-3. Nikunja.

[244] Judgment of the Supreme Court of India, 12th September, 2002, against the writ petition Civil) No. 98 of 2002.

with a book of Leviticus on account of its preoccupation with rituals and religious observance.[245] Our intention is not scoring merit in comparison, but to define fundamental differences of usage of 'law'.

By the time of Manusmṛti (commonly 200 BCE -200 CE), the word *dharma* amplified consisted of philosophical, religious and ethical treaties in the context of the social scheme. Philosophically, an object is said to have its *dharma* (*Svadharma*) in the sense that it has its own characteristic (*svabhāva*) which in other words, is called its nature and essence and its philosophical meaning is *dhṛ*. Accordingly the *dharma* a person is to correspond to his/her oblige innate nature or it should be his/her form; this seems to be the basic philosophical implication of Manu' usage of *dharma* in his social context of *Varna-āśṛama* (conduct for *Caturvaṛnas*) and the 'mixed castes.'[246]

Manu's usage of the word *dharma* is also implied as the 'ethical code' that belongs to the inner essence of a person's social relations. That is why *dharma* in Manu is primarily an ethical concept, even though it stands for morality as well. The key concept of Manu's *dharma* as summarized by Dr. Bhagavandas are as follows: that which holds a thing or things together, makes it what it is, prevents it from breaking up and changing into something else, its fundamental attribute, its essential nature, the law of its being, moral, ethical and legal duty, etc.[247] The theory of *dharma* according to Manu is not theoretical speculation, but the practical evaluation of life. It will be analyzed in depth in accordance with *saṁskāras*.

In further detail description of the Manusmṛti classified *dharma* into ten categories to lay out the inner essence of the laws. These are patience (*dhriti*), forgiveness (*kshama*), piety or self-control (*dama*), honesty (*asteya*), sanctity (*shauch*), control of senses (*indraiya-nigrah*), the reason (*dhi*), knowledge or learning (*vidya*), truthfulness (*satya*) and absence of anger (*krodha*). These are the qualitative aspects that fulfill the aim of observing the law to bind the divine and social realm together in individual life.

North Indian Christians can draw the insights fact from these aspects since they are not primarily propagating a particular faith system but to fulfill the responsibility of life in relation to divinity and society. The observance of *dharma* is not related to salvation but it is a path to improvise life from rudimentary state to a spiritual state. Re-culturation in India is possible if socio-spiritual traditions of Indian are not confused with dogmatic exclusiveness of Church.

---

[245] H. S. Vide Maine, Early Law and Custom, 5-6.

[246] Manusmṛti 1:2.

[247] Bhagavandas, *The Science of Social organization*, Vol. I, 2nd ed., (Madras: Theological Publishing House,1932), 48.

4.1.2.4. Modern Interpretation of *Dharma* in India

Since renaissance (from the beginning of 19th century), India started redefining term '*dharma*' within new global/Western context, mainly due to the new space of interaction. We also observe European category and its influence on Indian-Hindu leaders. M. K. Gandhi viewed *dharma* as the equality of truth and the ultimate reality. To Swami Vivekananda, *dharma* is a process that makes a brute-man into a God-man. He puts three aspects in the hierarchy: firstly, *dharma* which begins with rituals; then turns into morality and finally, becoming spirituality. Interestingly, he used *dharma* as a religion where Western impact appeared to have accepted as a category to many native thinkers. According to S. Radhakrishnan, the purpose of *dharma* is to achieve personal perfection and social efficiency. The word *dharma* in modem India is a synonym of 'religion' to a great extent. Prof. Hiriyanna points out that in ancient Indian philosophical usage, it denotes both morality and religion.

The possibility of *dharma* as an applied tool for re-culturation can easily break the doctrinal boundary of Christianity. As Greco-Roman philosophy used to explore the early Christian doctrines; so *dharma* can also do the same for North Indian Christian. As Dr. K. P. Aleaz, said that denying the spiritual framework available in India, Gospel would never be Indian. He continued in saying that Indian culture is integrally related to its religions.[248] And to him, the relation is the advaitic[249] therefore; the Gospel in Indian culture is the Gospel of interreligious harmony and integration.[250] The word *dharma* needs to be explained in accordance to apprehend the totality of Indian culture. It is adhered the fundamental plurality covering the vast circle of the socio-spiritual landscape of India.

The religio-political nationalism and later development of right-wing groups (since late 19th century beginning with *Arya Samaj*) further complicated the whole dialogue-possibility when they started consolidating all *Astika* traditions as Hinduism. The confusion of whether *Astika* traditions belong to only Hindus or belong to Indians is a persisting debate.[251] Largely *dharmic* culture is a flexible idea and path-breaking aspect in Indian culture and the

---

[248] C. Raja Gopalachari, *Our Culture*, 5th Edition, (Bombay: Bharatiya Vidya Bhavan, 1981).

[249] R. Panikkar, "Indian Christian Theology of Religious Pluralism from the Perspective of Interculturation" in *Religious Pluralism: An Indian Christian Perspective*, Kuncheria Pathil, ed. (Delhi: ISPCK, 1991): 269.

[250] Rasheeduddin Khan, ed., Composite Culture of Indian and National Integration (Allahabad: Indian Institute of Advance Study, 1987).

[251] Nikunja Vihari Banerjee, *Studies in the Dharmasastra of Manu* (Delhi: Munshiram Manoharlal Publishers Pvt. Ltd. 1980), 15.

Gospel re-culturation is possible if the dharmic culture is taken as a viable framework.

4.1.2.5. Law, Colonial Construction and Modern India

During colonial expansion, the idea of a new form of the nation-state and secular value along with dogmatic Christian universal values negated the existing other systems in the world and in India. The ancient laws are religiously categorized as Hindu law like Manusmṛti for an administrative reason. Scholars like Galanter and Derrett[252] viewed Hindu laws as obsolete and irrelevant whereas Masaji Chiba put his doubt on the civil law model in West and its value-neutrality and universal projection.[253]

Traditional customary laws in India are existing norms and practices, so visualizing India as Hindu (religion) is simply wrong. Indian civil laws (the Constitution) accepted the customary laws and its function for many ethnic groups. For example, most of the ethnic groups who are now Christian (largely tribes) in North-Eastern follow customary marriage, divorce, adaptation of child, property inheritance which contradicts modern civil laws (one nation one law) and even Christian laws are accepted, because those are important as the identity and culture of people that can't be replaced by modern civil law or Christian religious law after being converted. In that spirit, Manusmṛti can't exclusively be treated as Hindu religious law.

4.2. Significance of Manusmṛti and Torah

The history of ancient India and Hebrew people were shaped by Manu and Moses in great extent. The cultural history in India and Israel is in debt to these ancient laws, not because they are absolutely new innovative tenets in their time or the world had ever seen before their existence, but due to the initial contribution in formulating a new identity in their respective region and people. In a strict sense, they might not have introduced any radical new elements that did not exist before they formulated more systematically and placed them in a functional standard code of conduct. The perimeter of these two laws is much a unifying constitution that instructed a minute detail to highest governing nuance and rules. It can easily be said that they are both secular and religious in modern terminology. The reconstruction of the cultural identity of NIC would be incomplete without concentrating on both ancient laws.

---

[252] J.D.M. Derrett, Religion, *Law and the State in India* (London: Faber & Faber, 1968) and *A Critic of Modern Hindu Law* (Bombay: N.M. Tripathi, 1970) and also see, Marc Galanter, *Law and Society in Modern India* (Delhi: Oxford University Press, 1989).

[253] Masaji Chiba 1986.

Indian and Hebrew people are governed by a standing divine originated laws,[254] and Manu is understood as the first man who offers an oblation to gods (Rig. 10.63.7), similar to Adam. Divinity is an integral aspect of both laws, so people observe these laws in multiple forms like customs, culture, manners, religion, art, music, dance, morals, ethics, etc. To define the place and importance of these laws, it is consequential to investigate *dharma* in both laws. There are also counter the view that both laws are responsible for creating a social system of injustice, degradation of women, etc. If we compare ancient laws in modern context those weaknesses are well established. Even much later St. Paul's writing degraded women.[255] Mary Dale's feminist argument rests upon such religious texts. It depends on how interpretations are used as a norm to regulate religions community or they are subjective to the individual is a question. For example, taking some other verses, it may appear fairly well judgment.[256]Among earlier scholars, it is Friedrich Nietzsche attributed Manusmṛti even above the Bible and Christian traditions.[257] It is true that Nietzsche's personal standing on Christian tradition is complex; therefore his critical reading of Manusmṛti must be viewed within his own context. Whatever arguments are in place, there is no doubt that Indian and Hebrew people reflect ancient laws in modern life with some degree of evolution. Same is the case of the Law of Moses, the divine intervention to monitor the earthly activities by the given rules.[258]

> "Design, O divine one, to instruct us precisely and in due order about the Dharmas of each of the social orders (*varna*) and of the intermediate ones. MS. 1:1-2.
>
> When the LORD finished speaking to Moses on Mount Sinai, he gave him the two tablets of the covenant law, the tablets of stone inscribed by the finger of God." Exodus 31:18

In this research, Manusmṛti and Torah are not seen just as a sacred book of respective religion, but ancient laws (*dharma*) for people. Even though it is factually true that Torah exclusively belongs to Hebrew people, but for Manusmṛti, it can't be purely a Hindu religious scripture. Any assumption to take it just as a Hindu text would be a fatal academic error. Mostly Indian ancient books were free for all people of the land and they are regionally used

---

[254] Exodus 31.18 and Manusmṛti 1.1-2.

[255] I Cor. 14: 34-35.

[256] MS 3.55 and Romans 16:1-16, Galatian 3:28.

[257] Aaron Ridley & Judith Norman eds., *Friedrich Nietzsche: Anti-Christ, Ecce Homo, Twilight of the Idols, and Other Writings*, trans. by Judith Norman (Cambridge: Cambridge University Press, 2005), 57-58.

[258] Exodus 31:18 New International Version.

along with enormous local customs within dharmic openness. Hypothetically speaking, if European colonial rulers and Christianity do not arrive in India, such classification would not have existed. Our research argument thus does not hold religious/colonial sectarian categorization of ancient Indian literature. Torah has more exclusive usability, even though its teachings, ethics, morals, jurisprudence, etc., have been transmitted to other ethnic communities through religions like Christianity and Islam. For Manusmṛti, it is more a social reality in which people keep changing their religion. Such usability not only restricted among Indian originated religions but also influenced Christianity and Islam in shaping their social mobility in India. Therefore, the exclusive religious stigma on them can be seen either as an academic inaccuracy or propaganda.

4.2.1. Manusmṛti and Its Place in Indian Culture

Placement of Manusmṛti in Indian cultural history is a challenge in contemporary India, mainly because of the Western methodological approaches that are employed to classify all ancient literature with religion, denying unifying dharmic model as an authentic hermeneutical heuristic tool. The colonial construction of Indian culture was completely motivated by two ideologies: firstly, the grand European narrative of superior civilization on which a political theory was developed that undermined 'others' and secondly, the Christian doctrinal supremacy over 'other' religions. To consolidate political establishment, breaking the traditional bond and social mobility factors among other communities are used. As a result, Manusmṛti was categorized as the 'Hindu' law book, not for Indians. In the context of the resurgence of right-wing Hindu groups that are known as the Brahmanical Hindu ideology and their loyalty to Manusmṛti and on the other hand, Dalit movement, under Dr. Ambedkar that burned Manusmṛti as a symbol of protest against former groups. This paradoxical reality during the colonial period posed the challenges before us to take insights from such a book for Christian cultural reconstruction. Our thesis takes this challenge and invites for a wider forward-looking debate in future.

Importance of Manusmṛti is far wider than socio-ideological uprising or making it simply a Hindu religious text. The question would possibly be 'is it relevant in modern Indian or NIC'? Many would be skeptical. Divinity is a quest in Indian subcontinent and Western idea of atheist or secular is a confusing word to most Indians. In dharmic tradition, divinity is an empirical reality of life and Graham Chapman marked it as an essential cultural aspect[259] whereas Derrett opines that Western oriental interest on Manusmṛti including

[259] Graham P. Chapman, *The Geopolitics of South Asia, From Early Empires to India, Pakistan and Bangladesh* (Ashgate: Aldershot, 2000), 17.

other *śāstras* was very much artificial and romantic.[260] Someone can partially be agreed with him, on the ground of suspicion to define the interest of West because interpretation on the oriental subject is closely related to the colonial expansion. What is vital is not to find the reason of interest among the Western establishment, but to find out the importance of Manusmṛti information of Indian culture.

Analyzing the essential features of Manu's law (*dharma*) will help to get the fundamental nature of Indian culture.

i. Laws (*dharma*) in India were not a product of divine revelation or neither handed down (theoretically) through a single person, rather it is a process and subject to amend as per time demands (*kaladharma*). Manu, in such sense, provided the axis which provides a *dharmic* ground, drawn out of Vedas. It was not static, but subject to question, free for criticism; divinely oriented and at the same time drastically materialistic; and it ends with *moksha* (liberation) as final aspiration of human being. Culturally, present India does not contradict this *Manuvadi* (Idea of Manu) idea.
ii. The plurality that is known as 'unity in diversity' in the Indian context is another index of largely found in every Indian originated religious texts including Manu. This idea was not a mechanism that attempts to bring diverse groups together under one specific idea or system, rather in Manu, a human initiative to unify diversity stands opposite to the *sanātanadharma* framework which upholds the plural expression of One Single Truth. This concept is a reality in Indian life. It was understood as chaos to EWM which has a tradition to clarify and to codify and attempts to monitor the entire faith community under it. Manu expressed two aspects: internal unity and continuity of external manifestation. So plurality in India is both hidden and revealed. It accepts human potentiality to explain the divine subjects including God on the basis of personal experience. Since personal experience is exclusive in nature, so one differs from others, yet each expression is taken as divine or spiritual for welfare. The absence of heresy can be taken as the root of Indian plurality. Due to such extended plurality-absorbing possibility, conversion to Hinduism is still undefined, beyond legal ambit. It lacks 'entry-exit' monitoring mechanism[261] as Christianity used to practice with doctrinal backing.

---

[260] J.D.M. Derrett, *Religion, Law and the State in India* (London: Faber & Faber, 1968b), 316.

[261] Paras Diwan & Peeyushi Diwan, *Modern Hindu Law*, 9th edition, (Allahabad: Allahabad Law Agency 1993), 1-10.

Counter to the lofty view of divinizing a book or the person Manu above human level, placing him (and the book) back in 1700-1100 BCE[262] or in 200 BCE to 200 CE,[263] glorifying as mythical divine persona referring to Rig Veda[264] in *Dharmaśāstra*[265] is actually a limited opinion. The laws of Manu are recognized as the foremost code of sacred and civil conduct (*dharma*), not the absolute. Morgan agreed to such reference as Manu is mentioned in Vedas as the human being's first progenitor and medicine (not for health, but for the mind) to a human being.[266] Intentional misinterpretation Manu as a supreme guide for entire Indian culture by right wings Hindu groups (like RSS, VHP or their political outlet BJP) is a narrow sectarian ideology as Desai observed.[267] The hegemony Brahmanical interpretation has been always used for political motive even by the British to bring upper caste and European together on the ground of 'Blue Blood' and explained Manu as Brahmin, the part of a Supreme God. Dalit ideologists objected Manusmṛti on this point. When we argue on Manusmṛti as the formative cultural axis in India in this research, it does not qualify its supremacy over other *Dharmaśāstras* which are 136 in numbers including other contributors like Buddhist or Jainism, even later foreign cultures like Islamic and European. Largely śāstras within *dharma* featured essentials instructions on culture.[268] A myth around Manusmṛti has been wrongly developed during the colonial period after it was translated by William Jones (1794) and accepted by the British Govt. For implementing religious specific law as it was practiced in Europe. Questions may arise, then, how to interpret this ancient law. My personal observation is that no religious scripture is free from errors or above contextual limitation; therefore, it is not to dig out the limitation of this book, rather investigate how this book has contributed to providing a framework for Indian culture.

---

[262] Max Müller's date 1500 BCE, Thomas Oberlies's date 1700-1100 (Die Religion das Rgveda, 1998.158), Klaus Klostermaier even dated back in 4000 BCE referring to the late Mehrgarh Culture.

[263] Most recent date is 200 BCE to 200 CE, but William Jones put on 1250 BCE and Karl Wilhelm Friedrich Schlegel put on 1000 BCE.

[264] Rig Veda 10.63.7.

[265] Margaret and James Stutley, *A Dictionary of Hinduism* (London & Henley: Routledge and Kegan Paul, 1977), 161.

[266] Kenneth W. Morgan, ed., *The Religion of Hindus* (New York: The Ronald Press Company, 1953), 328-329.

[267] Satyajeet A. Desai, *Mulla Principles of Hindu Law*, 17th edition, Vols. I-II (New Delhi: Butterworths, 1998), 18.

[268] Nikunja Vihari Banerjee, *Studies in the Dharmasastra of Manu* (Delhi: Munshiram Manoharlal Publishers Pvt. Ltd. 1980), 1.

4.2.1.1. Manusmṛti and Samaj Dharma

In the process of creation and the extension of creation is the Brahman Itself, therefore, Manu conceived the idea of the ideal society as the 'Theogony of Brahman'. Proceeding from that idea, the *varna* was viewed to have a divine origin,[269] intended to protect the world here and beyond, and humanity to lead to prosperity.[270] The hierarchy[271] in Manusmṛti is the qualitative involvement of an individual within a social system that will ensure the survival and contribution to the society itself. Our modern system also functions qualitatively so far as profession is concerned, no birthright is accepted for job guarantee, and social justice is guaranteed. Sociologically speaking, Manu's division was for the Aryan community and it went on to include to other non-Aryan people groups in due time. It was a social evolution process which eventually ended in creating the extremely mixed ethnic groups in India.[272] It is not only the social system of *dharma* that holds various ethnic groups within a broader ambit, but also the role of 'Theogony' that acted in favor to incorporate and include non-Aryans. Manu might have constituted social order on the basis of the divine institute, but at the same time, he prescribed a kind of egalitarian concept that equates human being on birth (quantitative equality) and allows qualitative growth in life. Manu said that none born as *Brahmin*, but as *Sudra* (low) and it is the ability of an individual to become a *Brahmin* (*Divja*-Twice Born)[273] only by accruing knowledge/skills.[274] Even though *varna* (not caste) was discriminatory during Manu, the interchangeability[275] within *varnas* was a natural possibility since it was purely based on the education one received. The term '*Brahmin*' confirms the highest moral standard of law. It is true that the development of birthright was the idea of Manu.

The contemporary justice system is to allow everyone to use his/her capacity to explore himself/herself without hindrance. The modern social equality is not a birthright, but right after birth. Manu was not so far behind from the modern social idea.

4.2.1.2. Manusmṛti as a Possible Model of Re-culturation?: A Search

The content of the Manusmṛti elaborates a large number of issues beginning with cosmology, sociology, politics, jurisprudence, medicine, religious duties,

---

[269] MS 1.31.

[270] MS 1.31 *lokānāmtuvivṛdhyardham.*

[271] MS 10.4.

[272] MS 10.45-46.

[273] MS and Gospel of John 3:1-21. The flesh gives birth an ordinary person and second birth is spiritual is what Manu's concept of *Dvija*.

[274] MS 9.334-335.

[275] MS 10.65.

etc. Our research interest will deal only those issues closely associated with *saṁskāras* on which a re-culturation attempt would be made. We shall also try to investigate how these issues are still relevant to Indian culture in contemporary time and to what extend usability for NIC's cultural reconstruction as a new paradigm is feasible.

The Manusmṛti suffers from three basic allegations; there are:

i. Manu established and implemented the 'Birth-Right' of the *varna* system.
ii. Manu's providence of punishment for *sudras* is inhuman and favored *Brahmins.*
iii. Manu viewed women as something low and inferior, presently is gender justice issue.

These three accusations can be contested only if one takes *Smṛti* works of literature holistically. The accusations against St. Paul on the issues of women and slavery from selective texts may help to explain better. These are the limitation of this ancient book, but the contribution of this book in developing Indian cultural nuances is unquestionable. Since Manu didn't advocate any single principle that can be treated or used with absolute authority, the miss-used of this book is the subject of time.

4.2.1.3. Counter-Narrative to Manusmṛti

Evaluating and placing Manusmṛti in mainstream Indian culture is very controversial and widely debated. The social uprising against the caste-ridden social system with over 70% population as lower caste has a long history. Historically it seems to have begun during the rise of Buddha. Later in South India in 9th CE and in North India in 13th CE, an anti-caste uprising with an ideology of humanism under *Bhakti* (religious) movement can be taken as a first mass movement against Brahmanical Hindu traditions so against Manusmṛti. Earlier movements were religious and at a later stage, during British rule, it was a social movement. During the colonial period, caste was completely taken over by the British Government and used it into two ways: dividing Hindu society for political purpose and it was understood as the epitome of injustice in Hindu religious system, so the Gospel was presented as the only a liberative path for those people. In the late 19th century and early 20th century, socio-political movements opened a new dimension and emancipation, called Dalit movement. Among many, B.R. Ambedkar emerged as the central figure against Brahmanical Hinduism as well as Manusmṛti. According to him, social injustice in India largely relies on Manusmṛti, and he even burns a few copies of this book known as *Manusmṛti Dahan Din* (Manusmṛti Cremation Day) on 25th December 1927, stating 40 odd verses from Manusmṛti that are used to diminish lower caste community. Speaking on the burning of Manusmṛti later in 1938, Ambedkar said, 'The bonfire of Manusmṛti was quite intentional. It was a very cautious and drastic step but was taken with a view to forcing the attention of Caste Hindus... It is not that all parts of Manusmṛti are condemnable ...We made a bonfire of it because we view it as a symbol of injustice under which we have been crushed across centuries....'[276]

He even compared Manu and Nietzsche, in a context of creating a superior race over others. John Rawls categories it as 'against of human nature'. In very recent incident at Jawaharlal Nehru University (Delhi) students uprising (mainly Leftist and liberal wings), one of the slogans was '*manuual se chutkara*'(freedom from Manu Ideology) or highly polarized caste protest at Una in Gujarat on 'cow-meat', Dalit protesters are pointing to Brahmanical Hinduism and Manusmṛti as epitome against them.

Accepting such anti-Manu perception, one must not conclude that it is purely a sectarian book. In wider social landscape, Manusmṛti is not about the caste even though caste is the biggest social problem in modern India, but if one can analyze the cultural behavior (*saṁskāras*) of Indian people, Manu along with other law books will appear to be praxis and Manu may be emerged undoubtedly at the center-stage.

4.2.2. The Law (Dharma) of Moses: May It Provide a Model for NIC?

4.2.2.1. Law of Moses and Christianity

The use of the Law of Moses and its status in Christianity is a subject of long historical debate which is still unsolved. General theological and doctrinal position, somehow, distinguish the validity of two Testaments. In one hand, the confession of Church acknowledges that every word in the Bible is a revelation of God, on the other hand, due to the fulfillment doctrine in Jesus lowers the status of the Old Testament. This is, to me, a great dilemma and ambiguity in Church tradition. It is found that Jesus had ever permitted or supported or hinted such dichotomy. His fulfillment argument expresses a historical continuity and added deeper spiritual interpretation of existing scripture (Law of Moses). It is the Pauline writing which is more doctrinal in nature we notice a deconstruction process which further eventually gave birth of Christian dilemma on Torah status quo.

The very canonization which put both together as 'Holy Bible' did not resolve this persistent question of how to deal with the Old Testament. Hypothetically speaking during canonization period, if the Old Testament was

---

[276] Dhananjay Keer, *Dr. Ambedkar: Life and Mission* (Mumbai: Popular Prakashan, 1952, reprint 2005), 103.

taken as a secondary or supplementary scripture and the New Testament as primary scripture; the dilemma would not have aroused. The role of secondary scripture is found in all religions except Christianity (not considering catechism in that sense). Today such possibility is extremely hypothetical and some readers may take it as a heretic. Interestingly, it is Sattam Pillai who found the validity of the Law of Moses much closer to Indian culture (*dharma*). John Wesley comment on this issue gives us a new possibility when he said, 'Perhaps there are few subjects with the whole campus of religion so little understood as this.'[277]

4.2.2.2. Challenges to Investigate the Law of Moses

One of the major challenges of studying the Bible mainly Torah and extracting some elements (*saṁskāras*) from it and put them into our modern context requires methodological accuracy. Such challenge demands a further critical investigation because of its comparative nature of present research between Hebrew and Indian traditions aiming to synthesize probable cultural incorporation which suits for north Indian Christians.

The traditions which originated from the *Torahal* period can be harvested through close examination of the biblical narratives methodological consideration. The written records from the biblical text and extra-biblical narratives always do not confirm each other. In such circumstances the biblical narratives will be taken as a primary source for argument; even though it is fact that many socio-religious traditions which are documented in Torah have their roots outside Hebrew origin. For example, The Ten Commandments (Exodus 20) are found in the much earlier writings, known as the Hammurabi Code.

The social settings of ancient Hebrew people can be interpreted with the purpose of modern application and relevance. It is a fact that every aspect of life cannot be authentically established and almost impossible to apply a methodology which will provide a substantial, authentic picture of the 4000 years old Israel world. Having said so, the continuity of socio-religious traditions that have been proceeding towards the 21st century through a community that has been governed with a code of conduct is undoubtedly the product of Torah. This continuity which is a unique phenomenon of Hebrew people helps to actualize Torahal tradition pacifying time, place and the manner.

The comparative study of various texts in some cases provides the key to identify the actual meaning and the purpose of a custom.[278] In doing comparative work, however, it should be understood that no parallel is likely

---

[277] E. H. Sugden, ed., *John Wesley's Fifty-Three Sermons* (Nashville: Abingdon, 1983), 426.

[278] For instance, the poetic texts found at the ancient seaport city of Ugarit (1600-1200 BCE) are similar to in style and vocabulary to the psalms and the epic sections of the biblical text.

to be totally exact. Customs and traditions can remain unchanged for centuries, but every group of people; even in the same area is different in some way from its predecessors in the region. Therefore, it is necessary to qualify most statements made in comparing ancient and modern peoples with logic.

4.2.2.3. Law in Torahal Period

Exploring the socio-religious world of Israel, the biblical text, in fact, will supply the basic information to describe the aspects of the life of the Hebrew people. Questions such as what did they eat? What did they wear? How did they greet? How did they worship? It would be looked for an answer from the Torah, even though, to extract information from the Torah and apply on Hindu converted NIC with consistent explanation and practical utility to bring out constructive changes in their socio-religious life through a process of a meaningful re-culturation, would never be an easy task. The sole purpose of the research interest in ancient Hebrew traditions is to establish the research argument that many ancient Hebrew traditions which are part of the Christian Bible actually qualify some of the Indian-Hindu traditions. Therefore, those prototype/resemble customs in both Hebrew and Indian traditions can easily be accepted to the NIC with biblical origin to reconstruct the Christian culture in India more like Indian culture.

Like Indian society, Israel underwent various chances; its social attitude, customs chronological during Patriarchal, Settlement, Monarchy, Post-Exile, and New Testament period, and interestingly, a community, starting with pastoral nomadic culture of the patriarchs, eventually emerged as a nation-state, around an evolving identity what is now known as Jewish. For any research, harmonizing between ancient and contemporary needs specific objective. Since present research attempts to use very selective *saṁskāras*, so we apply limited investigation.

4.2.2.4. Law of Moses and Formative Factor of Hebrew Culture

Till the 17th century, there was a dogmatic approach to the Bible, particularly Torah, based on the theory of 'Verbal Inspiration'. According to the content of the Bible was regarded quite literally as the repository of God's message to the human race, as literal transcripts of His will revealed to worthy people called to elders, judges, and prophets. The role of these receivers was that of an 'obedient instrument' fundamentally passive as a mere mouthpiece of God. This attitude was so clearly shown in the Talmud, the first official Jewish interpretation of the Torah, where it is said: "The Holy One, Blessed be He, was dictating, and Moses was writing with a tear."[279]

[279] Quoted by Robert Gordis, loc, cit. 783.

But the critical study of the text in the context of its cultural milieu enabled the modern scholars to understand the Torah as a living and evolving law, keeping pace with new conditions and growing insights in the context of an emergent society. In India, even though early western scholars like Max Muller, categories the Manusmṛti as a Hindu Lawbook, whereas it should not/ cannot be limited as Hindu Law book with its confined application within the framework of the Western classification of 'religious' and 'secular'. These law books have actually helped the majority of the Indian population to evolve a cultural identity which affirms the Manusmṛti as the prime reference as Hebrew people do even today to Torah.

The period of the formation of the laws depicts approximately one thousand years of the history of the Jewish religious and social life. Then the total content of the moral and social ideas of the Bible presents itself as a progressive discovery of truth. The historiographical narrative of this progressive discovery of the 'Rule of Life' is the picture of social realization of the ideas of God, of people and of moral life in the cultural context of Hebrews. Hence as F. G. Bratton said, "...the Bible is not a pre-ordained supernatural deposit of truth, but a record of the experience of man in his long search for that truth."[280]

The unscientific linguistic observations of the Massoretes were replaced by the scientific grammatical studies of brilliant Jewish philologists following Judah Hajjuj, Abul-Walid Ibn Janah and by the notable commentaries of exegetes like Rashi, Kimhis, Abraham Ibn Ezra and others. Their scientific works attained a level of achievement that bears favorable comparison with those of our own times. Thus a new basis was laid for a 'human approach' to the Bible that would regard it not as the 'dictation to God' to man but as the 'record of man's to the aspiration to God'. Religious thinkers might still regard the Bible as the inspired word of God, but then man here has become the 'agent' and not merely the 'recipient' of the Divine.[281]

Thus this revolutionary literary attitude towards the Bible led to a new aesthetic appreciation of the Bible as a monument of the Hebraic social and cultural evolution. The Bible, therefore, presents the best 'expression of the national spirit of Israel during its most creative period.'[282]

4.2.3. Trialogue: A Model of Re-culturation and Credibility of Torah in Christian Life

Interpretation is subjective to the context hence it is true for our re-culturation to formulate a new model with a purpose. We have two ancient laws along

---

[280] F. G. Bratton, *The History of the Bible* (London: 1961), 19.

[281] Cf. Robert Gordis, loc. cit., 787.

[282] R. Gordis, loc. cit., 787.

with Christian tradition to deal with an objective conclusion which will take scriptures with significance. Three dimensions are important: firstly, how to read Jewish Torah, being a Christian;[283] secondly, how to read the Hindu Manusmṛti being a Christian and thirdly, how to read these two scriptures in the context of NIC. This is a risk-taking task which is subject to skepticism. In such a possibility, we are to apply a model 'Trialogue'. EWMM was a monologue, and from the monologue, now we have to shift to a 'trialogue', bringing three traditions together for re-culturation. To bring this possibility as reality demands the mental and academic neutrality and objective resolutions are to be given a prime priority to overcome the challenges. Jewish-Christian dialogue on reading scripture is explained by R. W. L. Moberly in his book *The Old Testament of the Old Testament.* He said that Christian should not denigrate the laws of Torah neither can it be read like the Old Testament, but *Tanakh.* His main interest is to explore the dialogue between these religions.[284]

The model has objectively assumed to dealing the question of re-defining 'identity' which would be scripturally supported in such a way that a balancing approach can be applied. The very identity of being an Indian may refer to a complex assumption. Since our aim is to deal a delicate and sensitive issue of possible futuristic culture for NIC within a plural cultural framework of India, so objectively exploring multi-layer interpretations to justify the concept of identity i.e. cultural. Identity, be it cultural or political, is a burning issue in our modern world. The monoculturalism verses cultural confederationism is emerging rapidly towards the opposite direction to define a local identity above a global one. In such a situation, any assumption needs continuous engagement with its opposite voices. Our re-construction for a new Christian identity would be treated by such yardstick.

When we were attempting to use three ancient scriptures, it is also to be noted that the cultural definition within India is getting a very narrow shape by the right-wing Hindu religio-political groups like RSS and BJP. The rigorous attempt to re-define Indian history and to establish a mono-culturalism based on Vedic tradition as the sole tradition of India is a serious concern and many Christians may take a confrontational position. If so, the possibility of suggestive re-culturation will be unwelcomed, even though research attempt indicates a crisis-solving in nature.

---

283 Richard S. Briggs & Joel N. Lohr, eds., *A Theological Introduction to the Torah: Interpreting the Torah as Christian Scripture* (Michigan: Baker Academic, 2012), 4.

284 R.W. L. Moberly, *Old Testament of the Old Testament: Patriarchal Narratives and Mosaic Yahwism. Overturesto Biblical Theology* (Minneapolis: Fortress, 1992, repr. Eugene, OR: wipf & Stock, 2002), 147-175.

Mark G. Brett[285] in his article "Nationalism and Hebrew Bible" narrowed down some possible assumptions. Firstly, he believed that Jewish and Christian would possibly accept a Hebrew Bible in which both visualize a common vision of God in spite of various approaches and interpretations and doctrinal adversary. To my observation, he is right in his assumption that allows both communities somehow to share a scripture (partly) and same God (except incarnation of Jesus) and a common history. This commonality must be seen as a positive sign to re-read the biblical narratives from a new light in our time.[286] Even though, the strong impact of fulfillment theory of the Torah (messianic redeemer) in the New Testament often overshadows the authority and place of Torah in Christian traditions, which is, to me, unfortunate, even though, the impact and use of Torah is found almost in all major *saṁskāras* in Church. Secondly, he observed that two communities (Hebrew and Christian) are relatively independent tradition but Christian identity cannot afford to ignore the Hebrew tradition, though the fact is, Christian will largely rely on the New Testament whereas Hebrew will be on *Mishnah* and *Talmud*.[287] I prefer to use the term 'dependently independent' to justify his logic. Taking a step farther, it cannot be wrong to say that hardly any tradition in modern time is completely independent of other: Christianity and Islam are directly depended on Hebrew scripture, apart from various indirect impacts. Sociologically speaking, the New Testament (life and teachings of Jesus and early Church history) is formulated within and in contrast (sometimes) to Hebrew traditions. Academically, the New Testament is an outcome of trialogue: Hebrew, Christian, and Greco-Roman. In our research context, the role of the Greco-Romanism is replaced by Manusmṛti oriented Indian culture. This analogy is a possible exit root for NIC from EWC[288] to become truly culturally Indian. Taking identity as a crucial challenge in our time within a 'double-defined' dimensions as Charles Taylor explained: multiculturalism (Western meaning: two paradox identities are at the same time in society) and uniqueness of one's social identity.[289] This gap could be bridged only through dialogue.

---

[285] He is the Professor of Old Testament at Whitley College, Australia.

[286] Mark G. Brett, "Nationalism and Hebrew Bible" in *The Bible in Ethics: The second Sheffield Colloquium*, edited by John W. Rogerson, Margaret Davies & M. Denial Carroll R. (Sheffield, England: Sheffield Academic Press, 1995): 136-137.

[287] In an age of post-Holocaust theology, it is especially important for Christians to appreciate the integrity of the Hebrew Bible and to avoid any pre-emptive Christological hermeneutics. See further M.G. Brett, The Political Ethics of Postmodern Allegory', in M. Daniel Carroll R., D.J.A. Clines and P.R. Davies (eds.), *The Bible in Human Society: Essays in Honour of John Rogerson* (JSOTSup, 200: Sheffield: Sheffield Academic Press, 1995), pp. 67-86.

[288] EWC: Euro-Western Christianity.

[289] C. Taylor, 'The Politics of Recognition' in *Multiculturalism and The Politics of Recognition*, edited by A. Gutman (Princeton: Princeton University Press, 1992): 25-73.

EWMM failed to realize the necessity of dialogue in India or elsewhere. Rejecting the dialogue-oriented progress of Christianity has overshadowed the contribution of Christianity in India' and highlighted more on foreignness and conversion. To reverse the old rejection model of EWMM, we have adopted a trialogue, advancing from the cultural dialogue, and therefore, trialogue is to be treated as a heuristic in our thesis. The universalism of EWM is largely being understood as a symbol of the colonial hegemony that denied local culture in Church and Christian life.[290] EWM visualized such native cultural identity as an eminent potential threat to establish their cultural identity (for example, Latinization of South Americans).[291] Such a policy is politically driven and applied to achieve a vested interested against humanity in general. EWC,[292] be it Roman Catholic or Protestant or recently Pentecostals) largely promotes a monoculturalism of their own kind and work against local culture. It may appear a bit academically unqualified, but NICs are culturally westernized and less indianized. Many independent individuals attempted to re-construct and got success to some extent and many stated to establish Indian Church like Bhakt Singh (1903-2000), Brahmabandhab Upadhyaya (1861-1907), Sadhu Sundar Singh (1889-1929), K. Subba Rao (1912-1981) and *Yeshu Darbar* movement (since 1992) in Allahabad, UP.

Now, it is the responsibility of NIC to envisage how to re-introduce the Torah to have a public discussion. For time being, let us assume that Taylor is correct to define multiculturalism,[293] but I defer in one point that NIC by same logic should have own culture. Multiculturalism is a state of freedom that accepts differences. NICs are Indian by origin and then Christian by faith. EWM had attempted to reverse it with faith first and the nation last. Here rests the fundamental question of cultural crisis and reason for re-culturation.

When European Christianity had suffered for their identity in post-French Revolution era, and when German philosopher Friedrich Nietzsche openly said, 'God is dead'; it contrasted to the Indian reality, religious traditions are not questioned with an intention to invalid its importance in socio-cultural life. It might be true that Church depended too much on the governance of Church and doctrines to assure the finality of life, not on dharmic law of Jesus.

---

[290] C. Taylor, 'The Politics of Recognition' in *Multiculturalism and The Politics of Recognition*, edited by A. Gutman (Princeton: Princeton University Press, 1992): 43 & 62. Cf. J. Derrida, *The Other Heading: Reflections on Today's Europe* (Bloomington: Indiana University Press, 1992), 19.

[291] J. Moltmann, 'Covenant or Leviathan: Political Theology for Modern Times' in *SJT41* (1994): 19-41 (esp. pp. 38-39), reflecting on the German experience under Hitler; see further Moltmann, *Politische Theologie-Politische Ethik* (Mainz: Grünewald, 1984).

[292] EWC – Euro-western Church.

[293] C. Taylor, 'The Politics of Recognition' in *Multiculturalism and The Politics of Recognition*, edited by A. Gutman (Princeton: Princeton University Press, 1992): 67 & 70.

Probably, it is true. On the question of the sustainability of *dharma* in Indian tradition, J. B. Pratt's observation might be right. He said, "If a religion is to live, it must adapt itself to new and changing conditions, if it is to feed the spiritual life of its children, it must have the sensitivity and inventiveness that shall enable it to modify their diet as their moods demand."[294] The *dharmic* culture is not static, neither it rejects or replaces something that is new but follows a constant process of supplementation. Therefore, *dharma* is still a very prevailing system in India and the spirit of *dharma* is Indianness.

Indian *dharmic* plurality goes beyond the define religion or can be said that it itself is a different model. When *dharma* in the Vedic tradition does not acknowledge a particular founder, book, savior, holy place, creed, rituals, and even though there are some prescriptions (*Visesha*) of *saṁskāras*, yet nothing is obligatory in right sense, then the Vedic tradition and its capacity to create space for other traditions is to be dealt with that spirit. *Vedic dharma* is not only Hinduism (in limited meaning) but a system for humanity, nature, and universe in Indian traditions. The *Sanatana Dharma* advocates collective research for 'Truth' and it does not advocate a particular idea and every human experience is questionable to correct to envisage the Truth. The human mind, by nature, is diverse and therefore diverse approaches are a natural process that is what *Vedic Dharma*. There is no presupposition of social conformity but provides the space for the individual inquiry to the 'Ultimate' through a system of his/her own choice. The British historian Arnold Joseph Toynbee (1889-1975) said that the *Vedic Dharma* not only exercises or concentrates on its own tradition but also complement other traditions too.[295] For many people it is 'tolerance', but I argue that tolerance may be practiced as a policy or doctrine (individual or nation), rather *dharma* is a system that does not interfere others affairs, does not justify or judge but acknowledge the new possibility. The Christian mission differs from such an open system. This exclusive positioning of Church secluded NIC from their heritage after accepting Christianity during the colonial period.[296]

The observation of many Christian scholars prescribes the *dharmic* culture as the best framework available to present the Gospel in India and the *dharma* of Jesus and *dharma* in India do not contradict but complement. Therefore, the research will apply the *dharmic* framework in re-culturation and therefore *dharma* and *dharmic* tradition would not be considered as a religion in entire research but would be taken as a model.

---

[294] J. B. Pratt, *Why Religions Die?*, 122.

[295] Arnold Joseph Toynbee, *Christianity: Among the Religions of the World and One World and India* (New Delhi: Indian Council for Cultural Relations, 1960), 42-59.

[296] R. C. Zaehner, *Concordant Record*, 22-23.

4.3. *Saṁskāras* and Sacraments

4.3.1. Definition of *Saṁskāras* and Sacraments

On the outset, we may make it clear that '*saṁskāras*' are not identical to 'sacraments' as it is understood and explained in Indian, Jewish and Christian tradition. *Saṁskāras*, in India, is a totality of life that governs the entire life of people, sacred and secular, even after death. In contrast to Christianity, Indian *saṁskāras* were never adopted by a council or codified in a single book (catechism); rather they are constantly evolving ritualistic tools in the hand all sections of society without diluting the basic imperative. Indian *saṁskāras* are a normative reality, not obligatory. Obligatory religious duties in the Semitic sense are unavoidable rituals which can't be questioned, altered without a decision of authority; whereas, *saṁskāras* are free from such jurisdiction. In India, everything a person does (for good) is *saṁskāra* and if one puts in a hierarchical order, some *saṁskāras* might be equated to Christian sacraments like marriage (*vivah*), baptism (*upanayana/diksha/suddhikarana*) or *antyesthi* (funeral) etc. Historically, religion plays a vital role in formatting people's culture. Therefore, it is rather impossible to separate one from others. Whether modern or primitive, many reflective behavior, ethics, morals, public and private life have religious roots and eventually, those with religious roots are codified as *saṁskāras* or sacraments and remaining is known as secular/civil customs/traditional norms. We shall discuss the various terms like 'Law', '*Saṁskāra*', 'Sacrament', '*Dharma*' and their meanings, and also to harmonize them in such a way that would provide a new *saṁskāric* model, meaningful and usable to NICs.

Therefore, it is an attempt to understand the status of *saṁskāric* life of NICs before and after conversion and to analyze the cultural shift in the new faith. It will also look the detail nuances of *saṁskāras* to support the argument why such re-culturation is a need and how de-culturation took place during the colonial period and in what extent the Manusmṛti along with Torah can provide a new *saṁskāric* model as a postcolonial aspiration.

This will also further undertake selective areas from both laws to address some issues such as i. how two different geographically developed ancient traditions could be compared; ii. What are selective areas for consideration and why such areas are significance into our research argument; iii. How those selective areas are to be used as a model for re-culturation for NICs. At last, the question would be asked in what extent such an attempt can provide a formidable new identity for NICs within Indian plural culture. Our research reasoning will consider the above categories while dealing with the issues involved in re-culturation for NIC and the postcolonial subaltern quest will guide the whole analysis heuristically.

Kathleen Bliss defines:

> Sacraments involve the worshippers more deeply than more highly verbalized forms of worship – but they become a mere indulgence in vague feelings of *numinosity* unless the worshipper understands their meaning as memorials of the issues from events and that involves the use of words.[297]

It would rather difficult to actualize the exact meaning of rituals apart from sacraments in the Christian context. It defines a manner of performing divine service,[298] the prescribed form of words of a liturgical function.[299] In today's Church traditions, the term 'ritual' has less usage, rather the term 'Order of Service' is more familiar. The sacrament is a more familiar term in Christian circle, originated from the Vulgate means '*mysterious*'. According to St. Augustine, it is 'the visible form of invisible grace or a sign of a sacred thing.'[300] To Thomas Aquinas, the sacrament is 'the sign of the same thing as far as it sanctifies man.'[301] John Calvin defines it as 'the term was applied to those signs which gave an august representation of things spiritual sublime.'[302] In Latin dictionary, two meanings are used to know its root; one is the security money deposited to a sacred place when there is a suit, and later loser's money be used for the religious purpose, and another meaning is the oath of allegiance of a Roman soldier before the King. In later history, there two meanings are combined as 'sacred rite'. Investigating much deeper meaning of sacraments, Calvin, in his book *Institutes of Christian Religion* said that nature itself can be considered as a sacrament with a selective note, 'And shall the Lord not be able to stamp his creatures with his world, that things which were formerly bare elements may become sacraments?[303]

4.3.2. Meaning of *Saṁskāra*

The nearest English word of the term *saṃskāra* may be translated as a sacrament.[304] *Saṃskāra* does not mean merely an outward rite or observance which is religious or held sacred. It has been defined as peculiar excellence

[297] Kathleen Bliss, *The Future of Religion*, (Penguin Books, 1972), 165.

[298] *Chamber's Twentieth Century Dictionary* (Allied Publications, 1965), 952.

[299] *The Oxford Dictionary of the Christian Church* (Oxford University Press: London, 1957), 1168.

[300] Ibid 492. John Calvin, Institutes....

[301] *Oxford Dictionary of Christian Church*, 1198.

[302] John Calvin, *Institutes of the Christian Religion*, Vol. II (London, James Clarke & Co. Ltd., 1949), 492.

[303] Thomas F. Torrance, *Calvin's Doctrine of Man* (Eugene OR: Wipf & Stock Publishers, 2001), 41.

[304] Pandey, *Cultural History of India*, 390 and see Pandey 11.

accruing from the performance of the rites ordained, excellence residing either in the soul or in the body.[305] The Sanskrit word *saṃskāra* is derived from the root '*kr*' with the prefix '*sam*' and suffix '*ghan*' added (*samskrghan*) and is used in different senses.[306]

Various systems of philosophy embody it to signify different meanings. For *Mimamsakas*, it is an attribute of sacrificial objects arising from sprinkling and the like; for the *Advaita Vedantins*, it is a false attribution of physical action to the soul; for *Naiyayikas*, it is a self-reproductive quality or faculty of an impression. In classical Sanskrit literature, *saṃskāra* has the sense of education, cultivation, training (*Raghuvamsa* V. 3. 35); refinement, perfection, and grammatical purity (*Kumara Sambhava* I. 28); impression, form, mould, and influence (*Hitopadesa* I. 8); a purificatory rite, a sacred rite or ceremony, consecration, sanctification and hallowing (Manusmṛti II). Thus it may be seen that the Indian (Hindu) sacraments aimed not only the formal purification of the body but also at sanctifying, impressing, refining and perfecting the entire individuality of the recipient, producing special merit in him/her,[307] i.e., a spiritual journey.

4.3.2.1. Etymology

'*Kr*' with prefix '*Sam*' and suffix '*Ghan*' = *Samskara* [*sam* + (*sa*) + *kr* + *ghan*]. There are much meaning of it, but it is clearly mentioned in Vedas, except '*samskrta*' means 'purification'[308]

Classical Meanings: The word started to use mainly various philosophical schools with different meanings. *Mimamsakaras* said it as 'ceremonious purification of sacrificial materials.'[309] In *Jamini*, it is 'purificatory rite.'[310] In *Naiyakaras*, it is 'self-reproductive quality.'[311] In *Advaita Vedanta*, it is 'the false attribution of physical action to the soul.'[312]

The *Advaita Vedanta* may stand opposite to the traditional practices since it believes that it is 'knowledge' that will bring '*mukti*' (salvation),

---

[305] *Viramitrodaya Samskara Prakasa* I, 132. See also Pandey, 17 and *Cultural History of India*, 390.

[306] R. B. Pandey, "The Hindu Sacraments (Samskārass)" in *The Cultural Heritage of India*, Vol. II (Calcutta: Ramakrishna Mission, 1937, repr. 1969): 390.

[307] R. B. Pandey, "The Hindu Sacraments (Saṃskārass)" in *The Cultural Heritage of India*, Vol. II (Calcutta: Ramakrishna Mission, 1937, repr. 1969): 391.

[308] Rig Veda (RV) V.76.2, *Satapatha Brahmana* I.1.4.10, MS II.26 Cf. R. Pandey, *Hindu Saṁskāras* (Delhi: 1987), 15.

[309] R. Pandey, *Hindu Saṁskāras* (Delhi: Motilal Banarsidass, 1969), 15.

[310] Jaminisutras III.1.3, 8.3, IX 2.9 also R. Pandey, *Hindu Saṁskāras* (Delhi: Motilal Banarsidass, 1969), 16.

[311] R. Pandey, *Hindu Saṁskāras* (Delhi: Motilal Banarsidass, 1969), 16.

[312] R. Pandey, *Hindu Saṁskāras* (Delhi: Motilal Banarsidass, 1969), 16.

not ceremony or *saṁskāra*. It also must draw our attention that one can defy *saṁskāras* (in limited senses), yet not called a heretic. This freedom is available in *dharma* that contradicts to Christian tradition because in Christian tradition the Council decides the final meaning of 'truth' and practices. In such a tradition, the individual actually has no or limited religious freedom. Even today, the Church used to control religious finality through the institutional organization.

4.3.3. Purpose of *Saṁskāras*

There were many purposes for the *saṁskāras*. It was used to turn away the unfavorable power when it was propitiated by a *saṁskāra*. Sometimes the gods were also invoked to prevent the evil influences reaching the recipients of the *saṁskāras*. It was also believed that every period of a man's life was presided over by a deity, and therefore whenever occasions arose, that deity was invoked to confer boons and blessings on the person concerned. Secondly, Samskaras also had a cultural purpose governing the evolution of the society, because they comprehend sacrifice and rites that have for their aim domestic felicity resulting from the gain of cattle, progeny, long life, wealth and prosperity.[313]

Thirdly, the performance of the Samskaras served the purpose of self-expression. The householder performed the Samskaras for expressing his/ her own joys, felicitation and even sorrows at the various events of life. The Samskaras also aimed at imparting to life a higher religious sanctity. Impurity associated with the material body real or imaginary is removed by the performance of the Samskaras. According to Manu II. 28, by the performance of the Samskaras, the whole body is consecrated and made a fit dwelling place for the soul. The Samskaras were never regarded as ends by themselves; they were performed to help the growth and ripening of moral virtues.[314] Each Samskara conveys to more than their constituents- they become for the sacramentally sanctified person an outward visible sign of an inward spiritual grace.[315]

4.3.4. *Saṁskāras* in Indian Scriptures

The Hindu/Indian *saṁskāras* (sacraments) are found in various *dharmasastras* but it is the *Karma-Kanda* (of *Gṛhya Sutras*) that is taken as supreme reference.[316] A number of *saṁskāras* vary in different *dharmasatras* and they differ from

[313] R. B. Pandey, "The Hindu Sacraments (Samskaras)" in *The Cultural Heritage of India*, Vol. II (Calcutta: Ramakrishna Mission, 1937, repr. 1969): 392.

[314] R. B. Pandey, "The Hindu Sacraments (Samskaras)" in *The Cultural Heritage of India*, Vol. II (Calcutta: Ramakrishna Mission, 1937, repr. 1969): 393.

[315] R. B. Pandey, "The Hindu Sacraments (Samskaras)" in *The Cultural Heritage of India*, Vol. II (Calcutta: Ramakrishna Mission, 1937, repr. 1969): 394.

[316] R. Pandey, *Hindu Saṁskāras* (Delhi: Motilal Banarsidass, 1969), 1-14.

16 to 108. *Gautama Dharmasutra* listed 40, *Vaikhanas Dharmasutra* listed 18, Jinsen in *Mahapuran* listed 108, *Sanyas Upanishad* listed 40 and Manusmruti listed 16. *Mimamsa Darshan* also proposed 16 *saṁskāras* as like Manu. In the process of developing a standard number of *saṁskāras* it is Manusmṛti that is taken as final. It proves the importance of this book in formulating the basic social behavior of people's life and custom. These *saṁskāras* at the end played a catalyst role to set a cultural pattern of the society. Below list can give a picture to argue why *saṁskāras* are not just sacraments in Christian sense.

Before Birth	Childhood	Educational	Family Life	Funeral
Garbhadhan (Ceremony to Conceive)	*Jatakarma* (Welcoming newborn)	*Upanayana* (Ordination)	*Vivah* (Marriage)	*Anthesti* (funeral)
Pumsavana (Fetus protection on 4 months)	*Namkaran* (Naming ceremony)	*Vedaranbha* (Beginning Education)	*Vanaprastha* (Taking the child outdoors for the first time)	
Simantonnayan (Satisfying the desires of the pregnant mother on 7 months)	*Nishkraman* (Taking the child outdoors for the first time)	*Samavarthan* (Convocation)	*Sanyas* (Renunciation)	
	Aanaprashan (first solid feeding)			
	Chudakarm (First head saving keeping a lock)			
	Karnavedhan (Piercing ear)			

They are believed to be spiritually sanctifying aspects and from conception in the mother's womb till death and even after death, *saṁskāras* are attached to Indian life. Many constituents of the *saṁskāras* were meant to be a means of intercourse with, and influences upon, spiritual beings that were believed to guide and interfere with the course of human actions.[317]

Some *saṁskāras* might have taken by the pre-Aryan tradition and made use in Aryan community after invading in the Indus land,[318] but many

[317] R. Pandey, *Hindu Saṁskāras* (Delhi: Motilal Banarsidass, 1969), VII.

[318] Pereira Theodore, *Towards an Indian Christian Funeral Rite* (Bangalore), 47.

contemporary historians refute the Aryan invading theory. To them, it was a colonial theory to legitimate European invading and put two invaders in same royal status (European and Aryan, and Aryan was taken as blue blood and Brahmin. All Hindus were not counted in this scheme of political theory).

4.3.4.1. Vedas

i. *Rig Veda*: There is no direct reference of *saṁskāras* in *Rig Veda*. But, *RV* has many hymns and rites that lay the foundation for later *saṁskāras*. It has an elaborated description of marriage (*vivaha*) conception (*garbhadharana*) and funeral (*antyasti*).[319] Except for word, practices are there and importance was given on their social meaning.[320]
ii. *Artharva Veda*: It gives more detail information on rites, ceremonies, mainly marriage and funeral.[321] It has also given importance on *Brahmacarya* (study life and celibacy).[322]
iii. *Brahmanas*: Here we get more domestic rites even though there are many occasional references to *saṁskāras*, mainly *Upanayana*.[323] Whereas *Aranykas* and *Upanishads* are concerned with philosophical speculation rather than rituals even though we get references to marriage, funeral, and daily study.[324] Apart from these, detail of *Upanayana*[325] and marriage and naming system[326] are also mentioned.

4.3.4.2. Smṛti Literatures

Sutra literature gives the earliest systematic account of *saṁskāras*. *Sutras* as a whole known as rituals literature and *Srautasutras*, *Gṛhyasutras* and *Dharmasutras* hold like one unit called '*Kalpa*' which falls under the six *Vedangas*. *Srautasutras* deal with *Vedic* sacrificial with rites.

i.i. *Gṛhasutras*: it gives more detail account of what is today known as *saṁskāras*.[327] Canonization of *saṁskāras* starts with wedding ceremony rites then followed by others. It also provides socio-cultural dimensions of *saṁskāras*. Since there are many *Gṛhasutras* affiliated with various *Vedic*

---

[319] RV I.89.9; II.17.7; VIII.35.10; IX. 9.11.67; X.162, 183.

[320] R. Pandey, *Hindu Saṁskāras* (Delhi: Motilal Banarsidass, 1969), 2-3.

[321] *Atharva Veda* XIV. 1.2.; XVIII. 1-4; III.23.

[322] *Atharva Veda* XI.5.

[323] *Gopatha Brahmana* I.2.1-8. *Sataphata Brahmana* XI.3.1.3.

[324] *Taittiriya Aranyaka* I.27; II.9.

[325] *Chandodyaga Upanishad* IV.4.14.1; VI.1.2.

[326] Chandogya *Upanishad*.15.

[327] R. Pandey, op.cit., 6.

schools of thoughts, we find diverse reflections on the purpose of their usability.[328]

There are other supplementary literatures that of *Gṛhasutras*, give an account of *Kaplas* (ceremony), *Parisistas* (supplements), *Krikara* (system of conduct), *Prayagas* (practical application) and *Paddhatis* (outlines). These instructions of *saṁskāras* are implemented as sacraments are practiced in Christian traditions. One can, in modern time, reject or minimize according to various reasons that decision is left to individual, family, priest, gurus, etc. Because of such flexibility, *saṁskāras* are surviving within socio-religion freedom.[329]

Therefore, the sacraments are dropped, altered, modified and this process is continuous. So we get different system within broader *saṁskāra* traditions in India and they are followed by people with a dharmic ambit. Every community, family, individual may differ within *dharmic* logic and freedom. It was hardly imposed on people as obligatory. In this respect, when EWM introduced new *saṁskāras* (sacraments), those appeared to be against *saṁskāric* cultural of India and it led to the conflict to dharmic nuances. There occurred a fundamental difference and cultural question. It also encroached the religious freedom for Indian Christians as well.

i.ii. *Dharmasastras*: During this period, the practice of *saṁskāras* was classified on the basis of *varna dharma*. It also accepted the birthright of *Varna* and as per birth, *saṁskāras* rituals were distributed. They were treated additional intensity as social conduct of an individual. The Present Indian culture reflects this tradition.

The first systematic attempt that has described the *saṁskāras* is found in the *Gṛhasutras*. In these *Sutras* we find a clear distinction between sacrifice in general and the *saṁskāras* performed to sanctify the body and perfection of personality. It is in the *Vaikhanasa-Smarta Sutras* that a distinction between the *saṁskāras* relating to the body and sacrifices, in general, is stated. The *Gṛhasutras* generally deal with the bodily *saṁskāras* beginning with *Vivaha* and ending in *Samavartana* (convocation at the end of education). The majority of them omit *Antyesti* (funeral), perhaps because of impurity and inauspiciousness attached to the dead. The number of *saṁskāras* in the *Gṛhasutras* fluctuates from twelve to forty-eight[330] in different traditions, and among them, sixteen are counted as main *saṃskāras* in Manusmṛti.[331]

---

[328] Ibid., 7.

[329] Ibid.

[330] R. Pandey, "The Hindu Sacraments (Saṃskāras)" in *The Cultural Heritage of India*, Vol. II (Calcutta: Ramakrishna Mission, 1937, repr. 1969): Ibid.

[331] Musashi Tachikawa, Shoun Hino and Lalita Deodhar, *Puja and Samaskar*, (Delhi: Motilal Banarsidass Publisher, 2001), 92.

These are called the *Smarta Saṃskāras*. There were many purposes for the *saṁskāras*. It was used to turn away the unfavorable power when it was propitiated by a *saṃskāra*. Sometimes the gods were also invoked to prevent the evil influences reaching the recipients of the *saṃskāras*. It was also believed that every period of a man's life was presided over by a deity, and therefore whenever occasions arose, that deity was invoked to confer boons and blessings on the person concerned. Secondly, *saṁskāras* also had a cultural purpose governing the evolution of the society, because they comprehended sacrifice and rites that have for the domestic felicity resulting from the gain of cattle, progeny, long life, wealth and prosperity.[332]

i.iii. The performance of the *saṁskāras* served the purpose of self-expression. The householder performed the *saṁskāras* for expressing his/her own joys, felicitation and even sorrows at the various events of life. The *saṁskāras* also aimed at imparting to life a higher religious sanctity. Impurity associated with the material body, real or imaginary is removed by the performance of the *saṁskāras*. According to Manu II. 28, by the performance of the *saṁskāras*, the whole body is consecrated and made a holy dwelling place of the soul. The *saṁskāras* were never regarded as ends by themselves; they were performed to help the growth and ripening of moral virtues.[333] Each *saṁskāra* conveys to more than their constituents and they sacramentally sanctify a person's an outward visible sign of an inward spiritual grace.[334]

4.3.4.3. *Saṁskāras* in Manusmṛti

4.3.4.3.1. Importance of Manusmṛti *Saṁskāras* as Cultural Framework of India

Saṁskāras have spiritual and social significance and they bring higher sanctity and make passage smooth for a soul to reach into another world. The entire life of an Indian (Hindu) is monitored by the act of *saṁskāras* from inception in mother's womb to death and even after death. Both spiritual and material aspiration of an individual is incorporated in such a way that life on this earth plays a vital role to fulfill the ultimate goal which is liberation/*mukti*. Indian (Hindu) *saṁskāras* are world affirming, not world-negating. In one hand a person seeks for wealth for social need, health, children for family and intellect for mental need, yet all are to be demanded with dharmic righteousness which will qualify and assure for *mukti*. They are also the way of expression of joy

[332] R. Pandey, "The Hindu Sacraments (Saṃskāras)" in *The Cultural Heritage of India*, Vol. II (Calcutta: Ramakrishna Mission, 1937, repr. 1969): 392.

[333] R. Pandey, "The Hindu Sacraments (Saṃskāras)" in *The Cultural Heritage of India*, Vol. II (Calcutta: Ramakrishna Mission, 1937, repr. 1969): 393.

[334] R. Pandey, "The Hindu Sacraments (Saṃskārass)" in *The Cultural Heritage of India*, Vol. II (Calcutta: Ramakrishna Mission, 1937, repr. 1969): 394.

and sorrow, gain and loss, life and death. It purifies the mind and body together in performing a particular rite.[335] Rishi Angiras said that *saṁskāras* develop individual personality and Rishi Gautama said that they lead to Brahman/ *Mukti* (salvation).[336]

It is reasonable to say that *saṁskāras* were developed, amplified, codified and given an institutional bias in the later period and as civilization proceeds they provide social stability.[337] They are broadly divided in three: *desk-karas* for region/country; *kula-karas* for family and *Jati-karas* for particular *varna/* caste.[338]

The purpose of *saṁskāras* is arranged to expel the entire inner energy of a person towards the creation of a perfect secular as well as spiritual life in such a manner that converts to overall social welfare. Max Muller said that the deep-rooted tendency in the heart of man to bring the chief events of human life into contact with a higher power and to give to our joys and sufferings a deeper significance and religious sanctification.[339]

4.3.4.4.. Socio-cultural Importance

According to P.N. Prabhu, an Indian-Hindu sociologist, "while the *varna* scheme approaches the task of regulating social life of the individual through the community as a whole in the main, the ashrama-scheme is essentially devised the same end but approaches the task from individual's side. And between these two stands the *saṁskāras* through which the individual becomes from state to state...thus the natural man is raised to the fullest social status step by step."[340] This Indian (Hindu) *saṁskāras* may be seen as so many stages for the individual in the process of his socialization.[341]

In that spirit, *saṁskāras* signify both social and individual importance and unify individual with larger society.[342] *Saṁskāras* point out the social ethics of the Hindus which maintains a proper balance between social and

---

[335] Shailendra Sendar, *Ancient Indian Rituals and their Social Impact* (New Delhi: Anmol Pub. Pvt. Ltd., 2007), 143.

[336] Ibid., 144.

[337] Ibid.

[338] Musashi Tachikawa, Shoun Hino and Lalita Deodhar, *Puja and Samaskar* (Delhi: Motilal Banarsidass Publisher, 2001), 91.

[339] Shailendra Sendar, *Ancient Indian Rituals and their Social Impact* (New Delhi: Anmol Pub. Pvt. Ltd., 2007), 144.

[340] Pandarinath Prabhu, *Hindu Social Organization* (Bombay: 1954), 122.

[341] McMullen Clarence, *Rituals and Sacraments in Indian Religions* (Delhi: 1979), 49.

[342] Pandarinath Prabhu, *Hindu Social Organization* (Bombay: 1954), 223.

individual good. In an integral approach to life, all these combine naturally and exist as mutual compliments.[343]

The Hindu *Samskaras*/sacraments form an important section of the *karma-kanda* because it is believed that the performer will be spiritually sanctified. The *Grhya Sutras* are the main source for most of the *Samskaras*. *Samskaras* are an outward expression of sacredness, aimed not only the formal purification of the body but also at sanctifying, impressing, refining and perfecting the entire individuality of the recipient, producing special merit in him, a spiritual journey.

4.3.4.5. Spiritual Significance

The entire life of an Indian (Hindu) except many tribal groups, is monitored by the act of *samskaras* from inception in the mother's womb to death and even after death. Both spiritual and material aspiration of an individual is incorporated in such a way that life on this earth play a vital role to fulfill the ultimate goal which is liberation/*mukti*. They are broadly divided in three: *Desa-karas* for region/country; *Kula-karas* for family and *Jati-karas* for particular *varna*/caste. *Samskaras*, as described in Vedas, has three aspects: *Karma* (action) *Upasana* (meditation) and *Jnana* (knowledge).

A lot of many saṁskāras (of Manusmṛti or Manava Dharmasastra and its "work of encyclopedic scope")[344] is no more applicable like of strict caste oriented profession but through social identity of caste is very a reality; *vanaprastha* is obsolete, after 60-65 years of age a partial withdrawal from family decision making is still practice, education system is completely replaced by the western system, but inviting *Kulaguru* for initiation of first writing for a child is prevailing desire. Even though the ancient *saṁskāras* are to be evolved with the change and demand of time, yet the general conduct of life are still kept a lot of ritualistic lineage to *saṁskāras*. It can't be denied that the Manu's *saṁskāras* are able to appeal to the contemporary Indians (Hindu), and that is the reason the Manusmṛti is the most referred and quoted scripture so far the social custom is the concern.

4.4. Christianity and Sacraments

The sacrament by its definition might sum up as a 'rite whose words and actions are bound up with God's saving activity in and through the church.'[345] Such an explanation must be properly expounded to express the doctrinal meaning,

[343] R. Sharma, *Indian Society* (Bombay: 1981), 26.

[344] Wendy Doniger and Brain K. Smith, *The Laws of Manu* (Penguin, 1991), 16.

[345] Jeffrey A. Truscott, *The Sacraments: A Practical Guide* (New Delhi: Christian World Imprints, 2016), 2.

since various denominations and traditions have been, in history, redefined its possible inner essence.

The Old Testament, as James White writes, has provided the background of present Christian sacraments to communicate God's act into a human level.[346] There are four aspects that are important for our theological attention: personalized theophany in which God appears to an individual like of Moses (Ex. 13.21); God's anointing power to an individual (Numbers 21.4-9); atonement of sin (Lev. 9) and thanksgiving (Ex. 12.24; Deut. 12.6-7; Lev. 7.11-21) and symbolism as God's action.[347] In the Torah, the ritual of *Kipper* (Lev. 16.30) generally means cover up one's sin, according to L. Kohler, this was the original meaning as to avoid or avert punishment.[348] Therefore, in a broad sense, purification, both body and mind for higher spiritual and social gain.

4.4.1. Torah and Sacraments

The Old Testament, as James White writes, has provided the background of present Christian sacraments to communicate God's act into a human level.[349] There are four aspects that are important for our theological attention: personalized theophany in which God appears to an individual like of Moses (Ex. 13.21); God's anointing power to an individual (Numbers 21.4-9); atonement of sin (Lev. 9) and thanksgiving (Ex. 12.24; Deut. 12.6-7; Lev. 7.11-21) and symbolism as God's action.[350] In the Pentateuch, the ritual of Kipper (Lev.16.30) generally means to cover up one's sin, according to L. Kohler, this was the original meaning as to avoid or avert punishment.[351]

4.4.2. New Testament and Sacraments

Taking above four basic aspects, it can be well established that Jesus' life and work have all these oracles means to communicate the act of God. Physical

---

[346] James F. White, *Introduction to Christian Worship*, 3rd rev. exp., ed. (Nashville: Abingdon, 2000), 177-178.

[347] Jeffery A. Truscott, *The Sacraments: A Practical Guide* (New Delhi: Christian World Imprints, 2016), 4-6.

[348] Ludwig Kohler, *Lexicon in Veteris Testamente Libros* (Leiden: E.J.Brill, 1953), 452. Cf. J. Barton Payne, *The Theology of the Old Testament*, 5th print, (Michigan: Zondervan, 1973), 249.

[349] James F. White, *Introduction to Christian Worship*, 3rd rev. exp., ed. (Nashville: Abingdon, 2000), 177-178.

[350] Jeffery A. Truscott, *The Sacraments: A Practical Guide* (New Delhi: Christian World Imprints, 2016), 4-6.

[351] Ludwig Kohler, *Lexicon in Veteris Testamente Libros* (Leiden: E.J.Brill, 1953), 452. Cf. J. Barton Payne, *The Theology of the Old Testament*, 5th print, (Michigan: Zondervan, 1973), 249.

means to actualize theophany (Jn. 9.6); his baptism and coming down of the Holy Spirit is highly empowerment act of God (Mt. 3.16, Mk. 1.10, and Lk. 3.22); saving authority of being the messianic identity (Mk. 8.1-10), the symbolism of suffering servant (Lk. 22.27) and incarnation (Jn. 1.14)

Even though sacraments are to reflect various religious and spiritual significances, eventually, within the new Christian community, it is a baptism that got the central status over other traditional Jewish sacraments. It is noticed that baptism (in rite and confession) appeared to be the hallmark for the new identity, ever since, baptism remains the most important among all others.

4.4.3. Sacraments in History of Church

It would be a bit obscure to state a very clear picture of sacramental practices in the first millennium in Christian Church in compare to contemporary clarity, numerically and doctrinally. Yet there are practices since Jesus' time in some form or other. In the writing of St. Paul, we first notice the sacramental formation mainly Holy Communion (1 Cor. 11:17-34). If we focus on language (v. 23, 'For I received from Lord...') it is not clear from whom he learned it, since he was not a witnessing person of Last Supper of Jesus. This text is the oldest instruction that lays a foundation of Holy Mass.[352] It was evident that in the first millennium, the main intensity was more on the meaning of sacraments, rather on numerical counting. It is interesting to observe that a comparative dilemma between Old Law (Jewish traditions) and New Law appeared as a strong praxis-making yardstick to bring down the numerical position of Church, and in Augustinian view affirms it, even if he highly considered 'Baptism' and 'Eucharist' as essential for every Christian to assure salvation.[353]

The earliest sacramental system has led down by Augustine of Hippo (354-430 CE) both theologically as well as rituals. To him, it is the 'visible word' (sacrament) when word added to elements.[354] Largely, this meaning is prevailing even today. He also clarified the difference between two Testaments, stating the former provides the promise to be saved and later gives us the savior. One argument of Augustine can be taken to encounter the traditional authority of a priest to conduct it. He clearly said that if someone other than (ordained) priest performs this rite (baptism), it is equally effective to the receiver. This argument can be further discussed while dealing **'baptism'** separately. This possibility is further explored by the various 'Little Movements' in India.

---

[352] Bernard Leeming, *Principles of Sacramental Theology* (London, 1956), 556.

[353] Josef Finkenzeller, *Handbuch der Dogmengeschichte* (Basel & Wien: Herder Freiburg, 1981), 59.

[354] Augustine of Hippo, *Treatise on the Gospel of John LXXX.3.* (ca. 416). Cf. Jeffrey A. Truscott, *The Sacraments: A Practical Guide* (New Delhi: Christian World Imprints, 2016), 9.

Augustinian theological stand on 'symbolism and signs' of sacraments continued to be the centrality in the post-Augustinian period until numerical finality (apparently) of 'seven' process began its formative journey after the middle of the 12th century due to the rise of mysticism and later reform movement. It is the 'Council of Trent or Concilium Tridentinum - 1545-63 CE' that sealed on 'seven' and prior to it, Martin Luther sealed (7>5>3>2) on 'two'; thus the Christian faith community was completely divided not only in number but also is theological logic and interpretation.

During medieval European Church, theologian like Hugh of St. Victor (1096-1141) who emphasized on three areas namely; similitude or like of the things signified, the institution to make this signification and ability to confer the thing signified on the recipient.,[355] but it is Peter Lombard (1096-1164) who first listed seven sacraments; whereas, it was Thomas Aquinas (1225-74) provided the fundamental theological argument in his book *Summa Theologica*. The central focus of his or his predecessors is on 'grace' that brings forth a new dimension over the Old Covenantal status qua. He also stated, like of St. Augustine, the efficacy of sacraments beyond the eligibility of a person, be it moral or spiritual. A sacrament, to him, even though conferred by a wicked or faithless minister, will be 'true'. Many people may not be agreed with such 'appeared to be radical' but theologically deep rooted meaning. Staking such possibility found in history, north Indian Christian may use is a model, allowing common believers to conduct sacraments to avoid 'strict' traditionalism and rites. The research's own experience of giving 'Baptism and Holy Communion', Dr. Gir's mission movement in Uttar Pradesh will be analyzed to find a new postcolonial possibility in the Indian context.

4.4.4. Sacraments in Protestant Tradition

Prior to the Protestant Reform Movement (16th century), theologians like John Wycliffe (1320-84), Jan Hus (1369-1415) or Erasmus of Rotterdam (1466-1536) have contributed the framework to revisit the old Christian traditions. This tradition was further accelerated by Martin Luther (1483-1546), Ulrich Zwingli (1484-1531) Philip Melanchthon (1497-1560) or John Calvin (1509-64) by exploring new biblical interpretations. Even though the socio-political context during the reformation ear can't be overlooked and the whole movement can be taken purely a religious reform based on the Bible (*Sola Scriptura*).

Protestant tradition, obviously, offered a model before north Indian Christians, especially for the FGC to explore the cultural ambit of their own to revisit the present rites in which 'faith' can be taken as the primary focus, not the 'rite'. Taking 16th-century socio-political context as pivotal urgency,

---

[355] Hugh of St. Victor, *On the Sacraments of the Christian Faith* I.9 (1140). Cf. Jeffrey A. Truscott, *The Sacraments: A Practical Guide* (New Delhi: Christian World Imprints, 2016), 10.

the post-independent India can also use the 'Post-Colonial' hermeneutic and methodology to create 'Space and Place' within the larger community through a cultural reconstruction. If European Christians have the religious freedom for their religious quest, then demand of north Indian Christian can be equally valid. Another aspect is that traditions (rites) and interpretations of scripture in Church history were never stagnant, it is open to the individual as a mark for religious freedom.

Interestingly, a paradigm shift in Lutheran logic is obvious from traditional understanding and practices of sacraments when he, after prolong New testament based argument, found only two sacraments to a new Christianity i.e., known as Protestant tradition. Martin Luther has, evidentially, provided 'divinely instituted sign and the promise of forgiveness of sin' as the *sola* evidence. Eventually, common people started adopting those new changes, both in doctrine and rituals.[356] He also agreed to develop the separate marriage rites and ordination, even though, to him, it could not be called a sacrament since they don't have divine saving promise.[357] Taking 'faith' as prime centrality for the sacramental justification,[358] Luther actually provided a possibility for Indian Christians (mainly FGC) to take 'faith in Jesus' as *sola* qualification to call a disciple and deserve the equal status within Christian Church, not the sacramental rites as unalterable justification.

Luther and Melanchthon may apparently have the similar idea on 'command and promise; through to Melanchthon, confession, absolution, and ordination could be taken as sacraments since they have same 'divine command and promise'. On the other, Zwingli emphasized more on spiritual aspects of sacraments; even though he had feared that rites (elements) may take over the spiritual institute of God. To him, the external element is unable to purify the soul and can limit the expression of freedom of Spirit.[359] John Calvin, on the other, took outward sign as an inseparable aspect of sacraments, '...outward sign by which the Lord seals on our consciences the promises of his good will toward us in order to sustain the weakness of our faith, and we, in turn, attest our piety toward him in presence of the Lord and of his angels and before men.'[360] The interplay between sacrament and the Holy Spirit is essential in

---

356 I Timothy 3.16, 4.4-5.

357 Martin Luther, *Babylonian Captivity*, LW 36.92.

358 Jeffrey A. Truscott, 'Luther's Pastoral Approach to baptism,' in *A Living Tradition: On the Intersection of Liturgical History and Pastoral Practice*, eds. David Pitt, Stefanos Alexopoulos and Christian McConnell (Collegeville: Liturgical Press, 2012): 139-40.

359 Ulrich Zwingli, *Commentary on True and False Religion* (1525), in *The Works of Huldreich Zwingli*, ed. Clarence H. Heller, trans., Samuel M. Jackson (Philadelphia: Heidelberg Press, 1929), 183.

360 John Calvin, *Institute of the Christian Religion* (1559), iv.14.1, ed., John T. McNeill, trans., Ford Lewis Battles, in LCC, 21.21 (Philadelphia: Westminster Press, 1960), 1277.

his an argument, to him, rites are empty if the Holy Spirit is absence. Even the Church of England on which the Church of North Indian is largely dependent doctrinally and sacramentally disagreed to accept that sacraments are just an outward sign. It sees it as the certainty of witness and effectual sign of grace and confirms one's faith in Jesus.[361]

Post-reformation period, the European history was dominated by enlightenment logic, to which, a challenge posited over the traditional value and further freedom of individual experiential religious (spiritual) value started redefining the sacramental interpretation. The person like Emmanuel Kant (1724-1804) minimized baptism just as 'intended to be holy' not actually happened and Lord's Supper is a moral expression of brotherhood.[362] That does not mean that they rejected the very sacraments, but surely downplayed the divine authority of those rites. Such outside Church interpretation has also deeply impacted when Anglican and Lutheran Church started focusing on the moral character of a person and personal introspection. The greater importance on 'confirmation' not on 'baptism' emerged as a higher spiritual reality of mature life.

Later in the 19th century, mainly in America, the tradition of the 'camp meeting' was a new start-up for Church to accept a 'revival' outside the Church control. Charles G. Finney (1792-1875) had systematized this tradition adding a whole of new practices like congregational prayer, emotional preaching, counseling for spiritual need, etc.[363] He interestingly said that the Church of the given age must find the means that suits best within the local context of the people. Looking at his statement and pragmatic approach, Indian Church and new converts are to given chance to define their spiritual need. Finney also mentions that Church tradition has always been going through changes in each aspect. The fallout of Finney's model, of course, devalued the previous position of 'elements' and 'word' in sacraments.

The emphasis on individual experience over Church tradition and the cultural setting of a particular place is, someway, getting importance in re-shaping the sacramental traditions of Church. The Protestant tradition is essentially a plural term and historically decentralized; therefore, re-constructing has become the spiritual trend of this tradition. What happened in European Church was a transformation within Christians whereas, in India, it is multi-faith social context with the complex religio-political nexus. The

---

[361] Church of England, *Articles of Religion* (1563), Art. XXV, in *Book of Common Prayer* (Oxford: 1784), SW, 20. For a modern Prayer Book containing the Articles see BCP 1979, 872.

[362] Immanuel Kant, *Religion within the Limits of Reason Alone* (1793), trans., Theodore M. Green and Hoyt H. Hudson (New York: Harper and Row, 1960), 187-88.

[363] James F. White, *Protestant Worship: Traditions in Transition* (Louisville: Westminster John Knox Press, 1989), 176.

freedom that protestant Church has been enjoying in Europe had lost its free spirit when they politically colonized other non-European countries. The socio-religious freedom of native believers was totally denied, and neither local believer had any right to ask freedom since the European Church and colonial power were inseparably one. Some freedom attempts like of Rev. Sattam Pillai (1850s) or Bengali Revival Association or in the 20th century many individuals took initiative to break away from European tradition but they were suppressed. Therefore, re-culturation through a valid re-construction of sacraments is to be a very legitimate religious freedom struggle for north Indian Christians.

4.5. Background and Reason for Sacramental Reconstruction

Rituals and sacraments have deep sociological and historical significance with its intrinsic theological connotations and rituals and sacraments have a historical, sociological and theological contextual reason of occurrence and also develop a cultural climate among people. Therefore, it must not be taken only a religious exclusively.

It is noticeable that in the historical development of *saṁskāras*, many older forms are replaced or altered to provide space for new expression. Christianity is no exception to it, like of Baptism; Holy Communication has also gone through the same process. Reconstruction of *saṁskāras* is to make *saṁskāras* relevant to the given context. When it comes to the culture of *saṁskāras*, they must be analyzed within a larger social context. For example, Muslim girls in Bangladesh are loving called by their mother as 'Lakshmi' (a Hindu goddess) as a symbol of good manner, prosperity and in this word, they are worshiping a Hindu deity, but wish to find qualities of Lakshmi in a daughter. Here a religious deity's quality goes beyond the religious usability and became a culture symbolism of people. In Indian saṁskāras, even though they have a religious origin. At end developed a culture for people. The rejection of the cultural meaning of saṁskāras would definitely enter into a cultural conflict and identity crisis for people who accept new faith. EWM failed to differentiate these two aspects of *saṁskāras*. The end result of rejecting *saṁskāras* only on the basis of the religious root has created a cultural identity crisis for north Indian Christians.

The most important reality in such a process is the tension between the meaning and mode of expression. Meaning is uncompromising essence of religion, signs, and symbols through which a ritual or sacrament is communicated its religious truth, are exclusively cultural. The cultural expression does not have any universal optic. Here lies the actual challenge of inculturation. The harmony between 'ours' vs 'theirs', as it happened in Indian Christian context, is a sustaining under current and in our present research we take up this challenge. Signs and symbols of one culture are not to be advised or forced to drop after conversion of religion. For example, changing name after conversion to Christianity has raised deep social identity crisis. The socialized religion is governed by a set of norms. Since a particular religion, in some cases, responsible for developing a junk of cultural matrix, like Indian culture and Hindu culture have a grey undefined area where Indian Christians are struggling/hesitating to inherit many of cultural aspects like a sign of '*sindur*' or white bangle for married women in Northern India.

Taking the inseparable relation between *saṁskāras* and culture, north Indian Christians are to be given freedom within the Church to re-define their cultural symbolism to find their social relevance.

4.5.1. Importance of Sacraments in Christian Church in India

The Church in India, fortunately, shows some positive sign towards rituals and sacraments after independence. The birth of CSI and CNI are the historical events in Indian Church history, not only in the unification of various denominations but also towards giving the much awaited Indian makeover through a process of re-culturation (though selectively), and to do so, the hierarchical episcopalism is reconstructed with local autonomy and cultural orientation. Dr. James Massey said:

> As a member of the CNI, and also as a member of the CNI Liturgical Commission, I can, with assurance and certainty, say this much that there has been, within the context of India, a concerted effort directed towards the intensification of the liturgical dimension of the Church.[364]

Even Roman Catholic Church has shown the same positive indication towards Indian-ness allowing local Indian (Hindu) cultural signs and symbols to be accepted within Indian Christian like of *sindoor,*[365] white bangle, using *sari*[366] in wedding, etc. There are many signs and symbols are even indicated in Gospels, yet they are not merely reflective aspects for theological or doctrinal interpretation but also have deeper application in the daily life of a believer, therefore, a wedding ring or *mangalsutra*[367] is not just a visible sign for a married couple, but assimilating process with larger social cultural reality of

---

[364] Clarence O. McMullen, ed., *Rituals and Sacraments in Indian Religions* (New Delhi: ISPCK, 1979), 53.

[365] *Sindur*: Red telecom powder especially as applied as a dot on the forehead or in the parting of the hair of married Hindu women mainly in Northern and Bengali Indian. Vermilion is another popular English meaning.

[366] *Sari*: The unstitched long cloths dress for women. Most popular women dress in Indian sub-continent.

[367] *Mangalasutra*: An Indian marriage chain given by bridegroom as the final seal of marriage during marriage ceremony. This seal will be with body always. Word meaning is –

India.[368] According to St. Augustine, when the word is added to the element, and then it has the power to cleanse the heart... not because it is said but because it is believed.[369] It clearly indicates the faith transform the sign's face value into a spiritual value. Since signs and symbols are very much cultural, for example, the egg is a bad Indian symbol, but good in many European cultures. For such complex reason, elemental re-culturation has become essentiality to communicate the deeper theological and doctrinal meaning of sacraments.

D. M. Baillie expressed his view saying that, unlike many Protestant traditions, 'instead of saying that sacraments depend on human faith, it is right to say that sacraments are to operate through Human faith.[370] The argument also goes further on the issue of human role whether the efficacy of a sacrament solely depends on the person or divine intervention is still on. The preparation of the first Lord's Supper by Martin Luther can further be impacted by this issue on a person's own holiness. The Westminster Confession of Faith stated its focus more on the role of 'Divine Grace and Act of Spirit' than human efficacy.[371]

The Baptism and Holy Communion, even though rejected by Quakers and Salvation Army, have great importance in the Church. Baptism, in Greek, is 'to dip or to wash', even though Jews have different washing rituals (Luke 11:38 and Mark 1:40), the root of Christian meaning goes back to John the Baptizer, by stating the forgiveness of sin through repentance (Mark 1:4). So for Christian baptism is not a regular washing ritual for religious reason, but deeper symbolic act to begin a permanent fellowship with God. It is a participatory act in the death and resurrection of Jesus.[372] This transforming doctrinal reconstruction is to be kept in reflective signs and symbols.

4.5.2. Some Contemporary Indian Trends

The Post-Colonial Indian, the Church started realizing her freedom (even though lately) by adopting and accepting many alternative possibilities which are to be explored in subsequent chapters. Those movement are like Sattam Pillai of Tamilnadu, who first use the Old Testament for re-culturation of Indian Church, since to him, the Hebrew Scripture has lot similarities to Indian culture, Ashram Movements, K. Subba Rao's movement has abandoned

---

good-wishing bond. According to Collins Dictionary, it is 'a necklace worn by a Hindu woman to signify that she is married.'

[368] Clarence O. McMullen, ed., *Rituals and Sacraments in Indian Religions* (Delhi: ISPCK, 1979), 57.

[369] St. Augustine, Institutes....493.

[370] D.M. Baillie, *The Theology of the Sacraments* (London: Faber & Faber Ltd. ND), 53.

[371] *The Westminster Confession of Faith* (Edinburgh: T & T Clark, ND), 143.

[372] John Calvin, *Institutes*... 513, and in *The Catholicity of Protestantism*, 110.

baptism rite because it creates social problem for many people since it is also contextual mixed with conversion. Churchless Christianity or *Yeshu Darbar* has opened the Lord's Table for all faiths.

Conclusion

MS and Torah are selectively used to find a model for NICs since MS provides the basis *saṁskāras* to India and the Torah gives the Laws to the biblical traditions. It is found to be possible that if the location of culture is to be taken as the important context for re-culturation, tradition, and customs of these books has the capacity to provide a new model because they have laid down the basic cultural norms for Indian and Hebrew people, therefore, re-culturation minus MS in India is abstract.

The concept of Dharma (cultural framework and doctrine that envisages the plural expression of One Truth) can harmonize Christian faith and Indian culture because Dharma is the axis of Indian culture which goes beyond the religious limitation. The SD of Indian rest and works only on the dharmic foundation that integrates diversity as the reality.

The reformation history clearly suggests that a path-breaking process is adapted to redefine the traditional understanding and practice of sacraments. The religious freedom during reformation and hereafter, also encouraged, me to take such free tradition to re-introduce in Indian post-colonial ear for re-culturation of Protestant sacraments. Since this tradition is the outcome of the individual quest, going beyond the institutionalized reformation, then, why not such tradition is to be taken as a viable model for re-culturation of sacraments for Indian Christians especially for new believers? If we take the individual experience as central of argument, then many of the Old Testament events would be very relevant, above supernatural value attachment into it. Serious introspection of Protestant tradition is in favor of creating a 'Space and Place' for every people within their cultural reality of life.

As in philosophy so in rituals and *saṁskāras*, life is regarded as a cycle. It starts where it ends. All the *saṁskāras* and allied ceremonies emanate from this. The *saṁskāras* covered all areas of life like social institutions, beliefs, sentiments, arts, and science. The *saṁskāras* were instituted to create the conditions required for the development of the Hindus in order to integrate s/he personality with the society in which s/he was born and with the world around her/him believed to be full of superhuman forces.

In sum, so far, it is a brief overview of the features and significance of a few important *saṁskāras*. Some of the *saṁskāras* have lost their meaning and utility in the present day's Hindu life and religious conduct. The main reasons for dropping some *saṁskāras* are i. there is freedom of selection for a Hindu to give emphasis or to keep a balance between belief and practices. Therefore if belief does not fit with the old practices, it is practiced which are to be modified. For this reason, some *saṁskāras* are either modified or dropped. ii. Many people or the followers feel that many *saṁskāras* are simply not needed s in the present life so is the reason for minimization.

Open Question for Further Debate

i. How far Manu's evolution theory would help to defuse social and caste discrimination in India, when the suffering community (low caste) thinks that MS is largely responsible for caste-injustice?
ii. How can egalitarianism both in Manu and Gospels help NICs to propagate a better and a just society in India when Nic [also IC] practices caste and elite division?
iii. How far Church would be a beneficiary from this re-culturation argument?

Chapter 5

Nāmakaraṇa Saṁskāra: Re-reading of Christian Naming Historiography in India: A Postcolonial Analysis

Introduction

Naming is an essential aspect of human civilization. It is simple but powerful since it carries a deeper meaning which not only identifies an object but at the same time it communicates a whole lot of complex features human existence and culturally it is a collective consciousness that goes beyond an individual. The primary purpose of a name is to identify an object visible and invisible. The Semantics of name is geologically located, linguistically expressed and more precisely a culture index of a particular community. The two major features that control naming system is language and religion. A naming expression can be changed as a result of the internal evolving process and it can be changed by some external forces: be it political, religious or cultural, etc. As culture always evolves, so the naming tradition is, but the factors that contribute to bringing changes of the traditional naming system, are important aspects to get our academic attention in the context of Christian names during the colonial mission in India.

The Western colonialism is a combination of political and religious ideology that holds Semitic religious bias and European cultural supremacy. One of the colonial-mission agendas was to create a new Indian community with European orientation. Among many applied tools to achieve the goal, changing names of native Christians converts was one such that was used rigorously to create a new culture. The linguistic change of name has created a confusion of cultural affiliation and their social mobility. It has given a new social identity that had colonial toned and had no communicative local meaning to locate someone within cultural mobility in Indian society. Hence, the linguistic dimension raised a new debate of 'native and foreign' that marginalized NICs (as well as others except for North-Eastern Christians) from Indian culture to a great extent. Therefore EWB[373] naming policy appeared to be one of the central issues for postcolonial Christian naming historiography and quest for Indian identity.

The objective of this chapter is to investigate the role of a 'name' in Indian cultural demography, limitedly focusing only on Northern India and to analyze the colonial mission's naming policy and its impact on NICs in the light of culture. There are four segments in this chapter, firstly, we shall try to elucidate the importance of 'name' in Indian society and social mobility; secondly, it will analyze the colonial mission naming policy and its cultural consequences, then thirdly, the tradition of Manusmṛti and Torah will studied to search for a model that emphasized naming not just a religious identity but a total persona that connects an individual with the whole: family, genealogy, ethnicity, physical and qualitative nature, cosmos, etc and lastly, the postcolonial response to reconstruct colonial naming system as a subaltern quest. The postcolonial methodology will be applied to search a new model which might possibly help to the NIC community for an integrated cultural reconstruction from within the *dharmic saṁskāric* tradition.

Within the *saṁskāric* tradition, name and naming are two different features: firstly, 'name' is a linguistic expression, right of family, placement in society, one's mobility, identity, genealogy, geographical location, etc and secondly, 'naming' ceremony. Our focus will be limited primarily on the first feature, because, name plays a larger social role than the ceremony which is an internal religious or family jurisprudence. The investigation will deal with the colonial naming system among NICs through historical data analysis in the last 100 years, divided them into 'pre and post' independent India. The characteristic of Christian tribal name mainly the Kuki and Mizo will be used for an alternative re-culturation model for NIC. The word 'proselytization' will be considered to investigate the colonial motif in the naming system. Applying the postcolonial methodology to reconstruct the colonial name-giving system is for social empowerment, cultural assimilation, and identity. Caste will be dealt with only to understand a social structure and mobility of Indians regardless of religion. Other issues in regard to caste are not falling within the ambit of our present research.

---

[373] EWB – Euro-Western Biblical.

5.1. Rationale and Importance of *Nāmakaraṇa Saṁskāra*

5.1.1. Naming Tradition and its Cultural Importance

In the era of globalism, local/national identity is a debatable issue. There are two strong opposite views: one group feels present world is heading towards an assimilating or melting down situation in which none can really hold or keep separated from the influence of others and other group is advocating and struggling to preserve the diversities of the globe, so that none should live in the shadow of extinction. In such a context, we shall be dealing a few questions related to the cultural role of a 'name' in the Indian context. Is this a serious issue which can make academic importance? We shall look into this question in this chapter. To search for its importance, I open up our argument by stating a character in Sigrid Undset's[374] novel *Den Brennende Busk* (1930), who named her daughter '*Sunlife*', inspired by an American novel. Later her daughter complained that it was not a real name and she preferred to be called '*Synne*', a short form of traditional name '*Synnøve*,'[375] a feminine expression in the Norwegian language. The little daughter's quest raises a central issue which acknowledges the role of local cultural and her very social mobility and integration. The index of the name, means, words and its meaning is the index of a whole persona that differentiates a 'person' among the mass. Opposite to that is a state of confusion to affiliate one with the whole.

This very simple example has an immense potential to explore why the category of the name has got an important place in our investigation in relevance to the cultural question of NICs.

'*Nama*' (name), a linguistic expression to identify an object, basically expresses a limited contextual cultural meaning, i.e., the location of identity. The socio-cultural parameter of a 'name' incorporates a number of issues like ethnicity, race, region, culture, genealogy, language, religion, etc. C.S. Song said 'naming' is a very powerful tool that can shape, control or exploit someone.[376] In another way, Merleau-Ponty explained that 'the word expresses thought, for speech is thought. The speaking subject takes a position within the world that is significant, and therefore, the subject becomes meaningful through language.'[377] He further said, "Language is not simply labeling of

---

[374] Sigrid Undset (1882-1949), Noble winner in Literature (1928), born in Denmark, lived in Norway.

[375] T. Hamsun, ed., *Knut Hamsuns Brev Til Marie* (Oslo: Aschehoug, 1988), 547. Cf. B. Helleland, C. E. Ore & S. Wikstrøm, eds., *Names and Identities*, Oslo Studies in Language 4(2), (2012), 273–284.

[376] C. S. Song, *Tell Us Our Names; Story Theology from an Asian Perspective* (New York: Orbis Books:1984), 90-91.

[377] M. Merleau-Ponty Barral, *The Role of the Body-Subject in Interpersonal Relations* (Pittsburgh: Duquense University Press, 1965), 195.

objects within the world, but rather, a 'double of being,' bringing both objects and ideas into the world."[378] His explanation has the contextual substance to re-examine the colonial mission's policy of naming.

The socio-cultural pattern of selecting a 'word' in any language (precisely in mother tongue) plays a very significant role in which, often, religious dominance has been a crucial factor. Since religion is a changeable social reality and ethnolinguistic praxis is more static then religion cannot be taken as a final yardstick to re-define culture especially as a policy that actually uses a mechanism to implement the agenda. The policy implementation is not spontaneous cultural change. Name in a particular ethnolinguistic group is actually an epitome of culture, expressed in diverse forms; oral, written, art, dance, music, etc. So a 'name' is not a word but the whole totality. The political establishment, if religiously motivated, often imposes the power to bring a new social order through naming-process. For example, Latin America by colonial Christianity or Islamic expansion is our historical prove. In the case of India, the advent of Islamic and later European/Christian religio-cultural genre, ethos and political system has changed the history of religio-cultural discourse.

5.1.1.1. Traditional Name in India: Family, Caste and Social Mobility

The name in Indian culture is a complex subject, but every conventional Indian name conveys important information. Due to diversity, India has no uniformity per se in the naming system, but plurality amplifies the deep-rooted socio-cultural affiliation of an individual. It is very apparent to identify a person only by name. The social mobility depends on the 'name' that he/she carries. It is like 'password' to enter into Indian system. For example, let us analyze the India cultural reality and its relation to names and to show how strong a name makes a person socially integrated, identified, mobilized and vice versa the tension as well.

[378] M. Merleau-Ponty Barral, *The Prose of the World*, ed., C. Lefort, Trans by J. O'Neill (Evanston: Northwestern University Press, 1973), 5-6.

State-Wise Caste Surname in Northern India

Sl. No.	Name of State	Name of Caste			
		Brahmin	**Kshatriya**	**Vaishya**	**Sudra**
1	West Bengal	Bandopadhay, Mukhopadhay, Chattopadhay, Mitra, Lahiri, Bagchi	Samanta, Konar, Panja, Jana, Gupta	Saha, Poddar, Sarkar, Ghosh, Kole, Mondal	Dom, Bagdi, Dule, Das
2	Uttar Pradesh & Bihar and MP	Mishra, Pande, Dikshit, Upadhyaya, Dube, Trivedi, Misra, Shukla	Chauhan, Tomar, Rathore, Sisodiya Thakur, Rajput	Yadav, Gupta, Saxena, Agarwal, Mathur	Choura, Chamar, Bhamgi, Pal Doni, Mehra
3	Rajasthan	Sharma, Yaishanava	Soni, Rathi, Gujar	Maheshwari, Khandelwal, Jaswal,	Singh, Meena, Meghwal
4	Gujarat	Vyas, Joshi, Desai, Bhatt	Solanki, Gohil, Rathore, Rana	Patel, Soni, Mehta, Goyal	Mordhara, Ramani, Kudla
5	Maharashtra	Kulkarni	Rao, Patil, Balaji,	Sindhe, Dateer, Dhage, Aswar	Pachrane, londe, Gujar,
6	Punjab	Jaitly, Trikha, Kumoria, Jinghan,Metra and Mohla	Bali, Vaid, Chhibber, Datt, Mohan, Lau and Bhimwal	Soni, Kohl, Kapur	Balmiki

Analysis: This table is designed on two matrixes: caste and state/region. The intention is to analyze how caste surname and regional social settings are closely associated with each other. Since the Indian state (province) was divided on an ethnolinguistic majoritarian basis, therefore, every state has its own characteristic. People's identity has caste and ethnolinguistic denominator. The inter-state migrated community also forms new 'group' in a new place, for example, Tamil people migrated in Mumbai, have developed a Tamil colony or Bengali colony elsewhere in India, so same caste from the different state does not actually integrate. Being an Indian or from same caste is not enough for social mobility, assimilation or integration. In such context, a name, especially a caste surname plays a very crucial role. The above table shows hardly two surnames are widely used across India. In some cases, even if, two surnames are found in two or more places, may not be from the same caste, like '*Singh*' has a different connotation in various places. *Singh* can be religiously '*Sikh*' (male) in Punjab and *Kshatriya* in Uttar Pradesh or lower caste in Bengal and Brahmin in Manipur. Caste-based surname demography in the table gives us an understanding of why the name, mainly surname is an important index for social mobility. It establishes a social right and social engagement of an individual. This surname also has a family genealogy which gives a family to define its place in society. The counter question may be asked what kind of modernity and progressive nature of Indian society has. If we take the western rationale of modernity as a finality, then it seems to be static. But, Indian modernity does not attempt to get rid of caste index. Since the era of Buddha, we have been noticing various movements (secular or religious) just to eradicate caste injustice, not the caste denominator (surname).

Caste does not offer any uniformity as a central system to operate entire India society, as a result, *Chaturvarna* (four caste name) index was further multiplied an ethnolinguistically and created enormous sub-castes within caste and this process has been continuing thousands of year. Since no Indian can speak to every other Indian due to linguistic diversity, the meaning of a surname in one language is often not understood by others. The linguistic localization even has made social mobility more regional. Therefore, for social mobility, only surname and caste are not enough, it needs linguistic clarity. Example, a Bengali and a Gujrathi, even from the same caste and religion will not engage in married relation due to its ethnolinguistic regional mobility. Further, Bengali Brahmins are often disliked or looked down by North Indian Brahmins, because of the non-vegetarian dietary habit of Bengali high caste. In Bengal (Kolkata) Gujarati people even have separate apartments to live due to dietary habit.

Commonly, Indian caste-regional psyche is deeply rooted that governs a person's subtle mind and controls the conduct of life. Within a state, the same caste has their different surnames which also play a role of intra-state caste mobility where sub-caste comes first. In matrimony, even *gotra* (the genesis of family lineage) is seriously considered in the way Israel tribe was divided and subsequently developed a family lineage. Interestingly this is a rude reality of contemporary India alongside her technological advancement. For such rigid regional identity, state-based political parties are restricted within that particular state or caste-based political parties are only able to mobilize vote bank within a particular caste group.

Taking global context in consideration, we can't deny the importance of surname, like of Germany or elsewhere, for any official document, family name option comes first, followed by the first name. In Germany, a person is not free to select any name, there are some restrictions. I remember a

Bengali female actor named 'Swastika Mukherjee'[379] was rejected by German Consulate in Kolkata to get a visa on the ground of the first name which has a political objection and black-listed. The *Swastika* is a very common female name among Bengali women and highly auspicious. The point that I am arguing here is not to question German law, but to show a name and social mobility is closely interlinked. For the same reason, Christians and even other people don't name 'Judas Iscariot' since it carries bad historical negativity only after the crucifixion of Jesus, not before. India Muslims does not name 'Mir Zafar' who betrayed local king and supported the British Army (East India Company) in the Battle of Plassey in 1757, after which India came under the British control (Beginning of Colonial Era). The Importance of a name is not just a 'name' but historiography of a person, land, people, etc. The unclear family lineage devalues human dignity even in our rational global world. EWM actually devalues the whole human persona and collective socio-cultural consciousness and existence of Indian Christians as an India culturally.

Indian Christians have been suffering from social integration, relational existence, and mobility due to the replacement of 'name'. Most Christians are struggling to specify their 'root' in their own community and it has forced them to live within tiny 'Christian Community. The colonial mission is the sole factor to develop such exclusive and disintegrated life. Dr. Ambedkar or M. M. Thomas points out such 'communal' nature and function of the Christian community. Surname replacement, in this light, has created a major cultural crisis that needs to be re-cultured from with Indian culture.

5.1.1.2. Composition of Name: Morphology and Semantic in North India

The setting and selection of words for a name corresponding to a vivid cultural landscape. The corresponding meaning includes the vast and diverse reality not only for an individual but also of the individual's racial, linguistic, religious, geographical, historical traditions along with numerical celestial and natural objects like stars, planets, animals, rivers, trees, etc. The Northern Indian name, generally, does not reflect any totemic genealogy. It actually has two segments.

The first part is a given name and the second part is a family name. There is also found a middle name which corresponds and glorifies the first word. Like 'Sankar Prasad Singh', here 'Prasad' qualifies 'Sankar', not 'Singh'. Presently middle name tradition is in decline. The first name can identify

[379] Swastika Mukherjee was denied German visa due to her first name in 2007. She was advised to change her name. She protested in public and question the logic of banning an auspicious Indian name. Germany even appealed an EU-wide ban to all Nazi symbols including swastika. Other Bengali women like Swastika Ghosh and Swastika Roy also expressed same problem to enter into Europe.

religion, region and in some cases *varna*. It also has a regional linguistic bias in semantics. For example, a name in South India usage of 'Krishnan' can easily be differentiated from North India usage of 'Krishna', even though both words have the same meaning. The second name i.e., surname, is very important in Northern Indian culture because regional, caste identity (*Jati*), family identity, social hierarchy, historical root are attached to it. Normally, Indian names are ethnic, caste and geographically oriented.

The caste based naming in our research argument does not deal with the problems of caste injustice in India. In fact after Ambedkar's movement, due to the caste politics and caste-based reservation in the Indian Republic, the caste has actually consolidated the social mobility in contemporary society. The caste-based name reflects this fundamental characteristic even in modern India. Therefore, any revolutionary reconstruction of the naming pattern (what European Missionary used) has, practically, uprooted a person from his/her social mobility and created a confused social identity which might possibly make him/her miss-matched and alien in his/her own society. Therefore psychological displacement and sociological alienation are the negative consequences of enforcement or adoption of Christian/European naming system during the colonial period.

5.1.1.3. Name and Regional Cultural Identity

The centrality of language in the field of identity is essential in cultural. It gives a visual picture of 'self'. The linguistic derivation in North Indian languages is generally from Sanskrit, but the linguistic expression has a regional flavor. The surname is also influenced by the regional languages even though different names express same caste profession i.e. '*Yadav*' in North and '*Ghosh*' in Bengal belonged to Milkman Community (*Vaishya*). Surname like '*Vedi*', '*Dwivedi*', '*Trivedi*' shows the merit of the study of scripture. The *Uppadhya* (religious Scholar) migrated to Bengal from North India; adopted a geographical prefix according to their new settlement, henceforth developed a new surname like '*Bango*' '*Uppadhya*'= *Bangopadhya*.

From the above examples, it is clear that the Indian naming system even if directly related to a particular religion (Hinduism); particular culture and *Chaturvarna*, it is immensely diverse. The failure to establish a name identical to a Pacific cultural root, not only disempowers a person socially and psychologically, but it also segregates one from the mass. Many Christian families and individuals are found to be suffering from cultural displacement because of adopting a new naming system from a different linguistic origin (Biblical-European) and as a result, most of the Christians have lost the social mobility within *varna* hierarchy and live within the small Christian community.

5.1.1.4. Name in Contemporary India

Whether name in modern aspired India is a serious issue for debate or does it have any academic consideration is to be analyzed. India has the largest number of the middle class (nearly 600 million) which looks for a better life with individual career-oriented reason but at the same time, another side of Indian society is still very conservative in nature and function. Taking diaspora (Indian) and those who accepted foreign nationality within a new social order where a new version of Indian socio-cultural caste-ethnic-linguistic characteristic is found. For example, in Germany there various Indian forums like Bengali, Tamil, and Malayalam, even though there is an Indian forum. Even it has deep-rooted religious symbolism like Bengali Hindu rejoice *Durga Puja*, not Tamil conducts *Pongal* or *Onam* by Malayalees. Even Hindu temples are functioning according to their regional ethnolinguistic bias. If we look into the naming pattern of the German Hindu temples, we may notice this reality like *Sri-Kamachi-Ambal-Tempel* Hamm (NRW) which is mainly for Tamil Hindu devotees. Indians in the Western world have not given up their regional and caste identity even if they are Indian. It would help to understand the ground reality of present Indian social mobility in the present context and from such reality what kind of socio-cultural suffering Christian community in North India has been facing is to be understood.

Back to Asian naming as the colonial reconstruction, we find two pictures: firstly, changing into European spelling and secondly changing the name itself. European rulers renamed many existing cities as per their linguistic expressional convenience with abrogated form. British named 'Burma' is now 'Myanmar.'[380] After 1948, Independent Govt. has changed many names of cities, streets, parks, etc. It was not primarily an anti-British move, but to bring back national cultural makeover as a postcolonial quest. India also has changed many names like 'Madras to Chennai', 'Bombay to Mumbai', 'Calcutta to Kolkata', Bangalore to Bengaluru' etc.

Why such a process is undertaken by colonial countries can be argued evidentially. Europeans did not begin their journey on the existing social order, but they attempted created a new social and administrative order and in doing so, the local/native system was lost its socio-political relevance and a new naming system was adopted from European linguistic phonetically order. It used Roman letters with European accent to a native name and it was written as they pronounced like '*Sri* or *Shree*' as '*Se*' or '*Barddhaman* as *Burdwan*' or '*Mysura* to *Mysore*'. Till date (Sep 2016) nearly 126 cities' name has been changed. Therefore, the name is a serious postcolonial quest in India. Subalternity, in this context, is very subtly penetrating element.

---

[380] 'Who, What, Why?' (26 September, 2007) 'Should it be Burma or Myanmar', BBC News.

In every such step of re-construction in the postcolonial era, two basic features are found: a postcolonial quest in a direct or indirect form and the rise of cultural nationalism. 'What does it serve in changing a name?' has been debated, but culturally it can be seen as a quest for identity. Asian postcolonial reconstruction is a process and name was the one central issue of debate.

5.1.1.5. Importance of Name in Indian Society

The name is an identity, bigger than its very limited application to identify a person. It is total wholeness in which one is known to this world. Placement of a person is a society like India is identical to his/her name. One's ethnicity, culture, language, geographical allocation and many such are interrelated to a name. For example, in Manipur the major groups Naga, Kuki and Manipuri live thousands of years together yet none adopted other's name and it gives their identity survived. Nagas and Kukis are Christian, still for ethnic identity is identical to name that they hold. EWM has marginalized this aspect in order to create an EW prototype here in India. In the case of NIC, subalternity was imposed through conversion based religious ignoring socio-cultural aspects of life.

5.1.1.6. Naming System

Naming and identity crisis is well-reflected in the naming selection among NICs. The pattern is different for one who is born in a Christian family and one who is converted. Within converts, Hindu and Muslim converts follow separate system for integration within Hindu converts. A new trend as a postcolonial quest is to give a family name (surname) with a Christian first name or sometimes an Indian middle name, i.e., Angel Priyanka Das, Peter Anil John, Alfa David Masih, Ashish Henry, Kalyani Renison Robinson. So, we notice that there is no fixed pattern for the Hindu converts in contemporary NIC, but in case of Muslim converts, accepting EW name of conventional non-religious Indian names are in use. Some Muslim converts even keep their previous name as well like Harun John, Pervez Khan. Most Muslim converts struggled to integrate with Hindu converts, therefore, a complete integration among two types of converts yet to take place. During matrimony, this issue of previous faith plays a role and it is fact Hindu converts used to avoid Muslim converts. Nearly 90% of Hindu converts expressed their reservation to marry the Muslim converts. To avoid such a situation, most Muslim converts accept EW or Indian names. Tribal community since their ethnic identity is the most priority fact of life, therefore, hardy it is noticed a complete change of name. They used to take the initial name as Christian like Charles Murmu or Marcus Baskey, keeping tribe name as it is and in case of North-eastern tribe's name, they didn't accept or wish to use any EW name. Very recently (last 20 years), few are using an EWB name as their first name before their traditional name like Mercy Nemneiching Haokip. Adopting a Western name is largely noticed in low caste converts rather than high caste converts. It was seen as the liberative tool from the oppression of high caste. In case of high caste converts, they retain the same caste name after conversion like Krishna Mohan Banerjee, Narayan Varma Tilak, Sundar Singh, Manilal Parekh, etc.

5.2. Name, Colonial Mission and Subalternity

5.2.1. Colonial Mission and Universalism Doctrine

Is there any universal concept which could bring all diverse traditions into one reconstructed framework where everyone would be absorbed willfully? Hypothetically assume such possibility in globalization, and then the question is who will develop that model and how it would be implemented convincingly? European mission and colonial power had a universal concept (even though European culture is diverse) loosely framed under a Greek philosophical framework, Roman political structure and Christianity (Roman Catholic and Protestant). Greek intellectual capability and Roman masculine power structure jointly transformed the simple movement of Jesus into an aggressive religio-political operative system which caused immense human tragedy, great judgmental in nature which has subverted the natural human diverse expressions until the French Revolution which was not only a protest against monarch but also against the Christian faith. Anything that was imposed by power is rejected by the quest for freedom and self-determination. As a result, Christianity in the Western world is minimized into a new low. This is the same reason why Christian was not seen as a natural alternative in Asia. West has a profound assumption of universalism which is ultimately aiming to bring the world into a 'single' operative system, be it salvation through Christianity or scientific secular process.[381] Rajiv Malhotra and Aravindan Neelakandan in his book *Breaking India* (2011) have dealt with the question of diversity in the context of the theoretical notion of Western Christian universalism. The divine mandate of the mission was persuaded through a masculine power struggle whereas Indian dharmic world view is purely spiritual and plural. Then these two opposite concepts and practices faced off and a massive conflict became a social phenomenon. Ultimate victim was, not Hindus, but newly converted Indian Christians since they were the 'object' to implement Christian universalism. The subalternity is to be understood in this context.

In contrast, Indian religious culture operates more within the dharmic system that accepts diversity as an operative tool. India had highly powerful dynasties but is hardly found any single political power took serious steps to impose their kind of totalitarianism to unify diverse India. We do not

[381] Rajiv Malhotra, *Being Different: An Indian Challenge to Western Universalism* (Naida: Harper Collins 2013), 307.

hesitate to acknowledge the massacre of Buddhist during Gupta period and the establishment of Brahmanical Hinduism which was also socially and religiously countered by South Indian *Bhakti* movement since the 8th century and in North from the 13th century onward. It is factual that dharmic notion is feminine and from such notion, the king Ashoka has taken over by Indians as the symbol of ideal ruler only after he renounced the military power and introduced 'non-violence' as operative political policy or Gandhi is known as 'Father of Nation' for the same reason. Muslim and European rulers compared this 'feminine' nature with their masculine power centeredness: both in the political and religious field. Because of this feminine character, regional diversity in India sustains throughout the centuries. EW universalism and its operative nature can be answered in the light of Indian operative system to get better insights in this regard. We assume that readers are aware of European Christian universalism or Hegelian concept of '*Weltgeist*'. Universal doctrine of Christianity projects 'Jesus Christ' as the 'only saving path' for the rest of humanity, and if so Indian dharmic traditions stand opposed to it.

From the above reality, we shall proceed into the area of 'name' and its cultural meaning. Before coming to Asian or Indian context, we can deal with the issue of 'name' in Europe in the light of Christian mission and universalism. Stephen Wilson in his book *The Means of Naming* (1998) has attempted to give a history of name in Western Europe since the Roman era to present time and he pointed out two factors, firstly the conventional system of name and how in modern time new name with spelling and vernacularization came in effect and such trend caused challenge to prosopography.[382] He argued that name reflects the fundamental features of society and culture. To entire Europe, naming system has a balancing act within local culture and Christian faith with its Roman lineage. It took a long period to harmonize and develop socially acceptable 'name-giving' collegiums. Christian universalism operated to change the faith and European cultural of 'name-giving' to bring sustainability into it. It is not too difficult for Europeans to locate a 'name', its place of origin, social status, etc., then how a NIC name like 'Vinison Dixon' or 'Thomas George' will be located within an Indian socio-cultural setting is a postcolonial question. Linguistic culture is denominator for an individual in his/her social life.

Subalternity is not a political or physical aspect but an operative mechanism which brings physical changes in social functional reality. EWM policy, by altering the name of local converts, took away their basic human right to name them. If universalism is kept in the realm of the thinking process, then the opportunity is feasible but physical universalism is an abstract that produces human conflict. Native Christian is in some way the victim but

[382] Stephen Wilson, *The Means of Naming* (London: 1998), x.

responsible for their present situation. Factually, subalternity is a given state of life, not self-created.

5.2.2. Caste and Mission Policy; A Subaltern Reading

5.2.2.1. Priest's Name and Proselytization

We would like to argue in the light of I Cor. 1.11-13 in which a priest centered believer's group was reported to St. Paul. The issue of 'egoistic' existentialism is human nature which not only gave birth to new parochialism but also brought internal rift in 'Body of Christ'. Coming back to the Indian context, such personal group and existence of a person (here it is a priest) is colossal. An ethical question can be raised on whether a priest should give his name on native converts? It is not the personal choice but a larger issue is 'new converts' were objectified. And then, therefore, the post-baptism 'name-giving' needs a deeper cultural and sociological consideration. C.S Song pointed out the cultural intensity of a local name which is, even though, replaced by a biblical name like Ezekiel.[383] We can analyze a few examples here like of Lucas, Dixon, Cutting, Brown, etc that are common among NICs. These are common surnames among colonial priest and it was given to new converts as a surname after baptism. Hence by this act, a native is 'objectified' and it was marked as his achievement. In Jesus' movement, human dignity was the central message which was commercialized within mission policy. Such names have no biblical or denominational root but show a personal 'cluster-making' attempt to count his success report. It can be looked within the context of the Hegelian concept of '*Weltgeist*' which advocates the supremacy of European civilization and Christianity.

During the interview, I asked the meaning to twenty such people who carry this colonial surname with them and none was able to give the meaning of 'word' used for their surname. Even when it is asked which social group they can be identified in present India and mostly replied, 'We are Christian.' This answer can be taken as a success of EWM policy to create a new colonial oriented community among new native converts. Those native converts understood their identity only through faith which is limited identity. M.M. Thomas and others were critical to such nature of Indian Christians and called them socially 'communal'. Those names have no Indian linguistic expression or correspond no meaning of cultural appropriation. Since it has no social mobility capacity, name-holder then sociologically takes refuse within faith identity as ultimate. They mostly live within colonial created world order, generally known as 'Campus Christian'. Subalternity of NICs in this context is an artificially created situation by displacing native from their root through replacement of name. Their identity and existence now depend on Church

---

[383] C.S. Song, Tell Us Our Names (New York: Orbis Books, 1984), 92.

authority. According to Antonio Gramsci, continuity of such negative identity is the sign of subaltern weakness when they accept 'elite' as superior, so to construct a new self-identity is challenging.

5.2.2.2. Egalitarian Logic: Contesting

One of the major arguments that put in favor of changing the name by the colonial mission is to eradicate caste injustice by deleting their caste surname. It was thought to de-notify one's caste identity hence he/she will be assimilated with the masses. On face value, such initiative was a positive move and it is also true that caste injustice has forced nearly 70% of people in dismay throughout the century.

Culture has two features: one that controls the conduct of life and others gives a cultural consciousness. By replacing the name, none of these can be changed, so attempting for an '*ekklesia*' community rationally was not possible by changing the name since cultural consciousness is an invisible aspect to change. Anti-caste movement has 2600 years long history in India, but what EWM attempted does not reflect any historical study of Indian society. Socio-religious movements against caste were actually against injustice, not caste as the social denominator. If we take Buddhist, South and North Indian *Bhakti* or modern secular or political movement are basically against injustice. Physical change like name replacement is apparently easier, but changing caste consciousness needs a psychological transformation and higher level of humanitarian awareness. We can't preconceive that all who have an upper caste surname are anti-low caste or vice versa. Second lager issue is social evolution which can be ideological even foreign ideology like democracy, Marxism, etc., but evolution must be from within, not external. EWM naming centered egalitarianism suffers from either one. It was a forceful and imposed on someone who, in the process of entering into the egalitarian faith community, actually entering into a state of subalternity since s/he has no freedom to define the 'self'. For example, in Goa, someone 'Govinda Parrikar' now 'Antonio Gonsalves' or a girl in Andhra Pradesh 'Sagarika' now 'Ileana D'Cruz' is not transformative in nature but in other way trans-de-formative. What purpose do these EW names serve, except carrying a colonial historical legacy?

The egalitarian logic further suffers when Christian mission accepts caste to reach different caste groups like Robert de Nobili adopted Brahmin culture to reach out Brahmin. It is also true Indian converts did not give up or the colonial mission failed to eradicate caste from the newly created Christianity community in India. In many places in India mainly in South India, caste is equally strong in Church like the Hindu community and in many places we noticed high and low caste Church and cemetery. It evidentially stands opposite to the egalitarian logic.

5.3. Naming Tradition: In Indian and in Hebrew Tradition

The name is a sign of social consciousness. In Indian and even Hebrew civilization, naming was taken with seriousness: socially, culturally and religiously. Both traditions categorized 'naming' within *saṁskāras*. Brahaspati, one of the Indian lawgivers' remarks about the desirability of naming, "Name is the primary means of social intercourse, it brings about merits and it is the root of fortune. From name man attains fame. Therefore, the naming ceremony is very praiseworthy."[384] In the same way 'meaning' of a name is carefully used for a person, because it would be with him/her and generation next. It has a historical continuity; therefore much attention has given in Manusmṛti and Torah in this regard.

5.3.1. The Origin

It is generally found that name giving is often connected to religion. The child is frequently named after a god who seems to be regarded as its protector or it is named after a saint whose blessings are sought for it. Secular ideas are also responsible for determining names. It denotes a particular quality. New names are also given to a novitiate when one enters a secret society.[385] The adoption of the father's name is also found in India. Thus, there are so many factors working behind the system of giving a name to a person.

5.3.2. The Vedic Period

In ancient Indian literature like Rig Veda,[386] Aitareya[387] and Satapatha Brahmanas,[388] name-giving is mentioned with certain sacredness. The very common trend was to take two words in which later used to denote success and distinction in life. Usually wards are chosen on metronymic manner, for example, in Kaksivanta Ausija,[389] the first word is the popular name and the second name is derived from Usija (the name of mother); in Bṛhaduktha Vāmneya[390] the second name is derived from Vamani, in such cases, however, it should be noted that parentage name was not necessarily a common feature. A person could be named even after a remote ancestor. Some local names, although not prescribed by scriptures, are found in the Brahmans, i.e., Kausambeya (named after Kośambi) and Gangeya (named after Ganga).[391]

---

[384] Brahaspati, quoted in *V.M.S.* Vol. I: 241.

[385] H. Webster, Primitive Sacred Societies, 40 ff.

[386] Rig-Veda X. 55. 2 & 71. I.

[387] Rig-Veda 1. 3. 3.

[388] Rig-Veda 6. 6. I. 3 & 9; 3. 6. 2. 24; 5. 4. 3. 7; Br. U. 6. 4. 5.

[389] P. Br. 14. 11 17.

[390] P. Br. 14.9.38.

[391] P. Br. 8.6.8.

Besides these incidental references, one positive rule is also found in the Satapatha Brahmana for performing the naming ceremony of a newborn child: "one should give a name to the newborn son."[392]

It is evident that in the Vedic era, naming was a custom not ceremony. We don't find Grihasutras (except Gobhila) utter many Vedic references. Getting gradual social importance, in Dharmasastras, Nāmakaraṇa *Saṁskāra* was explored in detail. This exploration later provided a wider cultural format and somehow unified with a system within *saṁaskāras*. This ancient form of naming has its role in the contemporary naming system in India since in later stage the Vedic tradition was elaborated, explained and brought within *saṁskāras* that gave sustainability of antiquity.[393]

5.3.3. The Composition of the Name

The first question which has been discussed from the tie of *Grihasutra*[394] is that a name should have two syllables, beginning with a sonant, with a semivowel in it, with the long vowel or the *Visarga* at its end, with a *Krt* suffix, not with a *Taddhita*. In the opinion of Baijavapa, there is no restriction of syllables. "They should give a name to the child containing one syllable, two syllables, three syllables, or an indefinite number of syllables,"[395] whereas, Vasistha restricted the number two or four syllables and asks to avoid name ending in 'i' and 'r'.[396] In modern time, if a family keeps a home priest or consult Guru, such specific nature of selection is practiced, otherwise, people go by dictionary meaning or personal liking.

Sutras including Manusmṛti advised an even number of syllable for girls name ended with 'ā'. Manu further added the pacific qualifications for a girls name, "it should be easy to pronounce, not hard to hear, of clear meaning, charming, auspicious, ending in a long vowel and containing some blessing."[397] A girl must not have awkward like, "a constellation, a tree, a river, a mountain, a bird, a servant, and a terror."[398] Manu even went further and pronounced a decree of prohibition to marry a girl who has awkward names. It is not a model that Manu alone prescribes for Aryan or larger Indian. Girls name in the world generally objectified with a soft object like Apollo (music/poetry), Diana (Moon God), Venus (love and beauty). India is not exceptional in this regard.

---

392 Satapatha Brahmana 6.1.3.9.

393 MS 12.3.

394 Paraskara Grihasutra 1.17.1.

395 Vīramitrodaya Samskāra Prakāśa Vol. I, 241.

396 Visiṣṭha Dharmasūtra iv.

397 MS. 2. 33.

398 MS. 3. 9.

In another way, a man's name has a masculine flavor. This observation has a biological reason. Since body and act are inseparable then name used to follow to identify the natural character. That does not mean works are to be strictly divided on gender, but gender has a role.

Present Indian name can be classified into four categories: according to asterism under which the child was born, the deity of the month, the family deity, and the popular calling. This system was not fully developed in the pre-*Sutra* or the *Sutra* period. The system was fully worked out by the later *Smṛti* literature due to the development of religious sects and astrology. The sectarian rise gave birth to the family deities. Astrology brought the people under the influence of the astral world, and every period of time was believed to be presided over by a deity or a spirit. The gods of days, months, etc., arose out of this belief. Since every month denotes to a celestial deity, a name selection is also influenced by it, then followed by a family deity from own *sampradaya* (sect).

The popular name was meant for general use in society and was very important from the practical point of view. The rules of the composition given above were consulted in framing this name. The formation of a name relied on the culture and education of the family and desired to be auspicious and significant.[399]

The gender difference was a wider issue that was considered not only the physical appearance of male and female but also the distribution of work. It was understood the natural object and nature of the human gender must go hand in hand. Men supposed to do harder work, whereas women are to do the tender works. This is why the female name ends with a vowel either 'a' or 'i'. Another important criterion for naming is related to fame, wealth, power, etc. Lastly, the name also suggests a person's caste hierarchy.

Therefore it is almost clear that naming in Indian culture was not taken only to identify a newborn baby rather a serious socio-spiritual matrix. Even today, *Nāmakaraṇa* does not lose its importance in Indian cultural life in a contemporary context.

5.3.4. Naming in Torah

5.3.4.1. Biblical Period

The identity in Hebrew tradition is always a crucial issue with much religious overtone and therefore, the name of a person is believed to have control his or her soul and destiny (Ber. 7b). Manusmṛti does speak in the same line of thinking. Therefore, the selection of an appropriate name is a critical decision. "One should ever examine names, to give his son a name worthy for him to become a righteous man, for sometimes the name is a contributory factor for

[399] Vīramitrodaya Samskāra Prakāśa Vol. I, 241.

good as for evil.'[400] A symbolic change of name often accompanies a change in personal status, such as relating to adoption, marriage or conversion.[401]

In Torah, we don't find any specific strict family lineage. A Hebrew name is given to a boy on the occasion of his *brit milah* (circumcision) and to a girl when her father was honored with an *Aliyah* in the synagogue shortly after her birth. A person's complete Hebrew name is his/her first name (and middle name) followed by *ben* (son of) or *bat* (daughter of) and then the first (and middle) name of the father (and in some liberal circles today, often also that of the mother). If the father is a Kohen or Levite, the child's name ends with the word *Ha-Kohen* or *Ha-Levi*, respectively. Even today, these Hebrew names are used during Jewish ceremonies and rituals when called to the Torah for an *Aliyah*, on the *Ketubah*, and in a special memorial prayer like a funeral.[402] Tribe identity for Hebrew and *varna* identity for Indian may bring a similar semantics and in both, divinity, family genealogy, virtue, fortune is countered with high extreme. Interestingly, the culture of these two ancient civilizations has been evolving without changing the basic fundamental nuances of religio-cultural leniency. It is important for our research to evaluate Indian (MS) or Hebrew (Torah) traditions to argue the basis of selecting these two books for the reconstruction of NICs. Indian and Hebrew people are living in the 21st century with the century-old traditions as the system of inner function of society. From such context, Western society might have evolved in a different way to some extent, even though not completely.

5.3.4.2. Cultural Diversity of Naming System in Torah

Like of any traditional society name reflects a larger picture of the people that includes diverse aspects like family lineage, role of family members, clan, gender, religion, language, climate, nature, adjectives of qualities: good and bad, political history, art, and many abstracts wishes: hope, wish, blessing, animal, birds, etc. Israel being a traditional community like of Indian society, does reflects the above diversities. Culturally it is right of a family to give a name for their newborn. It was never the authority of the priestly class as we see during the colonial period around the world. The colonial mission has taken away the basic self-determine right that exists in Indian and Hebrew culture despite changes due time. And name in such context was taken up by the colonial mission to de-cultured people who were converted to Christianity. Subalternity is analyzed from this perspective. There are traditions that are

---

400 Tanhuma Ha'azinu 7.

401 Ellen frankel & Betsy Platkin Teutsch, *The Encyclopedia of Jewish Symbols* (Northvale: N. J. Aronson, 1992), 117.

402 Wayne Dosick, *Living Judaism: The Complete Guide to Jewish Belief, Tradition, and Practice* (San Francisco: Harper, 1995), 289.

to be explained why changing in the naming system has actually created a cultural crisis and if it was not a spontaneous internal change.

5.3.4.2.1. Women or Mother's Right

A Right to name is another issue to discuss here. During the New Testament period, we noticed that name is given during circumcision (eight days after birth)[403] and traditionally it was chosen by his/her mother. Earliest record on the Torah (in Genesis), it is Eve who has given a 'Cain' to her son (Gen. 4.1) and in Gen. 35.18 Rachel named her son corresponding her situation. In Indian tradition, a mother has the right to name her kids. Shu'a names her son Shelah.[404] Sometimes first kid's name given by father[405] and second kid's name is given by the mother and it continues alternatively. It is her family right and symbolism in the social order. Jewish society has a lot for a mother in practice that empowers her and positioning her credibility in the functioning culture within a family and then it transformed into a social culture.

5.3.4.2.3. Religious Meaning

Reading Exodus 33.12 & 17 that speaks about the relation between a person and his/her faith like Nathan - 'he has given' or an individual is known by God.[406] It also carries the genealogical record of a clan or community. The establishment of this lineage is the essential identity of Israel people. Altering this system is actually ending with the existential crisis of people. Such names have theophoric execution in the social order. Commonly, a Hebrew name reflects the divine revelation or anointment and it is to believe that the energy of God posses through the name to the body. In the earliest record in Genesis, it is God who instructed to name.[407]

5.3.4.2.4. Circumstantial Meaning of Name

Many names in Israel tradition explain the events during birth. Such name later appeared to be a metaphor in culture, remembrance of sacrifice, etc. The name of Cain means 'acquired' shows the circumstance of Eve's pregnancy. Since Rachel died during her delivery, her son carries this sad event, so his name is Ben-Oni (son of my sorrow) and later Jacob has changed with a positive name Benjamin (son of the right hand).[408] Many other names like the mother of the only daughter known as *Za'uleh* (irritating) on forth birth or *Tamâm* (Enough)

---

[403] Lk. 1.59; 2.21.

[404] Gen. 38.5.

[405] Gen. 29.34.

[406] Gen. 32.30; Ex. 3.13-15.

[407] Gen. 2.19-20.

[408] Gen. 35.18.

on eighth birth. Those names speak about the situation through life is passing through, expressing the uncertainty of life, not necessarily divine in nature but agony.

5.3.4.2.5. Totemism

Many names are taken from animal to express both good and bad natures of a person. Deborah means 'bee' might be she was as busy like a bee. Rachel means 'sheep' or Yona is 'dove' or Caleb is 'dog'. These names may appear to be carrying tribal totemic tradition but it may also mean their relation to the enemy or very nature or character or right after birth someone saw a particular animal at first. Elôn means 'oak-tree'

i. ***Cross-culture Name***: Israel people used to avoid foreign names but it is noticed that close to the Christian era there is a change in the pattern of naming. In Luke's Gospel chapter 1.57-64 gives a new pattern when repeated use of one name from mother or father side is given priority. During exile Arabic name like Martha, Tabitha became common. Later Greek or Roman impact is found like John Mark, the Greek form of Semitic name like Jesus or Maria.
ii. ***Re-naming***: Re-naming in Israel is found in many occasions like Jacob's name was re-named as Israel since he wrestled with God.[409] Abram and Sarai became Abraham and Sarah[410] Many a time it may be due to various dialects that caused the changes the name, but when it comes to culture, it denotes an event of life that speaks a history of people and a person. Those changes are part of the cultural history of people. There are few re-namings that indicate the forceful implementation of one culture on others like Joseph was re-named as Saphenath Panea[411] or Daniel and his friend's name were changed.[412] This forceful name changing was the stereotype during the colonial mission in India when the name change was a consequence during faith change.

Many Biblical names have deep significance related to an event that accompanied the birth, the life of the parents, their hope for newborn fortune, or simply an expression of thanks to God for the blessing of a child.[413] The sons of Rachael and Leah were named in response to the rivalry of the sisters for Jacob's love. (Gen. 29:32-35, 30:6-24). Thus Leah called her first son Ruben

[409] Gen. 32.29; 35.10.

[410] Gen. 17.5 & 15.

[411] Gen. 41.45.

[412] Dan.1.6-7.

[413] David C. Gross, *The People's Almanac* (New York: Hippocrene Books, 1988), 566.

(see a son), saying, "The Lord has seen my affliction... now my husband will love me."(Gen. 29-32). After years of barrenness, Rachael named her firstborn 'Joseph' (May he add) saying, "May the Lord add another son." (Gen. 30:34). As Rachael was dying in childbirth, she named her second son 'Ben-oni' (son of my suffering). Fearing that this name may bring misfortune to the child, Jacob changed it to 'Benjamin' (son of my right hand Gen: 34:18). When Pharaoh's daughter adopted a Hebrew child, she found in the Bulrushes along the Nile, she named him 'Moses' (I drew him out of the water, Exodus 2:10) in Hebrew, even though it had Egyptian root referring to Sun god, 'born of Ra'.[414]

The Biblical names often contained some form of one of the names of God in the parents' effort either to praise God or to secure divine protection for their child. Among these is El; abridge forms of YHWH, such as Yah and Yehu; Melekh (king); Bar (Master); Shaddai (Almighty), etc. Many Biblical figures received the new name after divine encounter such as Abram became Abraham (Gen. 17:5) and Jacob was renamed as Israel (Gen. 32:19). Comparatively, it can be discussed with a new name after renunciation (*sanyasa*) in India or change of name after appointed as Pope or even in monarchical installation as king.

In the early Biblical period, first names were uniquely coined at the child's birth and considered his/her exclusive possession. For example, the names of Patriarchs and other major figures are never repeated in the Bible. This even applied to royal family, in which none of the 21 kings of Judah was named after David.[415] Some children were named for animals and plants, such as Rachel (ewe), Jonah (dove), Deborah (bee), and Tamar (palm tree).[416]

5.3.4.3. Talmudic Period

The Talmud complains that "most Jews in foreign parts (Diaspora) bear heathen names (have the same names as the Gentiles)" (Git. 11b). Faced with the prevalent tendency of Jews adopting foreign names, the Rabbis stressed that one of the reasons why the Israelites were delivered from Egyptian bondage was that "they did not change their names." It is unclear whether they were attracted to the change from a previously given Hebrew name to a gentile name-a custom that was decried as a sign of deliberate assimilation or the initial giving of non-Jewish names, such as Hadassah-Esther; Daniel-Balshazzar; and his three friends Hannaniah-Shadrach, Mishael-Mishach, and Azariah-Abel Nego. Under Hellenistic influence, it apparently became a widespread custom for an individual to have two names, one Semitic (Hebrew

[414] David Lieber, ed., *Etz Hayim* (Philadelphia: Jewish Pub. Society, 2001), 323.

[415] David C. Gross *The People's Almanac* (New York: Hippocrene Books, 1988), 566.

[416] Hayyim Schauss, *The Lifetime of a Jew* (Cincinnati, Ohio: Union of American Hebrew Congregations, 1950), 13.

or Aramaic) and one Greek. An example such as Hasmonean rulers as John (Yochanan) Hyrcanus, Judah Aristobulus, and Solome Alexandra, as well as the five sons of Mattathias (e.g., "Judah, called Maccabeus"; 1 Macc. 2:2). Some names were direct translations from the Hebrew, such as Philo from Yedidiah and Theorus from Nathaniel. Other Talmudic era names were authentic Hebrew appellations that were Hellenized in form or spelling, such as Joseph becoming Jose and Shimon changing into Simon.[417]

The Rabbis recommended that children be given names of major biblical figure the patriarchs and matriarchs; several of Jacob's sons; Moses, Mariam, and Aaron; and various judges, prophets, and kings. There is really puzzling to see the absence of use of early biblical names like Abraham, Israel, Moses, David, or Solomon after Rabbis. Similarly, the names of the prophets are also rare among the Talmudic Sages. Instead, obscure biblical names became fashionable because of the accomplishments of those who bore them, such as Hillel and Gamaliel. New non-biblical Hebrew names were developed, such as Akiva, Meir, and Nachman; others were chosen from Hebrew words with positive associations, such as Chaim (life), Simcha (happiness), and Ari (lion). The Talmud prohibited giving a child the name of a wicked person (Yoma 38b), but this often appears to have been disregarded. Several high priests were named Ishmael; some rabbinic scholars were called Menachem (a biblical king who 'did what was displeasing to the Lord'2 Kings 15:18).[418]

Observing such diverse changes in word and pattern of Hebrew names, one can argue EWM's new naming pattern for native Christian can also be seen under this light. The differences between twos are to be noted. For Hebrew, it is normally an evolution from within and not a change by a forceful foreign power. Self-determination is what Hebrew people enjoy to adopt their own process of change, and for NIC, naming was the matter of subjugation and hence subaltern.

5.4. Name and its Implication: A Cultural Analysis and Challenges in India

Indian names are predominantly formulated in accordance with the few fundamental aspects. Those aspects are related to a broader cultural plurality of the social fabric. Firstly, it is the Varna (*Jati*) that reflects in semantics. In due course of time, the traditional role and its attachment to a particular caste profession are largely diluted and a new democratic (British pattern) form which aspires for equal right to live and select occupation is in functional

---

[417] Hayyim Schauss, *The Lifetime of a Jew* (Cincinnati, Ohio: Union of American Hebrew Congregations, 1950), 568.

[418] Hayyim Schauss, *The Lifetime of a Jew* (Cincinnati, Ohio: Union of American Hebrew Congregations, 1950), 566.

mode. That is why all Indian citizens are free to occupy a job on merit, not on caste. During colonial rule, there was a hope in the mind of Europeans that the caste tradition would cease to exist with the influence of European rationality, but the new European mechanism failed to eradicate the *varna* system. The reason partly was the misrepresentation and interpretation of *Varna* (caste) which was viewed as just a system of social injustice. It is factual that social injustice is the outcome of this system, not the system itself. When we take social injustice as tantamount, then our argument denies its cultural identity mapping index. The caste rigidity is often explained by orientalists with a fragmented truth. The numerous sub-castes are actually originated through cross-caste mixing that proves another factual history.[419] The Dalit movement mainly in South India, after achieving partial freedom from the domination of high caste, holds their caste identity intact. Removing injustice and taking out caste identity is dialectical. Secondly, the semantics of the language in India is to reflect the regional characteristic which is identical to the ethnolinguistic culture of people.

This regional identity is the strongest social affiliation in India. For example, even in Germany, there is Tamil association, Bengali association alongside to Indian association. Thirdly, within a region/state the family lineage is defined by a name. It has a very important factor for their social mobility like marriage, sub-caste demarcation, etc., and fourthly, the reservation system of the Union Government. Indian Government at Centre or in States has a reservation for different caste groups for social development and to implement justice. Since Christian and Muslim in principle do not practice caste, hence, do not enjoy reservation schemes. In November 2015, the head of RSS, Mr. Mohan Bhawat vaguely expressed his wish to review the caste reservation during Bihar state election, and RSS backed political party BJP was lost miserably (got only 53 seats out of 243). It indicates the depth of the caste-hold in Indian society. The caste *swabhiman* (caste pride) is a predominant factor and such is the truth even among Christians. Therefore, the caste name is people's social identity and part of the modern democratic process.

Here the missionary went wrong in evaluating what caste based naming system was all about. Attempt to bring justice by eradicating or replacing a caste 'name' shows that EWM's analysis either had a vested interest to project it 'only a symbol of injustice' to win lower caste for Christ or methodological and hermeneutical error to analyze Indian social system correctly.

There are two basic segments of EWM naming giving a pattern that to be addressed: firstly, the semantics of name which has four categories: i. wholly Indian names including caste surname; ii. a mixed name with Indo-

---

[419] Subodh Kapoor, ed., *The Hindus: Enclclopaedia of Hinduism*, Vol. V (New Delhi: Cosmo Publications, 2000), 387-388.

Euro-western-biblical word; iii. purely Euro-western biblical name and iv. North-Eastern tribal Christian name and secondly, the rituals of naming rite which is lesser important in our research. Empirical data will be supporting our argument here.

5.4.1. Naming Trends among Indian Christians

The convention of names in Indian is identity oriented i.e., ethnic, regional, religious, etc. Nearly 95% of Indian people use the conventional naming pattern that can be easily traced to his/her location. A name has generally two parts: given name and family name. Family name also has a regional linguistic pattern.

5.4.1.1. South India Specially Kerala Christian

The Name in South India has its own cultural structural nomenclature which is little longer (number of words) than other parts of India since it includes more detail family genealogical information of a person, even the place of birth.

In South, grandfather/mother's and father/mother's name and a family name along with a given name form a new name. This system is typical for Syrian Christians; for example, a Christian name in Kerala is like 'Madathumchal Koshy Varghese Mathew'; so semantic is, first word 'Madathumchal' is the family name which is essential for social integrity, marriage, baptism, burial, etc., second word 'Koshy' is given name; third word 'Varghese' is from grandfather (father side, if first son, mother side if the second son) and last word 'Mathew' is from father. For a girl, it is from the mother's side. Syrian tradition in Kerala does not use 'surname' to identify the caste, yet new name pattern is Christianized with the tradition of affirming their caste status.

Generally, the Syrian Christian (including CSI, Mar Thoma, etc.) in Kerala belongs to high caste. If there are more children, then each child carries a unique balance by taking names from both father's and mother's side genealogy in the sequence of birth of a child. Kerala Christians in two thousand years provide a successful model of a name for native Christians. Unfortunately, in the second wave of Christianity carried out by the European Mission and later USA Christian mission agencies failed to understand the importance of a name and overlooked the St. Thomas tradition due to the supremacy of Roman Catholicity and later the Protestants over native culture and traditions including Christian traditions. The Synod of Diamper (1599) is proof of it.[420]

---

[420] Interviewed to Mr. Regi Varghese, Dr. John Varghese Mathew and Mr. M. J. Thomas. All three are theological fraternity in India and from the Syrian tradition of Kerala.

5.4.1.2. Northern Regional Name and Cultural Construction-Re-Construction

Names in North India have more direct caste expression. Generally, it has two or three words, in which the last one is a surname and also caste indicator. The confusion comes when the same surname is used by different caste-like 'Singh' in North India can be high caste as well as low caste. In such a case, only local people are capable of identity. Like 'Ghosh' in Bengal can be farmer, milkman or Brahmin. People ask their family lineage (*gotra*) to classify a person. Asking *gotra* or surname is a very common matter since people social mobility is greatly dependent on it. Let us analyze the list below:

Sl. No	Name (All are Christian.)	State/Region
1	i. Pradeep Kumar	Chhattisgarh
2	i. Bhoye Jignesh Bhai - Traditional ii. Gameti Smitaben Vinodray – Traditional (F) iii. Rana Gorden Joseph - Mixed iv. Christian Ivans Joel - E-Western	Gujarat
3	i. Gaurab Das - Traditional ii. Mark Abhishek Das - Mixed	West Bengal
4	i. Avinash Kumar Gailey - Traditional	Uttrakhand
5	i. Rohit Chauhan - Traditional	Rajasthan
6	i. Yakoob Masih - Mixed (Urdu)	Punjab

Analyzing these few names may establish ample academic argument, such as Bhoye Jignesh Bhai is purely a Gujarati name (North-Western India). Using '*bhai*' is the hallmark of this community for man and if she is women, '*ben*' will use used, like, Gameti Smitaben Vinodray. 'Gameti' is the family name applied as the first word for all members of the family. De-culturation arises when missionary changes such semantics and used EWB words such as Christian Ivans Joel for same Gujarati converts. In the interview, Mr. Ivans failed to integrate himself with his family lineage,[421] so, generally confined within the Christian community, limited social mobility, psychological displacement has taken place. Another name like of Rana Gorden Joseph (Gujarat) is using three words like tradition, but only 'Rana' identifies his social status as a family name. The other two words have limited used and marginalized usability. Coming to the naming pattern in the Eastern part of

[421] Interviewed to Christian Ivans Joel (from Gujarat) on 12th August, 2014. His family was converted during by the EWM.

India like Bengal, it is noticed that surname classifies one's social position and obviously religion. The Bengali Christian names are more cultural in the pattern; hardly complete change with EWBN[422] was in use. The reason was the British policy that prevented mission to work for the first 100 years and subsequently, renaissance took place that gave rise of nationalistic pride among Bengali. Giving an EWBN first name is noticed, like Mark Abhishek Das or Joseph Ghosh. Mostly Bengali Christian wishes to keep a cultural name from the beginning of Christianity. This trend is partly reversed among Roman Catholic converts and Anglo-Indians. The Roman Catholic policy was much more Zionist in spirit, whereas Anglo-Indians were forced to develop their own culture due to their formation from the 'un-married' progeny.[423]

Talking to **Mr. Rohit Chauhan**[424] in an interview, being a first generation Christian and from high caste in the postcolonial period, he wishes not to change his surname 'Chauhan'. He also expressed his desire to use a Christian identical name in next generation along with Chauhan. It indicates a new trend among new generation Christians that is slowly denouncing the colonial legacy as the ultimate Christian identity for native Christian. The memory of the colonial legacy is surviving among old Christians who hand over this legacy to the next generation through family tradition and Christian culture that exists among them. New generations, who are coming from Hindu or other faith communities, the colonial Christian is a remote reality of life. On the what is impacting is the charismatic movements mainly USA origin and their policy is much similar to the colonial policy with a new makeover.

It is undoubtedly true that the colonial naming policy to form an egalitarian society was a questionable decision which was not taken in consultation to native Christians. Therefore, EWM in India was not simply the expansion of faith, but it can easily fall in the category of 'proselytization.'

---

[422] EWBN: Euro-Western Biblical Name.

[423] Un-married progeny: many of EW people during colonial period took local woman for physical need, and the children out of such un-married couple mainly formed the larger Anglo-Indian community in India. Those people were given father's name and surname but had no right to acknowledge 'that man' as 'father'. Child and woman were given some amount money. They were completely separated from main-stream society, and form their own colony which still exists. During India's independent they were special reservation to send their own political representative to Local Assembly and the Parliament of India. They eventually accepted Christianity and mostly speak European languages. After independent, their self-glorified status started diluted losing their colonial patronage. We can vaguely compare with Samaritans during Jesus' time.

[424] Mr. Rohit Chauhan is form Rajasthan, now living in Uttar Pradesh, is the first generation Christian, told that he would not change his surname, since it is a social value and statuesque. Chauhan is high caste, and dropping it means lowering himself as well his family. This symbolism is very essential reality of Indian life (12th Nov, 2015).

5.4.1.3. Impute of a *Khristabhakta*[425] (Believer of Christ)

Here we will analyze a few questions that are put to one of the leading *Krishtabhaktas* from Assam (Eastern part of India). Since they are no more isolated but very much part of Christian reality in India, the views are taken for a serious consideration in this research.

Q.I. Name change after baptism was common colonial practice, what is the main purpose of doing so?

Answer: No, it is not at all right. Many tells of Saul changed to Paul but the Bible is clear, it records "Saul was also known as Paul" (Acts13:9) for us to learn. We also know that in Eastern tradition, we have more than one name for a person.

Q.II. Many people are given a typical Western name like Mr. Vinison Dixon or Lorance Matthew etc., do you think by doing it, we are de-rooting a person from his/her culture?

Answer: Knowingly or unknowingly, this all goes back to the civil law of 1865 for the Christians. It is extraction from all that comes along with your birth identity. We have indeed knowingly or unknowingly become the channel of de-rooting a person from his/her ethnicity and depriving parents, grandparents the joy of giving the child his/her name. It is a direct insult/neglect of the social system and family traditions. This is so unbiblical.

Q.III. Do you believe that cultural name helps a person to be in culture with new faith?

Answer: In 1Cor.7 Paul says, "Be at the same place when the Lord called you" then how much more our names that our parents and dear ones gave us! Indeed, it helps a person with his/her ethnic identity. A name defines a person's community, tribe and lot more in our country. How can Western perspectives ever understand this? But again, there are people who would not like to be called by their original name for that reminds them of the caste system-the Dalits, S.C, S.T or O.B.C. I would say these are more political issues and

[425] Kristabhakta: From late 19th century and early 20th century, mainly in Bengal, being disillusioned by the colonial presentation of Jesus/Christianity and their kind of religious discourse which stood opposite to Indian traditions, many like Brahmabandhab Upadhyaya, R.C. Das developed worshiping community outside conventional Church (new known as Churchless Christianity). It is to believe that Indian has nearly 1 million *Khristabhaktas* outside Church. Conventional Church is still struggling to acknowledge them as real Christian. But on the other they do not look for recognition and live a follower of Christ, living same as before conversion. It is deity change not cultural change. Yeshu Darbar is one such powerful movement in North India. They actually take the spiritual aspects of Jesus, not rituals and remain culturally Hindu/Buddhist/Jain etc. More and more new generation converts are heading towards such cultural life.

issues of the heart rather than of the Kingdom of God. I believe our names bound us closer to our culture, people, and community. Keeping our original names help us to be rooted within our community and therefore be a better witness of the Lord's love in this journey of life.

His answer reflects the importance of this issue that is dealt with here in our research. The name is not just to express faith, but to be with community/ nation and culture. On the same reason, North-East tribes didn't change the name at all after conversion, yet they are Christian like any other in the world.

5.5. Caste and Mission Interpretation

Like many confusing translations of Indian words like of Dharma, *varna* that was misinterpreted by European orientalists. One such error is *varna* became caste. Scripturally, *guna* (quality) was the basic logic of *Varna*, but not caste as it was depicted the symbols of injustice. Manu's *varna* was *guna* oriented social distribution of labor. And in that sense, the meaning of '*sudra*' denotes a person who lacks the minimum quality to work or a newborn baby whose quality is unknown.[426]

Mission and European orientalists altered *varna* with caste and presented it as a symbol of religious discrimination within Hindu. So, Hindu as a religious practice, legalized an injustice or legitimizing it for the vested interest of upper caste, was the main presupposition of European orientalists. Therefore, this manufactured theory had provided a platform to fight against Hinduism to place Jesus as a social savior.[427]

The desire to establish an 'Ekklesia' as the 'Kingdom of God in Jesus' for native converts was taken as the policy of missionary. The caste was seen as a system of the injustice of Brahmin. Even though there is a truth in it, but this observation by European mission cannot be taken as an ultimate interpretation of *Varna/jati* system in India. The Colonial Government and mission agencies were convinced that caste must be eradicated, and in doing so, hope was, more people will be joining in Christian fold which would give social sustainability to the colonial rule, hence name change was an objective resolution. Two basic features are noticed in the name changing policy: firstly, for high caste converts and secondly for low caste converts. High caste converts were reluctant or refused to drop their name, for example, Krishna Mohan Banerjee (First Indian Anglican Priest in Kolkata) or Kali Charan Banerjee in Bengal, Manilal Parekh (Rajasthan), Subba Rao in Andhra Pradesh. They even raised their voice against such uncalled for policy and marked this policy as anti-

---

[426] Manu Smṛti, edited and translated by Pushpendra Kumar, as *Hindū Dharmaśāstra*, 1st edition, Vol. II (Delhi: Nag Publishers, 2011).

[427] Ajay Kumar Jaitly & Madhu Rani, eds., *Cultural India* (Delhi, Chennai, Patna: Globus Press, 2012), 87-104.

culture and unbiblical. For low caste converts, the name change was made compulsory or they accepted colonial logic of egalitarianism.

5.5.1. EW[428] Name and the Role of Caste

What happened during the Muslim rule, the same was repeated during the colonial rule, i.e., the de-valuation of the low caste Indians. In my observation, they were not treated with complete human dignity, even though in principle both of them propagated egalitarianism. The forcefully proselyting policy was imposed without their consent; therefore they have been suffering from a massive de-culturation. The name is one such area.

Typical Euro-Western or Biblical Names

i.	George Tomes	Uttar Pradesh	Methodist
ii.	Racean Mirock	Uttar Pradesh	CNI
iii.	Christian Ivans Joel	Gujarat	Methodist
iv.	Vinison Dixon	Gujarat	CNI
v.	Alfa David Masih	Jharkhand	Lutheran

These are the tip of the iceberg of what happened to low caste Christians in the name of egalitarian Christianization. Most of the people after fourth or fifth generation, now, they forgot to whom they supposed to integrate, what was their ancestral root, a region of origin, local affiliation, etc. The natural consequences are 'uprooting' from cultural soil. And this is exactly what mission policy was intended to achieve.

In my observation, most of the Christians are semi-refuse in their own homeland. And name played a role, separating one's social root. There two angles of it: one when a priest gives his first name and added a modified biblical name, for example, John *Masih*. 'John' can be from Bible or from the priest's name and a modified name 'Messiah' as '*Masih*' (savior), so there are many NICs who are carrying '*Masih*' as a surname. The use of this word '*Masih*' as a surname in different parts of Northern India.

A List is given:

Akhil Masih	Uttar Pradesh	Uday Masih	Bihar
Alfa David Masih	Jharkhand	Yakoob Masih	Haryana
John Masih	Punjab	Manish R. Masih	Delhi

Some other surnames that are common like '**Lucas, Dixon, Cutting, Brown**', etc. among NICs. Those words are used mainly to replace Indian surname. The consequence of such attempt falls on cultural ambit on which an Indian citizen, regardless of religion, must have the right to live and inherit as

[428] EW: Euro Western.

the natural national. Since the right was denied, mainly to those traditionally weaker sections, who were assured to have 'right' after conversion, what they never enjoyed since they were not treated equal to white EW people, but what pragmatic really and truth are that they were denied their right to choose. It is obvious that EWM did not count NICs as the 'free and new religious community', but subverted as a 'captive' to the colonial power. In the postcolonial period, the anti-caste political movements (North or in South) like BSP, DMK, etc. did not feel to replace the surname as the means to achieve their emancipation from caste injustice but focused on the replace the religion if indeed needed as an option to achieve their goal. It is what had made Dr. Ambedkar appeared to be the ultimate hero for weaker sections of India including for the Dalit Christians.

Mission policy, unfortunately, was neither successfully able to present Jesus as an alternative for weaker people of India, nor they were able to separate themselves from colonial power to prove their religious transparency beyond hidden and vested colonial interest.

5.5.2. Tribal Name, Identity, and Cultural Questions

For an endogamous community, the linguistic name is not related to faith but it is a mark of community. A name plays various intra-community practices, moral and ethical norms, for example, among Kuki (A North-East tribe who are completely Christian with a population of nearly six hundred thousands) tribe, two persons having the same name are natural friends and through them, both families are connected. They are by custom help each other when they need. It upholds some social responsibility and service to people. In 2003, our bus broke down in a remote hill at night. Finding no option to travel home, my wife started searching the same name as her brother has in a nearby village and we found one person. Night at 10 pm, we knocked at his house and my wife said that she was the sister of 'Kaikhomang' and bus brake-down. An elderly person much older to her brother welcomed us, cooked and morning we left their home. It may be silly in the modern world, but why not the Church also attempts to preserve such lofty tradition. Just change a name can make a huge social disorder and disintegrate a community.

If we accept that EWM was only to form an egalitarian society; then there should be a social study to know the people. Just to pre-assume that every single convert should accept EW Christianity and alter their social order to fit into the colonial system, was actually de-humanizing the very existence of a particular group. In contrast, the central Indian tribal Christians were given an EWB first name but not a tribe name which is their social identity, just as caste name for Hindu converts. A tribal name like Timothy Hemrom, Nepolion Hasda or Charles Murmu is common. When it comes to North Eastern tribal Christians, mission policy was completely rejected by local converts and hardly first name or even the surname/clan name is to be found till the date. Since we are taking Kuki tribe as a counter-argument, let me place some names like Mr. Kaikhomang Khongsai, Mrs. Hoikhonem Lunkim, Ms. Nemneilhing Haokip, etc. They are typically Kuki expression and they are not even influenced by other groups with whom they have been living hundreds of year. Presently, it is seen some youths adopt Biblical/western names as the first name, and followed by a clan name, but thus far no record can prove at least a single Kuki who has dropped his/her clan name even if 100% people are now Christian since 1910.[429] There is even less than 5% who willfully use the biblical or Western name only as a first name or nickname.

The clan and sub-clan or tribe names along with their traditionally three syllables first name semantics that has never changed. Same is true for other North-Eastern tribes like Mizos or Nagas. The exemption of tribal name by EWM may raise the suspicion on their motif to Christianize India Hindu and replace India culture by Western culture just as it was done in Latin America and many of Western African countries. Such an assumption is not taken a pure academic hypothesis, but it can be explored further to analyze whether there was any specific policy for Hindu converts or not.

5.5.3. Post-Colonial Naming Trends and Freedom of Religious Expression

In our empirical data survey, one new trend has emerged which is clearly separate Christian history of Indian into two periods: one since the 16th century the arrival of European mission and other, from the rise of Indian freedom movement since the beginning of 20th century. The Indian freedom movement had influenced those people who were fighting to bring Church out of the Western setting and put it on Indian cultural settings. As early as the 1850s, we see the protest of Rev. Sattam Pillai and ultimately separated from Colonial Church and first ever started the indigenous Church in Tamilnadu in 1858. Later, Brahmabadhav Upadhyaya, Sadhu Sundar Singh or Bengal Christian Movement, etc., are few examples. The political freedom struggle in this context infused the psychological empowerment to take it as an open revolt against the colonial Church authority. Native Church was completely de-voiced by the colonial mission and did not count native demand legitimate. Since Edinburgh Conference 1910, a voice from Third World was at the front, and eventually the Tambaram Conference 1938, we noticed many objective resolutions in favor of colonized Churches like of India. Bishop Azariya's was a pioneering voice. The rise of national awakening had made some sort of cultural revival among the Christian community as well. Our limited use of

---

[429] Tongkhojang Lunkim, *Multiplying Pure Meitei Churches in Manipur Valley* (Imphal: The Upper Room Press, 1986), 23.

this vast area will be limited to new naming trend since the 1900s and more prominent in the post-colonial period.

Let me place some families who are Christian at least 4th or 5th generation to analysis this trend and at the end put postcolonial converts to establish this argument.

5.5.3.1. Case Study No. I of Hindu Orphan

Rev. Amit Thomas' Family[430] (Bihar State): Andrew Thomas (first Christian as an orphan, the early 1900s) > Arvind > Anil (Naveen, Andrew & Noel) >Amit > Anand & Arman

Analysis: Mr. Andrew's real name is not known now and he was converted as a Hindu orphan, therefore, EWB named him Andrew and it separated him from his community/society hereafter. The given name derived from the pastor including the new surname 'Thomas'. His son was given Indian name 'Arvind' as a new trend and freedom of choice is noticed. Mr. Arvind named his four sons half Indian and half Christian name. Mr. Arvind's son Anil also followed the same and named his son Mr. Amit and Mr. Amit's two sons are named Anand and Arman (an Urdu word). They allow the new family surname 'Thomas' to continue. In my interview, he expressed that typical EWB names were not the best choice of ours and name 'Anand' was given by his grandfather. According to his opinion being a pastor in NIC, surname changed was deeply motivated with an idea of proselytization to debar someone from his/her own cultural root. For orphan kids, no missionary ever thought of an upbringing in Indian culture. As a result, many are still suffering from social integration.[431]

So, a re-culturation model is on practice in double dimension: freedom to adopt any names either Christian or India. In this new trend, Christians are either take an Indian name which has biblical value or meaning or takes the name from the Bible for religious identity. Most non-biblical Western names were mistakenly known as Christian names in India both by Christians and other communities like Napoleon, Franklin, etc.

5.5.3.2. Case Study No. II of Hindu Convert

Evangelist Amit Chandra Das' Family[432] (Assam State): Ram Ratan Christian (converted in 1917) > Mr. Samuel + Mrs. Puspojine Das > Mr. Aren + Mrs. Manju Das > their children: sons – Amit Chandra & Abed Das and daughter Sara Das.

---

[430] Rev. Amit Thomas interviewed on 25th April, 2014.

[431] Rev. Amit Thomas, a pastor of Evangelical Church of India, faculty in Allahabad Bible Seminary, in the Dept. of Theology, have his Ph.D. research on 'Alternative Church Movement like of Yesu Darbad in Allahabad.

[432] Amit Chandra Das, Evangelist, Presbyterian Church of Mizoram, interviewed on 23rd July 2014.

Analysis: Two major reverse trends are found in this family: firstly, EW missionary dropped their family name (surname) and in place using 'Christian' which is a non-corresponding meaning in society or in language. It was the mark of the old fashion mission policy of proselytization. Next generation, in the 1940s, they brought back family name 'Das' to integrate them in the community. Not only with Christians, but with their parental family who is Hindu. So, the limitation of religion in social life obviously acknowledged. Mission agencies were overdriven by the idea that religion as the final index to social re-arrangement. Presently, this family has the freedom to use biblical names for faith identity and a family name for socio-cultural life.

5.5.3.3. Case Study No. III of Hindu Convert

Ms. Jinatama Dighal's Family[433] (Odisha State): Mr. Lakapati + Mrs. Shishaphula Dighal (postcolonial Christian)> Mishra + Geetanjali Dighal > their children: son – Deepak and daughters – Jinatama (20 years now) & Deepika

Analysis: The case study of this family gives a postcolonial trend. This family came to Christianity after independent of India, so no pressure from the Church to change of name was noticed. After independent, most of Indian Church under the Constitution freedom religion and Indian secularism, one only can request to a new convert whether he/she wishes to have any Christian name or not. It is noticed like this Dighal's family, many new converts after 1947; wish to continue their cultural and tradition caste names. I was also requested during conversion (in 1991) to change the first name that I refused to do so. By their family name and name's selling, it is known that they are from Odisha, a Hindu converts and caste affiliation. This model is predominant among new converts in the postcolonial period.

In September 2015, while teaching 25 pastors and evangelists from newly converted Christians from Hindu community, primarily from a low caste, but not a single one has changed their name, neither they wished so. It proves a point that a cultural awareness and a new interpretation of the Gospel that it is the change of heart, not cultural or religion has slowly taken control of mission in India. Name semantics speaks a lot to substantially establish our argument.

---

[433] Ms. Jinatama Dighal, Missionary, Church of North India, Odisha Diocese, interviewed on 9th August, 2015.

5.5.3.4. Case Study No. IV of Muslim Convert

i. **Rev Samuel Andrew Noel's family[434] (Uttar Pradesh State)**: Ranjan Khan > Indriyus Khan, changed after conversion into Andriyas Noel (from a Canadian Pastor's name) > Samuel Andriyas Noel > his son Arpit Andrew Noel & daughter Angel Priyana Noel

ii. **Rev. Vinison Dixon's Family[435] (Gujarat State)**: Great grandfather – Mr. Beli who was converted in Anglican Church (was orphan), then EWB names like Samuel, Dixon (from a pastor) added to names as first and surname in place of Beli. Rev. Vinison Dixon and his wife Mrs. Louisa Edward have given cultural names like son Anugrah and daughter Avani.

iii. **Mr. Parvez Rafique Khan's family[436] (Uttar Pradesh State)**: Rafique Khan (1st convert) > Mr. Parvez Rafique + Anupama Khan > their kids: son-Sonit Solomon & daughter – Selja Khan

Analysis: Interesting features are to be noticed among Muslim converts both in colonial and post-independent India. Hardly Muslim converts actually objected to EWB names as replacement of their traditional Islamic names. There are two basic reasons to be analyzed here. Firstly, since Muslim and Hindu relationship was low and has a huge trust deficit, even after becoming converted into Christianity, old religious tension continues to accept each other. Truly, even today, most of the Hindu convert Christians avoid the marital relation to Muslim convert Christians. This tension plays a role in naming semantics for Muslim converts. It is observed that Muslims are more prone to change their names and the reason is to integrate with majority Hindu converts in the new faith. In another way, Christians in India are culturally dominated by India-Hindu traditions. Secondly, the alternative way of naming is an adaptation of Sanskrit-Hindi originated words or EWB names for their new identity. Above all three family trees support this logic. Down the line, they slowly absorbed in majority culture or local Indian culture. For example, Mr. Parvez Khan opined and admitted the mistake of not changing the surname 'Khan' which has become the obstacle for his social integration and victim of recent global and Indian socio-political tension with Muslims. He said that his children face more difficulties in daily basic being mistakenly taken as Muslim when we are Christian. It is observed that Muslim converts hesitate to disclose their pre-conversion religion as Hindu converts openly do. It is

---

[434] Rev. Samuel Andrew Noel, Senior Pastor in Evangelical Church of India, Allahabad diocese, Uttar Pradesh, interviewed on 20th August, 2015.

[435] Rev. Vinison Dixon, pastor of Church of North India, Rajasthan Diocese, interviewed on 11th September, 2015.

[436] Mr. Pravez Rafique Khan, Assistant Liberian, Allahabad Bible Seminary, interviewed on 12th September, 2014.

deeply psychological and it affirms a persistence Hindu-Muslim religio-social conflict within Indian Christians.

5.6. Church of North India[437]

Taking the traditions of the Church of North India as our focus area, it is important to mention that Christians in the Northern region are very loosely divided among denomination. The demarcation among them is just administrative. I am not talking about liturgy or doctrinal position of a denomination which is a very serious issue in European Churches; whereas Protestant Churches in Northern India are closely interdependent and even intermingle. For example, all protestant Churches including Syrian Orthodox Churches have accepted 'One Theological Institute' to train their pastors and missionaries, known as the Senate of Serampore College (since 1818). Indian Protestant Church run seminaries accept any qualified faculty of Senate of Serampore and every denomination sends student to different seminary. For example, I teach in Allahabad Bible Seminary where faculties are from the Church of South India, Church of North India, American Baptist, Restoration Church, Mennonite Church, etc., but it is run by the Evangelical Church of India. This picture must be kept in mind when the analysis of CNI is applied to the entire NICs. It is important to note this scenario at this juncture.

Let me bring here some reflection from two CNI pastors to understand the whole cultural situation as they deal in Church and in society.

Rev. Praveen Massey[438] explained that the CNI has no standing rule or tradition to select the words for the name. During the colonial period, European name was given by Pastors to the new converts and their children. Dropping the surname, taking Pastor's, surname, using the mixed name, etc. were normal practice. But after independent, in Anglican tradition as well as other North Indian traditions, common people prefer more Indian name which carries Christian values like Samarpan (surrender), Priti (compassion), Anugrah (grace), etc. After the formation of CNI, Indianization is emphasized for cultural re-orientation of Church. On the question of how to choose one's name and in reply he mentioned that in the post-colonial context, CNI as well as other North Indian Churches favor keeping a balance between Indian culture and Biblical tradition, and wish to separate from the Euro-Western culture.

---

[437] Church of North India: It has come in existence on 29th November 1970 when 6 denominations merged together. This is the second such unification after Church of South Indian in 1948. CNI and also CSI have denounced the previous denominational identity and form a common doctrine and liturgy, even though they are much close to the Anglican Communion. It is surprising to many Western Churches to see the possibility of such kind. CSI and CNI are the largest Christian groups in India.

[438] Rev. Praveen Massey, the Pastor of Miurabad Church of CNI, Lucknow Diocese, interviewed on 4th September, 2015.

The names directly related to gods and goddesses of other faiths are almost avoided. Answering to the question whether any impact of previous faith, he said that there are two trends: firstly, the Hindu converts started to go back more of Hindi words with Christian values and secondly, Muslim converts prefer Biblical names. It is interesting to observe that many of the lost cultural aspects, even though originated largely from Hindu tradition are re-introduced in Church. Indian Christians are more or less influenced by Hindu culture. That is why Hindu cultural influence is not taken as a sensitive issue. There is a cultural comfort zone which Muslim converts do not enjoy in society since the traditional Muslim name itself is a mark of social segregation.

There are few other reasons for leaning towards Indian names: i. CNI by constitution accepted the cultural reconstruction, limiting extra-episcopalism, adopting freedom. ii Many children are complaining against social difficulties of their typical Western or awkward names to harmonize in social engagement. iii. Government or public official dealings also become difficult (occasionally or regionally) to correspond non-native names.

Evangelist Rathod Pitarsan Ravikiran[439] observed that the Gujarathi tradition and Christian consciousness in another way which qualify the caste arrangement and regional bias settings. He said that 80% of present Gujrathi Christians wish to have at least one word among traditional three words naming semantics. Local Christians are deeply proud to keep state identity in a new fashion. He also noticed that Hindu converts (first generation) keep more of a cultural name than traditional Christians. Surname changes are found more among lower caste converts for two reasons: to hide low social status and high caste will hardly change their surname because they feel losing social status.

5.7. Egalitarianism Logic and Reality of Caste-Based Christianity in India

Socially, the condition of Christian Dalits is not getting any better even within the Christian community, and this problem faced by them is openly admitted by Roman Catholic and Protestant Church leaders. For example, Archbishop George Zur, Apostolic Pro-Nuncio in his inaugural address to the Catholic Bishops Conference of India, (CBCI) meeting held in Pune during December 1991, made the following observations:

> Though Catholic of the lower caste and tribes form 60 percent of Church membership, they have no place in decision making. Scheduled caste converts are treated as low caste not only by high caste Hindus but by high caste Christians too. Though Dalit

[439] Evangelist Rathod Pitarsan Ravikiran, is from CNI, Diocese of Gujarat, interviewed on 26th August, 2015. He is mainly working among adult school and college going students last 5 years.

> Christians make 65 percent of the ten million Christians in the South, less than 4 percent of the parishes are entrusted to Dalit priests. There are no Dalits among 13 Catholic bishops of Tamilnadu or among the Vicars-general and rectors of seminaries and directors of social assistance centers.[440]

It was supported by the President (Archbishop Alphonse Mathias) of CBCI.

The Bishop of the Church of South India, M. Azariah observes:

> The Scheduled Caste (Dalit) Christians are thus discriminated against and opposed by fellow Christians within the various churches for no fault of their own but the accident of birth, even when they are 2nd, 3rd or 4th generation Christians. The high caste Christians who are in a minority in the Church carry their caste prejudices even after generations, unaffected by Christian belief and practice.[441]

5.8. Re-construction of EWM Tradition: A Postcolonial Cultural Quest

5.8.1. Theology of Mission: A Postcolonial Interpretation to Name Giving Culture of EWM

Identity is essential to the existence and every object is therefore identical by its name. It is the most powerful aspect of this universe. The Bible affirms this theological nuance as divine ability as a sign of existential nature of creation. A name is a location of a human being and also other creatures within the space on earth. It also depicts the cohesive natures within the objects, and therefore, unjustified alteration of this system would be conditioned as 'injustice' in the biblical process of justice. In Genesis (second creation narrative) 2:5-25 invites us into a new theological debate in the third world from within a postcolonial reading. C.S. Song explained it as '...a name stands for the totality of the being denoted by it, and ...it represents the power of the name-giver over the totality given ability its name. It is a formidable power that is associated with this God-given ability of name giving.'[442] In biblical theology, a 'name' is not just a 'name', but it is substance. When God authorized Adam to name each object, it appeared to be an identity in particular. God did not authorize Adam to name a human being, except his family. The theology of naming, therefore, rests upon the family hereafter. The family is empowered to continue this process

---

[440] James Massey, *Dalits in India* (New Delhi: Manohar, 1995), 82.

[441] Ibid.

[442] C.S. Song, *Tell Us Our Names: Story Theology from an Asian Perspective* (New York: Orbis Books, 1984), 91.

through generations which are carried forward significantly not only in the history of a particular family but also a symbol of their spiritual genealogy. Taking an example of Matthew chapter one (genealogy of Jesus), apart from various interpretations, the theological significance is very much evident to establish the religio-ethnical identity of Jesus. It is an applied truth for every community. If any human being is in a position to give a name, he/she controls and contributes his/her socio-religion-ethnical-cultural totality.

In the West, Christianity adopted an alternative *saṁskāra* for them, then, a new identity emerged over the old. Old is now an obscure reality of the past, mainly in the context of the non-Western world. It is indeed a revolutionary step that raised serious cultural question where Christianity and it's Gospel mean to change inner heart (change of inner life) or physical life which has socio-cultural expression. The book of Acts Ch. 15 provides us a completely different mission model that accepts the assimilation of culture by denouncing circumcision for gentile. Then it may worth asking a question to the motif of EWM which failed to create cultural 'space' for gentiles (Indian here). The Postcolonial theological question may ask where 'physical' conversion in any way the intention in Jesus' mission or it was primarily spiritual in nature and content. EWM in Asia and Africa fully exploited the name-giving power. They explored, conquered, and gave a 'name' for converts. And by giving a new alien (linguistically and culturally) name, they controlled them. Song has raised a theological question to the mission of EWM, "Is theology doing equally well in restraining this name-giving power in its own house?" Christian mission takes Matthew chapter 28:18-19 as mission commandment, and propagated the 'good news' in the name of Jesus. Since the inception of the Christian faith, the faith-exploring mission has been carried out in the name of Jesus. The name is the centrality of the Christian mission. After 2000 years it is still the same.

Ironically, EWM had attempted to conquer Asia and Africa in the name of Jesus, after achieving success, they took away the names of people, hence uprooted them from culture permanently. Preconceiving the mighty military power and European civilization as a final yardstick; mission implemented a rigorous christening project (baptism, conversion, and proselytization) that entered into the socio-cultural life of millions and destroyed their very existence or re-constructed into a point of no-return by giving a new alien name. For example, Song used the testimony of an African convert to argue the importance and distortion of EWM name giving catastrophe.

> My own father's African name was Mangombe, meaning 'one who owns a large herd of cattle.' When he became a Christian, he was baptized, Charles. My mother's name was Pfumai, meaning 'may thou be wealthy.' When she became a Christian, she was given

> the name of Helen.....In most cases, names were chosen by the evangelist or missionary with no regard as to whether the family, for whom the name was initially significant of course, could even pronounce it at all....My own name Ezekiel...is pronounced and pronounced in about ten different ways by my people.[443]

Such is the reality in India too, and the conditioned 'people' are voiceless, so subalternity prevailing into a given condition of EWM. Spivak raised a question 'Can the subaltern speak?.'[444] Question is valid, '*Can Indian Christians speak*?.' Our focus is to explore the contextual possibility whether NICs have any space to speak and re-construct their identity with a postcolonial motif? A native name is an absolute fine, and it is not only the question of a new Christian faith identity but a larger cultural issue: a history of a person, family, pride, social mobility are inter-related. Faith during EWM often minimized other identities in the level of 'nothing'. A native name could be a useful tool for a mission for Indians, it is a medium to the link between past and handed down to future. It is not an identity of an individual, but an aspect of their whole world view and social wholeness.[445]

The very subalternity is practically enforced by giving EW name and by doing it, EWM makes a person from 'somebody' to 'nobody' and left to live almost within a cultural vacuum. Taking biblical account of Jesus in Matthew 7:21, when he explained that for salvation, it is not the name, but the faith of heart that matters. The problem of EWM is not the name as a surface value, but the doctrinalization of European Christianity and culture (Weltgeist-World Spirit, Hegelian construct), presumed it as an absolute matrix for the rest of world. The 'worlding' and 'othering' is what Spivak explained as the centrality of cultural conflict in subaltern India Christians. She raised a question of 'worlding' of the 'native' or the formation of the 'other' by the European self.[446] In colonial missiological epistemological trajectory which sets the narrative for 'other' and thus, in place of 'other', mission agents are to speak for/as natives. Ritu Birla said it as 'quit-other.'[447] In the Indian context,

[443] C.S. Song, *Tell Us Our Names: Story Theology from an Asian Perspective* (New York: Orbis Books, 1984), 92.

[444] Gayatri Chakravorty Spivak, "Can the Subaltern Speak? Speculations on Widow Sacrifice" in *Wedge* 7/8 (1985): 120-130.

[445] C.S. Song, *Tell Us Our Names: Story Theology from an Asian Perspective* (New York: Orbis Books, 1984), 92.

[446] 'Wordling' is Spivak's term for the process whereby a conolizing agent assimilates a subject people through acts of epistemic violence, such as naming or remapping. Spivak, A Critique of Postcolonial Reason, 211-212.

[447] Ritu Birla, "Postcolonial Studies," in *Can the Subaltern Speak? Reflections on the History of an Idea*, edited by Rosalind C. Morris (New York: Columbia University Press, 2010), 252.

native identity was re-constructed by EWM, not in consultation to native, but as if it was the ultimate divine authority to construct 'others' as a process of biblical epoch-making. Here comes the authoritarian index of 'worlding' and clash of civilization. Euro-centrism of Christian faith and mission released the political power to execute the 'biblical order' of Matthew chapter 28:18-19 with European clothing.

Looking at the historiography of native Indian Church, it is still the history of Europe/West, and it is the extreme evidence of 'quit-other' and situation of subalternity of Indian Christians as an object of history, not the subject of history.

5.8.2. Globalization Logic of the West

Look what is the contrast between India and West, for example, India hardly (never in history) attempted to melt down the various diversities and form one single identity (culturally or religiously), instead accepted plurality as the meeting point of diversity. Name places a vital role to give existence to this plurality and cultural diversity.

A culture is a common property of a community and it cannot be decoded with new language and symbolism with the radical application of structuralism to create a new organizational identity. Merleau-Ponty explained, "For to name a thing is to tear oneself away from its individual and unique characteristics to see it as representative of essence or category." Just as the object is brought into existence through naming, thereby *becoming* the name, so too the individual *becomes* its name; the name determines what the individual is.[448]

5.8.3. Cultural Questions

5.8.3.1. Social Question and Re-culturation

Western Name

- Roman Catholic Tradition: Compulsorily complete new European name given (Goa) more a Portuguese name like Romeo D'Souza, Oscar Fernandez and also Latin name. Protestant name like Luke Matthew etc.
- Mostly protestant tradition: Since there is no central body for them, name ceremony and selection both are traditionally established by the denomination, but a mixed name is commonly followed by a complete Western name.

Mixed Name

- Confused one social identity

[448] M. Merleau-Ponty, *Phenomenology of Perception*, Trans. By C. Smith (New York: The Humanities Press, 1962), 176.

- One faces various social questions to prove his/her identity
- Departs from the traditional system
- Does not correspond meaning to others in India except Christian community i.e., Hephzibah (2 Kings 21:1 & Is 62:4). Language in society and study provides the meaning of names and gives psychological feeling in calling, therefore, complete foreign names create confusion. The name is not only to remember or to identify a person but also to understand the value attached to the name. In the Bible, the name was very important for its corresponding meaning, not just a 'word'.

Exception: North-East Tribal Christians hardly use Biblical or European names. They follow cultural and traditional name to uphold their ethnic identity which is known mainly by names in a pluralistic context. An altering cultural name is actually taking away one's social identity.

i. Kerala Model: In a naming ceremony in India, elements used like honey, leaf, uncooked rice, turmeric, gold, dresses are highly symbolic. The name selection also reflects the local culture like, for the first boy, child's name will be from the father's father and for the first girl child, the name is taken from the father's mother's name as her first name. If he is the second boy, the mother's father's name will be given to him. If she is the second girl, she will be called by her maternal grand mother's name and so on. The surname will be always the father's name. Today the communities used to include a pet name before the ancestral name.
ii. North-East Model can be used to co-existence a balanced identity between the Christian faith and culture.
iii. For converts must not be intimidated or insisted or proposed or forced with a name which is alien to him/her or family or society. Child of Christian family can avoid typical European names or unmatched combination of traditions: Indian, biblical and Western.

5.8.3.2. Problems and Perspectives

- Indian name appears to be Hindu or attached to Hindu meaning
- Pressure more on new converts either to change and hide behind a twisted name like Krishna to Kris or Ken; use Indian name just abbreviation Sitaram just as S. or Krishna Jeevan as Jeevan K. (related to conversion)
- Mahalakshmi after conversion became Rebeca (related to conversion)
- Confusion over Indian and Hindu name

- **Miss-concept**: Biblical, Western and Middle East names: Yakoob (Arabs) in Bible Joseph or Parvez (Persian) looks like a Muslim name
- The whole European names are known as Christian names by Christians and non-Christians

Conclusion

An Indian name is religiously, linguistically, regionally, caste-wise, ethnically structured and by imposing the EWB names, converts have lost social relevance because it has no communicative meaning and identification index with 'others'. Names were not chosen or made optional before converts, it was just put on them and this process has de-humanized native as 'object' of the colonial Church property. It has disempowered them socially and subjugated them under the Church. So, name-subalternity is a serious issue that is found here.

There is a postcolonial trend among new converts mainly in rural Indian indigenous movements outside of mainline Church that upholds the Indian names with the biblical meaning and they only avoid the typical religious names of god and goddess or in the most cases, the name change does not take place at all. Yet, a dilemma of identity being Indian and being Christian is prevailing (Mimicry of Bhabha). A balancing naming system is yet to develop among NIC [IC]. The hybrid (of Bhabha) name that is composed of one biblical word and one Indian word is an emerging trend among many traditional Christians.

In Manusmṛti, *nāmakaraṇa* is considered as *saṁskāra* due to its social and family importance that connects a person with the whole social system and individual finds its place within the cultural mobility of society. It is not only a word but denominator in which one integrates oneself with the rest of social conduct.

This *saṁskāra* is the most prevailing cultural and religious observation since the Vedic period and eventually transformed as the culture of people. It is religious but right to a family to observe, name a person. In both ancient systems, *nāmakaraṇa* is the fundamental religio-cultural rite through which one is included with family and into the society.

We find three features during the colonial period: firstly, Hindu converts in which high caste rejected the EWB naming pattern and low caste converts who were forced to adopt or given a new non-Indian name which actually worked as the catalyst to create a cultural displacement from their own culture and community relationship vertically; secondly, naming policy applied for central Indian tribal converts, in which, surname change is not noticed and thirdly, the tribes in North-East where name was at all took place.

The CNI being autonomous Indian Church, it has adopted the policy of 're-culturation' and has been encouraging many changes towards new cultural orientation including naming custom. North-Eastern tribal naming customs can be taken as 'model' to argue that accepting 'a new religious identity' does not demand to change old names or accepting different names. An alternative naming semantics within the Indian linguistic system like Bhavani Charan Banerjee as Brahmabandhava Upadhyaya, Sundar Singh as Sadhu Sundar Singh can be explored as a new naming tradition among NIC.

Open Question for Further Debate

1. How necessary in this global world to follow a traditional name and what purpose does it actually serve?
2. In this global world when information and technology have brought people so close to one another, then what constructive input does the ethnolinguistic name serve?

Chapter 6

Saṁskāra of Purification & Conversion Issue: Encountering Jesus 'With' and 'Without' Baptism: An Indian Response

Introduction

We begin our argument stating what Jesus commanded to his disciples in the Gospel of St. Matthew 28:18-19 and what St. Paul stated in 1 Cor.1:17. First one is known as the Great Commission of Jesus Christ to carry forward a particular mission and the second one talks about the priority of preaching Gospel and baptism. Two apparently may appear as contradictory if deeper and inner meanings are not be subsided by a single baptism oriented interpretation and the mission of God that lead 'conversion'. The spiritual aspiration of this particular command is noble. Anecdote of this noble demand eventually and historically has converted into religious legality to qualify or disqualify someone's relation to Jesus, Christianity, and church. This command is directly responsible to develop the sacramental rite of 'baptism and conversion' as a scriptural end-goal; whereas St. Paul sets an alternative end-goal which might contradict the first notion. Eventually, this rite has become a statutory sacramental obligation, 'the gateway' to Christ, salvation and institutional church. EW universal approach is questioned by many Asian, African Christians and secular leaders. There is also an attempt, initiated by many Indian Christian leaders like Manilal Parekh, K. Subba Rao to re-construct baptismal rite within Indian context or to repeal it altogether. Ankur Barua[449] in his book *Debating 'Conversion' in Hinduism and Christianity* argues for contextual paradigm change mainly

[449] Ankur Barua, *Debating 'Conversion', Hinduism and Christianity*, ed., Govin Flood, Routledge Hindu Studies Series (New York: Routledge, 2015).

within Indian pluralism. He located the whole debate within the geo-cultural ambit of India. The postcolonial aspiration is actually 'geo' limited in nature, hence often rejects the Christian obligation to Baptism rite which is actually conversion, not only from one faith to other but also one culture to other.

Dealing the issue in relation to 'baptism and conversion' and its sociological implication within the complex plural dimension of India, we would like to raise some pertinent questions to deal with this statutory rite with special reference to the NICs.

i. Why baptism is such a contentious socio-religious issue in India?
ii. Is it possible to examine the obligatory status of baptism to follow Jesus and the Church?
iii. The public opinion of baptism is negative and it is often linked with proselytization and conversion, so can we examine and search for an alternative form within Indian context?
iv. Since baptism and after-effect of baptism have failed to negotiate to the plurality of India, them, why not an alternative means be searched?

J. Jayakiran Sebastian also raised such questions and insisted to examine this rite.[450] Issues are to be examined from the socio-religio-cultural context of India to find a cultural answer. The editorial of *Religion and Society*, it is written:

> If the baptism is to be retained in Indian Christianity, the Churches that retain it should be constrained to find in it (or for it) a meaning that is strongly supportive of Christian life and faith. Otherwise, its liability to the Gospel in India can hardly justify its continued practice.[451]

We are highly considering the 'People's Voice' within a 'Space and Place' model as to analyze the doctrine and rite of baptism that would expand and enhance the *Samaj Dharma* as Christian reality of life. The 'People's Voice' is the postcolonial hallmark in the postcolonial arena. Re-culturation is possible only when reconstruction accommodates the aspiration of those people who follow it. During colonial ear, native Indian Christians were never consulted, asked for, and rather thrashed upon a European Christianity with unquestionable purity. Hence, NIC became 'object' of the Church, not the

---

[450] J. Jayakiran Sebastian, "Baptism and the Unity of the Church in Indian Today", *Baptism and the Unity of the Church*, eds., Michael Root and Risto Saarinen (Grand Rapids: William B. Eerdmans Publishing Company. 1998), 197.

[451] "Editorial" in *Religion and Society*, Vol. 19, No. 1 (March 1972): 4.

subject. NC[452] eventually denigrated as subaltern Christian under a superior EW Christian authority. Religion must listen to the voice of people because it is primarily for people, not for the authority. Therefore, the 'People's Voice' is our primary resource (survey and empirical data) that would be applied to investigate the ground reality of baptism rite from two major segments: BC[453] and FGC.[454] An attempt will be made to evaluate various texts of Manusmṛti and Torah on initiation and purification *saṁskāra* and will examine whether insights from those customs can be useful to redefine the present practice of baptism in form and content. Various North Indian Christian little traditions would be considered to see their credibility to provide an alternative model or not. The objective resolutions as the contemporary alternative models, their feasibility, usability, and challenges before North India Christians are to be undertaken.

6.1. Locating Debate

Locating debate is important to explore an in-depth analysis. Our debating issue is 'conversion' which is the result of obligatory rite 'baptism'. Another term which must be incorporated along with the central issue is 'proselytization'. This debate in India has been continuing since the beginning of the colonial period. During renaissance in the early nineteenth century, mission motif was seriously questioned. Three groups are involved in this debate: Christian mission apologists, Hindu converts (FGC) and Hindu intellectuals; and since the late 20th century, this debate has taken over by secularist, right-wing Hindu, journalist, political activist and others. This debate has been gaining momentum in recent time (since 1990 due to the rising popularity of right-wing Hindu groups like of RSS, VHP and a new narrative of cultural nationalism), even though the central issue was almost the same since Raja Ramhoman Roy had raised this debate in the 1820s. Therefore, our debate is in some form of continuity of 200 years old debate that included many contemporary Christian movements like *Yeshu Darbar*. Baptism and conversion issue is always located within the plural culture of India and socialization of faith *Samaj Dharma*; be it religious or purely cultural. The scriptural argument does not give uniformity, for example, the baptism of Jesus, not a socio-cultural conversion but when we take Paul's writing in II Cor. 5.17 (NIV) that says, 'Therefore, if anyone is in Christ, the new creation has come: The old has gone, the new is here.' If we take 'old' as the whole cultural life of the past, then social conflict is unavoidable but at the same time the baptism of Cornelius (Acts 10), no cultural conversion

[452] NC: Native Christian.

[453] BC: Born Christian, means Christian who are in faith generations.

[454] FGC: First Generation Christian-a person joining in Christian fold from the other faith tradition for first time.

is mentioned. More evidently, in Acts 15, Gentiles were permitted to be in their culture (no circumcision). This is what the central question of many Indian Christians like Manilal Parekh, S. Sundar Singh who interpreted baptism is an inner spiritual renewal, not outward cultural change. St. Thomas' mission in India emphasized on inner change and that was reflected through the mode of Indian culture. According to Dr. Samuel George, it is the conversion of the inner heart (conversion within).[455] The spiritual and socio-cultural paradigm has got central imagination in the Indian mind. Locating it within Indian postcolonial society will also help us to analyze whether or not North Indian Christians are in a position to implement the reconstructed proposals as a subaltern quest or colonial subalternity is an existing reality which holds colonial narrative as superior which, according to Homi Bhabha is a subaltern 'mimicry'.

6.2. Baptism-Conversion in Biblical Tradition

6.2.1. Baptism-Conversion and Its Root in Torah

Jewish community like of Indian community has been practicing various social and religious rituals. Most of them have been connecting one with a broader socio-cultural functional system. Religion has obviously contributed many such rites into the system. Baptism, as it is practiced and interpreted in the Christian tradition, is not-existence in Jewish tradition.

Yet, Christianity accepts the Old Testament as the formative background and the whole revelation and ultimate fulfillment in Jesus are established as a continuity of God's plan for salvation, taking logical journey beginning from the Genesis. Directly, 'baptism' is not found in the Torah, but the ablution rites[456] are very close to baptism, i.e., a rite of purification with water and even food.[457] The symbolic meaning attached to it like of dying of old and rise as new and initiation are common practices among Jewish, mainly among Qumran community. The New Testament practice of conversion (baptism) is not a new rite, but modification of a Jewish tradition. The Hebrew term '*hub*' connotes the meaning of conversion that is to 'return' or 'turn away' (Jeremiah 7.9).[458] It has a socio-religious paradigm too. In Exodus 33.11, 'would return to the camp' is ethnologically social. It is not the change of social life, but a decision that demands an ethnic and moral reconstruction. This ethnic-moral dimension continued in the life of Jesus and the early Christian movement

---

[455] Samuel George, Conversion with 'In' for Missions with 'Out' in *Journal of Mission and Intercultural Studies*, Vol.3, No.1 January-June (2016): 39.

[456] Lev. 16.15.

[457] Ibid., 17.15.

[458] Samuel George, Conversion with 'IN' for Mission with 'OUT" in *Journal of Mission and Intercultural Studies*, Vol.3, No.1 January-June (2016): 39-40.

until Jesus' followers separated from Jewish tradition. Whatever the meaning of baptism within the Church, its root in the Old Testament is undisputed.

The Hebrew word '*tabal*' in Torah[459] (in Septuagint translation), the applied meaning is connected to ritualistic purification through a bath or ablution, and the Greek word '*bapto*' also means 'to dip' in water. However in the Jewish tradition, purification is to be conducted for various reasons, since the level and layer of impurity are attached to daily life from dawn to dusk. The ritual purification in the Manusmṛti is very similar to Hebrew tradition. Mostly those purificatory rituals are a daily routine of life: applied for house-holder and public servant like temple priest, king, etc. Another Messianic meaning is 'repentance'; factually the baptism of Jesus is conversion through repentance, not a change of religion or cultural detachment.[460]

The underlying truth is a concept of 'sin' and its consequence is to be removed. Interestingly, 'sin' is not what Christianity advocates. 'Sin' sometimes is known just an 'unclean' state of body or food like taking bath after intercourse, during or end of menstruation of a woman, before entering to temple work or not eating certain meat or bread for Sabbath, etc. Christianity has minimized such daily purificatory rituals and attached to 'sin and salvation' mandate with deeply metaphysical sense.

Eschatological aspect in the Old Testament is also very strong where God brings forth political freedom when the nation as a whole falls below the moral law of God. It is somehow similar to the concept of the New World in the New Testament or *Satya Yoga* in Indian tradition. Of course, this NT or Indian idea goes beyond the geopolitical reality and explains the salvific plan of the entire creation. The Indian idea is inclusive in nature even though the Hebrew concept may not necessarily inclusive or to say, conditionally universal, whereas Christian concept is more anthropocentric reality confined and implemented only through the 'baptism'.

6.2.2. Baptism in the New Testament and Early Church

The Christian baptismal rite is closely connected to the baptism of Jesus by John the Baptizer (Matthew 3.13-17, Mark 1.9-11, and Luke 2.21-22). It was perhaps an extension of Hebrew water purification rite and the intention of John was a moral-spiritual call to the individual. Baptism of Jesus was a socio-religious rite which is a part of his culture, society, religion and family tradition. Yet, the Matthew 28.18-19 was interpreted as the centrality in the mission of Church and later doctrine of baptism has converted as one of the

---

[459] Gen. 37.31, Lev. 14:6 & 51.

[460] James J. Walter, "Conversion" in *The New Dictionary of Theology*, eds. Joseph A. Komonchak, Mary Collins and Dermot A Lane (Bangalore: Theological Publications in India, 2014): 233.

prime sacraments. Trying to visualize the baptism from Acts 2.42 and 4.32 and also in John 4.24, it is simply the rejection of sin, not the rejection of culture or society. Baptism is neither world-denial nor the metaphysical aspiration. Another meaning that dominated early Church was the eschatological hope of coming of Messiah and such an idea, mainly among Palestinian Christians, shaped the practical life when they were just waiting for the end time. Many contemporary Pentecostal also advocate immediate 'end time' message. This also makes many people to think only life after death. The whole spirituality is somehow negated the contextual reality of life.

The sacramental status of baptism is found in the Tertullian writings but it was the work of St. Augustine that defined it as the visible signs of an invisible grace. According to Jenson, it is the 'visible words' come into life with grace from above. Embodied the exclusive elements adding to this rite, and baptism overshadowed a simple religious rite (water) for moral-spiritual (free from sin) corrective objectivity, and now appeared to be the license to have fellowship with 'selective' people who are now known as Christian. This view is prevailing among many Indian Christians even today.

But, the dominating Christian concept of baptism is an outcome of the Hellenistic Christianity that doctrinalized it as death and rise of Jesus in connection to the new birth and new life. The contrast of 'new' and 'old' life, eventually took a new meaning of 'other faiths' and then, the 'old' is tagged as 'sinful' and the 'new' is spiritual, so rightful.[461] This meaning actually has infused a deep sociological complexity and categorized entire humanity into 'saved and profane'. 'Setting apart for God and setting apart from God' praxis, literally, has set a negative notion against Christianity in India. The exclusive nature of Jewish against what Jesus had launched a movement was lost its momentum being exclusive again. Negate your own (past) was appeared to be the yardstick to qualify closeness to Christ. In Indian reality, this Hellenistic tradition via European Christianity causes the cultural de-rooting and social alienation or foreignness to NICs.

The use of the cultural resource is one of means of Jesus to communicate his message. De-culturation was an absentee de facto during Jesus and first generation Christian, neither cultural imposition was practiced. Culture, being a positive tool, makes his message easy to transport to people.

Baptism-Conversion has two symbolic aspects: firstly, rejection of 'sin' and secondly, rejection of the 'old'. The rejection is a persuasive notion of the gospel, and in the Indian context, rejection of 'sin' symbolizes Indian religions (mainly Hinduism) and rejection of 'old' is culture. Individual call of Jesus is to be free from sin, has converted by subsequent Church leaders as withdrawal from the past social pattern of life (called out) and entered into a new life

[461] "Baptism, Eucharist and Ministry" in *Faith and Order*, No. 111 (Geneva: WCC, 1982): 2.

(European Christianity). Gospel as spiritual *marga* for salvation is to be kept in individual level to make it relevant in India. Social life can't be replaced by faith. Social life is an unending reality of life which religion can contribute or enrich. EWM wished to offer an alternative culture along with faith, and it appeared to be fatal. Look, hundred years of African black and European white in the USA, even being largely Christian, failed to assimilate in each other due to ethnocultural differences.

6.2.3. Protestantism and De-centralization of Baptism Tradition

The plurality or freedom to re-interpret rites and doctrines is fundamental in Protestantism that accepts the interpretation of an individual as a final authority within a decentralized system. It was a deconstructing process that provides a formidable model to re-construct baptism as well. Such reality may provide a reason for 'subaltern quest' in the plural religio-culture tradition of India. Therefore, any new suggestion in our research would not be taken as contradictory to the history of Protestantism, but the extension of the tradition, hence, objective resolution at the end can't be critiqued as a radical absurd.

Since Martin Luther broke away from the Roman Catholic authority, the Church lost her absolute monopoly to exercise religious authority or on the other way, a more de-centralized system became a reality. The pre-Lutheran Church was largely an institution, but, it is from Luther when an individual appeared to be an institution. Thereafter, sacraments, rites, etc. have been undergoing various changes due to an individual's new interpretation. We shall, therefore, examine whether such individual freedom model would a viable model for re-culturation of baptism for North Indian Christians as a Postcolonial quest for identity.

So far baptism is a concern, Luther, (away from Roman Catholic tradition), emphasized that baptism communicates the inner divine grace of God, reducing the ecclesiastical importance of the past, taking it as a command of God,[462] putting spirituality as centrality, not the rite per se.[463] He also believed that it is a private ceremony, not a ceremony of Church, and immersion in deep water (German word '*Taufe*', 'deep')[464] in presence of priest and godparents was advocated. John Calvin (1509-1564) interpreted baptism as a re-birth into a new life and fellowship of Christ.[465] He believed baptism is not just an outward sign of inward change (of Zwingli's view) or a conveying grace (of Luther's view), but inward mortification and signifying grace. What is a

[462] Matt. 28.19 & Mark 16.16.

[463] Martin Luther, *Small Catechism* (1529), BC, 360.12 and *Large Catechism*, BC 465.74.

[464] Martin Luther, *The Holy and Blessed Sacrament of Baptism* (1519), LW 35, 29.

[465] John Calvin, *Institutes of the Christian Religion IV.* 16.2 (1559), ed., John T. McNeill, Trans., Ford Lewis Battles in LCC XXI (Philadelphia: Westminster Press, 1960), 1326.

more fascinating aspect in Calvin for our research re-culturation is his idea of 'conductor of baptism' which denied the role of an ordained priest is obligatory and emphasized on the importance to the recipient.[466] The priesthood of every believer of Luther is much closer to it in some way. John Wesley (1703-1791) in his book *A Treatise on Baptism* (1756) analogically used circumcision same as baptism, the New Covenant. The role of Trinity became central to wash away original sin,[467] a sign of born again to become holy.[468] The impact of the new social context of England has provided as a new hermeneutical tool for his interpretation and understanding of baptism.[469] Latter the Pentecostalism in early 20th century in America initiated by Charles F. Parham (1873-1929) and others have been emphasizing the act of Holy Spirit as essential sign of baptism, reducing the importance of water as secondary, drawing theological logic from Wesleyan Holiness, often baptizing in the name of Jesus in place of Trinity is also practiced.[470]

Drawing reference from above brief discussions in the protestant history, three facts have emerged: firstly, the role of the individual as the sole authority to interpret and introduce a new sacramental tradition; secondly, the ecclesiastical nature of Church has changed with a democratic administration; thirdly, no rite and doctrine is believed to be final.

Our research will draw its logical strength from this de-centralized, individualistic model to introduce some suggestions at the end.

6.3. Baptism-Conversion in Indian Context: Importance, Critic, and Challenges

Setting a socio-cultural debate on the issue of 'baptism and conversion', Joseph Mattam said that most of the Christian groups believe that the sole and ultimate purposes of mission activities are 'baptism and conversion'. The theology of the mission affirms that baptism is a response to God's grace after being realized one's guilt through repentance. Therefore, it is positive in nature. The history of the church while practicing this noble rite, failed to avoid the eventual conversion as an end result of baptism rite. This rite is problematic in Indian context due to its exclusive nature that advocates no possibility of salvation outside Jesus or Christianity. Such positioning denies India's pluralistic religious culture and co-existence. For example, Gandhi viewed conversion as the deadliest poison against truth, even though he holds Jesus in

---

466 John Calvin, *Institutes...* IV 15. 22. LCC XXI, 1323.

467 John Wesley, *Treatise on Baptism* II. 1-5, *Works of Wesley* X, 190-92.

468 John Wesley, "The New Birth" IV. 3, *Works of Wesley* 2, 198.

469 Jeffrey A. Truscott, *The Sacraments...* op. cit. 59.

470 James F. White, *Protestant Worship: Traditions in Transition* (Louisville: Westminster John Knox Press, 1989), 194-201.

high extreme but not the baptism oriented proselytization. The fellowship of Indian Missiologist, in their Fourth Annual Meeting (on 24-27 August 1995, Pune) took the questions raised by Mr. Arun Shourie on the motif of Christian conversion from socio-religious and cultural perspectives. To Shourie, the conversion is a method to exploit the unjust demography of India population by Christian missionaries. He also raised a suspicious hypothesis to assume the doubts on the nationalism of Indian Christians. Shourie's controversial assessment can be challenged or contested, but his merits would be not be overlooked.

From the collective opinion, it is possible to visualize that a deep problem with baptism conversion has crippled Indian perception. The role of Church, instead of becoming an instrumental for change, appeared to be a force to develop a community within Indian society on a doctrine of baptism assuring salvation, hatred to other faiths, rejection to own culture, accepting symbol of Western culture and imperialism. Parekh said that the Church through baptism has come to mean absolute severance from one's own community.[471] Baptism, as its present usage, appeared to be mere ecclesiastical rite and an instrument for proselytizing and thus having it very little spiritual significance. This rite has been used to achieve a cheap goal by the Church.[472] His above projection of baptism must be critically examined, not straightway rejected. Church through baptism separates people. The role of Church, to Parekh, is not to isolate people but help people to grow spiritually i.e., Hindu would be a better Hindu.[473] Late Rev. Titus (a Methodist priest from Bihar) shared at *Sattal Christian Ashram* in 2010 how European mission used to monitor and control the social life of native converts through Church authority.[474]

Searching for a reason of baptism controversy, it is apt to analysis mission strategy of EWM which is largely believed that, 'if anyone says that baptism is optional, that is, not necessary for salvation, *anathema sit.*'[475] The world is divided in to 'saved' and 'unsaved' or 'believer' and pagan'. Indian dominating culture is attached to paganism, so newly converted Indians are subjected to be replanted into 'so-called' European system, separating from their social reality. The Baptist Confession formulated at Amsterdam in 1611 C.E. stated:

[471] Manilal C. Parekh, "The Spiritual Significance and Value of Baptism" in *National Council of Churches Review*, 44/9 (September, 1924): 324.

[472] Manilal C. Parekh, "The Spiritual Significance and Value of Baptism", op. cit., 328-329.

[473] Manilal C. Parekh, "An Autobiographical Sketch", R. H. S. Boyed, ed., *Manilal C. Parekh – 1885-1967 & Dhanjibhai Fakirbhai – 1895-1967: A Seclection* (Madras: CLS, 1974), 27.

[474] Rev. D.P. Titus shared his experiences being a pastor in the colonial Church before 1947 at Sattal Christian Ashram during Summer Retreat Program, May-June, 2010.

[475] D.C. Scott, "Baptism in Indian Context –An Event of Separation or Human Solidarity?" in *The Christian Century*, January (1990): 103-108.

Every church should receive all its members by baptism upon the confession of their faith and sins wrought by the preaching of the Gospel, according to the primitive institution and practice. And therefore, churches constituted in any other manner or of any other person, are not according to Christ's treatment.[476]

Several assumptions clearly underlie these statements from two very different traditions within the Church.

i. That, baptism is a 'necessary' and 'required' rite due, presumably to an imperative from our Lord, and therefore, every church should be constituted solely of baptized members. The exception to this is contrary to Christ's ordinance.
ii. The act as such is essential both for individual salvation and for membership in the Church.

The fallout of such position is double folded: firstly, baptism and its rite are essential imperative that constitutes a Church and secondly, Church stands exclusively only for those people who accept that rite. By doing so, in India, Church isolated herself from the rest of the society, so her congregation. Baptism, understood in this sense, is not only a religious community but also a social bipartisan force. This is, of course, not to deny that at all times and in all places, the 'sword' brought by Jesus is a dividing factor in a world of sin. When Christians, like their Master, are committed to working for a new just socio-economic order, for the integrity of all creation they will necessarily cause divisions and persecution. While we Christians positively avoid divisions based on caste, class, race, gender, and so on, we welcome the division that comes from a radical commitment to following Christ.[477]

6.4. Conversion: Indian Theological Response and De-construction Attempt

Proceeding from the above discussion of Protestant tradition, we now analyze the baptism-conversion from the writings of Indian thinkers. The central controversy since EWM entered in India is due to its primary focus to extend the European kind of Christianity in India,[478] and in guise, supported the extension and sustenance of the colonial power. The 'baptism-conversion' has

[476] D.C. Scott, "Baptism in Indian Context –An Event of Separation or Human Solidarity?" in *The Christian Century*, January (1990): 103-108.

[477] Ibid.

[478] Roger Gaikwad, "Rethinking Theology in India for the Twenty-first century: Ecclesiastical Perspectives" in *Rethinking Theology in India: Christianity in the Twenty-first Century*, eds., James Massey & T. K. John SJ (New Delhi: Manohar, 2013): 331.

not only given the negative perception of Hindus but also to Indian Christians. Pre and post-colonial writings will be able to reflect the shades on this issue.

6.4.1. Earlier Writings

Brahmabandhav Upadhyaya (1861-1907) said that Christianity in India must remove European clothes and put Indian garments to be acceptable to people.[479] Sadhu Sundar Singh's (1889-1929) of *Gospel in Indian Cup* or E. Stanley Jones' book *The Christ of the Indian Road*[480] communicates a message what the Bishop of CSI, Madras, Rev. Sundar Clarke in his book *Let the Indian Church Be India* expressed saying that Indian Church is far behind from being a truly Indian, be it liturgy, appearance or existence.[481] These are the statements indicate towards a serious sociological problem of Indian Church. Manilal Parekh,[482] (FGC from Jainism) may be the first truly advocated that baptism must be used only for *Sadhana* (spiritual) *Dharma*,[483] not against *Samaj* (social) *Dharma* (*Svadharma of Manusmṛti*). In his observation, this rite is a tool to campaign against *svadharma* (*varnadharma*), confusing with the caste system by EWM and exploited (Robert de Nobili[484]) it for the preaching of quality. His idea is much similar to Churchless Christianity in India.[485]

The spiritual dimension of Church is doctrinally overshadowed, and it is further complicated with the denominational rivalry. Example, Upadhyaya was convinced by the Roman Catholic Church that his former baptism in Anglican rite was wrong and second baptism was given.[486] A separate culture, doctrine, and practice have divided Indian society and its geopolitical impact has deepened beyond the faith.[487] Anto Karokaran (Indian Missiologist) believed

---

479 Brahmabandhav Upadhyaya, "The Clothes of Catholic Faith" in *Sophia*, Vol. V, No. 8, 9 August 1898: 124.

480 E. Stanley Jones, *The Christ of the Indian Road* (New York: The Abingdon Press, 1925).

481 Sundar Clarke, *Let the Indian Church Be Indian* (Madras: The Christian Literature Society, 1985), 2nd Print, 2.

482 Manilal Chhotalal Parekh (1885-1967), born in a Jain family in Rajkot, Gujarat, India, baptized in the Anglican Rites, known Indian Christian Theological, founder of Hindu Church of Christ, worked with Gandhi. His model is to create more space to accommodate people to Jesus within Indian reality.

483 Krickwin C. Marak and Plamthodathil S. Jacob, eds., *Conversion in a Pluralistic Context: Perspectives and Perceptions* (Delhi: CMS/ISPCK, 2000), 56.

484 Robert de Nobili's decision to adopt Brahmin social life was a missiological decision, not the love of local culture. He did it to reach out high caste and convert them in to Christianity.

485 Manilal C. Parekh, *Christian Proselytism in India: A Great and Growing Menace* (Rajkot: Harmony House, 1947), vi-vii.

486 Sunand Sumithra, *Christian Theologies from an Indian Perspective* (Bangalore: Theological Book Trust, 1995), 66.

487 H. Grunder, "Christian Mission and Colonial Expansion" in *Mission Studies* XII/23, (1995): 18-21.

that baptism being used by the colonial authority to consolidate Indian converts reorienting them within the Western culture by using the strength of Church institution, and it leads to a permanent threat to the societal identity, integrity and right to exist.[488]

6.4.2. Contemporary Writings

6.4.2.1. Kalagara Subba Rao[489]

His life and ministry are one of the most fascinating chapters in the history of Christianity in India. Subba Rao sought to proclaim a Christ disentangled from controversy, doctrines, rituals and denominational rivalries, and believed in renunciation to be a disciple of Christ. C.D. Airan writes, "Mr. Subba Rao is an advocate of religiousless Christianity, in which the Lord Christ is the center of life and the indwelling Christ who uses our body and mind as his channel of Grace and Healing Ministry."[490] Regarding baptism, he is very critical and in his 'Outpourings of My Heart' he wrote that baptism does not qualify anyone for admission into the school of Christ; rather it is the conversion of heart which is the true baptism. In his book *Retreat Padre,* he questioned the cheapening of the Gospel by Padres (priest) who have made it a business. This is to say that he sees baptism as a ritual that has been used to legitimize unjust and unnecessary structures within the church with which he did not want to associate.

He objected to the high importance of baptism for salvation as a decisive factor to hell and heaven. Mere baptism in water, as he said, will not be able to serve the spiritual purpose. To him, it was a policy of priest and numerical competition for better status within his organization.[491] For him, baptism can't purify someone externally, so it should not be essential.[492] The objection of Rao is to be seen from the context of *Sadhana Dharma* that is a cultural expression of baptism. Making it an external essential rite, to him, it has lost its spiritual meaning and appeal.[493] According to Rao, this rite is used just as a *mantra* to

---

[488] Anto Karokaran, "Cultural Alienation of Converts and radical Inculturation of Faith" in *Mission and Conversion: A Reappraisal*, Joseph Mattam, ed., (Mumbai: St. Pauls, 1996): 154-155.

[489] Kalagara Subba Rao (1912-1981), born in local landlord Hindu family, in Andhra Pradesh, never took baptism, but a preacher and healing ministry, and planter of his type of Church. It is known as the new movement that is still functioning in various part in India.

[490] C. D. Aairan, *Kalagora Subba Rao: The Mystic of Munipalle* (Vijayawada: N. Kutumba Rao and Co. n.d.), 13.

[491] Kalagora Subba Rao, *Retreat Padre*, 2nd ed. (Machilipatnam: n.p. 1972), 18-19.

[492] Ibid.

[493] Rao Sahib K. Subba Rao, *The Outpouring of My Heart*, edited and translated by C.D. Airan (Guntur: Srimathy Parripati Sita Mahalakshmi Sayanarayana, 1964), 6-7.

mislead[494] since faith in Jesus and admission to a Church is rested upon the ceremonial rite called baptism. Subba Rao stood within a parental cultural context (Hinduism/Indian) and refused to be baptized since it provides only to be a member of an organized church. Being a believer of Jesus, he felt no importance of the priest or baptism rite.[495] Rao is true in the context of mass-conversion in Tamilnadu and North-East India.

6.4.2.2. M.M. Thomas

M. M. Thomas' (1916-1996) understanding of the Church and baptism is much radical. To define baptism and Indian society, he plainly said that Christian community of India is functioning as a communal group which is formed through conversion within the context of proselytism in which the baptism rite is used as a mark (like circumcision) of transferring from one community to another community.[496] He saw the main problem in Indian Christianity, being pietistic individualism which emphasizes dogmatic belief and the communal tendency of the Christian community which has isolated them from the rest of the society.[497] In the light of Thomas's observation, the baptism appeared to be a stumbling block in the religious and ideological pluralism of India and this is why Church has failed to invite common people, except the Christian community.[498] To him, Christ-centered fellowship would be secular, means religious without being communal which is a direct product of baptism-conversion for Indian Christians who are socially isolated.[499]

6.4.2.3. Some Other Arguments

When the Westminster Confession states that baptism is not to be administrated to anyone outside of the visible Church,[500] it actually empowered the Church as the sole religio-spiritual authority. *Samaj Dharma* stands opposite to this idea. The difference between the temple and the Church is so high, simple

---

[494] Kalagara Subba Rao, *Three Letters: Become Christ, Don't Pray, Man Created God* (Secundrabad: n.p., 1965), 8-9.

[495] C. D. Aairan, *Kalagora Subba Rao: The Mystic of Munipalle* (Vijayawada: N. Kutumba Rao and Co. n.d.), 15.

[496] M. M. Thomas, "Baptism, Church and Koinonia: Three letters and a Comment" in *Religion and Society* 19/1 (1972): 73-74.

[497] M. M. Thomas, *Salvation and Humanization: Some Critical Issues of the Theology of Mission in Contemporary India* (Bangalore/Madras: CISRS/CLS, 1971), 12-13.

[498] M. M. Thomas, *The Church's Mission and Post-Modern Humanism: Collection of Essays and Talks 1992-1996* (Tiruvalla/Delhi: Christava Samithi/ISPCK, 1996), 153-154.

[499] Sebastian C.H. Kim, *In Search of Identity: Debate on Religious Conversion in India* (New Delhi: Oxford University Press, 2003), 100.

[500] Westminster Assembly of Divines (1643-49): The Westminster Confession with Shorter and larger Catechisms 28:8 London. Question No. 95.

inculturation does not make any cultural re-orientation. How an Indian would be a better cultural Indian with selective adaptation from his/her own culture? Is it not true that the whole society belongs to his/her? Deny to that natural of belongingness is a societal crime that the Church committed be separating converts from social life. K. S. Rao, in this context, said that he would have forgotten Jesus if he continues going to Church.[501] It indicates towards the internal impression of the Church that stands opposite to India *Samaj Dharma*. In Indian religious tradition, religious institution has limited authority or no authority over one's freedom to accept or to reject or to alter a particular religious system. The Church in India looks more political than spiritual. In his article "Baptism: A Scandal or a Challenge" Joshua Russell Chandran (1918-2000) opines that tradition of Church presented a sectarian identity of baptism and it can't be regarded as pure religious rite since it has its socio-political implications, therefore baptized members used to form a communal structure within Indian plural system. Many expressed it as harmful for India, therefore, a radical paradigm shift in obligatory baptism is essential.[502] Giving a reminder to Indian Christians to the nation, he said that baptism should not alienate the people from anything of abiding value in their tradition or heritage.[503]

The socio-cultural consequence has prevented many people to avoid the baptism rite, yet follow Jesus (unbaptized believers[504]). This has raised a crucial theological issue in the life and mission of the Indian Christian and Church. Church's stand is always ambivalence to address this issue. R.C. Das, after working 46 years in the mission, said that the church is like a club of few registered members with a subscription. He also viewed that there was no need of baptism for salvation.[505]

There are others like William Miller, Manilal C. Parekh, or Kaj Baago who rejected the present idea of church and try to fit Jesus within a cultural setting and negated the validity of baptism to acknowledge Christ. Others ecumenical thinkers like S.J. Samartha advocated an accommodative model to unite the diverse faith groups who acknowledge and understand Jesus from the different standard of theology. This group prescribes non-communal forms of Christ-centered fellowship outside the visible, institutional church where

---

[501] Kaj Baago, *The Movement Around Subba Rao: A Study of the Hindu-Christian Movement around Kl. Subba Rao in Andhra Pradesh* (Madras: CLS, 1968), 11-12.

[502] J. R. Chandran, "Baptism – A Scandal or a Challenge" in *Religion and Society* 19/1 (March, 1972): 51.

[503] J. R. Chandran, "*I Believe...*" *Christian Faith Re-articulation*, 2nd ed. (Bangalore: SCMI, 1998), 82.

[504] Herbert E. Hoefer, *Churchless Christianity* (Pasadena & California: William Carey Library, 1991), xv.

[505] H. L. Richard, ed., *R.C. Das: Evangelical Prophet for Contextual Christianity* (Bangalore/Delhi: CISRS/ISPCK, 1999), 141.

baptism should not be an issue.[506] Indian Church must find the new way to face the growing challenge of unbaptized followers of Christ, living as Churchless Christianity. It would be a religious luxury to ignore a million such followers.

6.4.3. Sociological Aspects of Baptism and Conversion: An Evaluation

According to Julian Saldanha,[507] the conversion was purely strategic and politically interlinked in pre-independent India and different methods were applied to baptize people and to bring them into Christian faith (being converted). Not only social demography such as caste system but also EW mission, to him, explored the possibility various natural calamities like famine, flood, etc., to preach and convert, presenting the Gospel as a solution. J. E. Clough being disagreed to natural calamities theory said that many marginalized groups were willing to take baptism and join into Christian faith. Even though various reasons were stated like B.N Banerjee (a Hindu Brahmin) opines that it is the dignity and self-respect that instigated for conversion, not poverty. Interestingly, hardly poor Brahmins do the same who faces natural calamities.[508] Geoffrey. A. Oddie thinks that baptism-conversion has many reasons from spiritual to the material.[509] One is always there in perception level among academicians to grass root village people that acknowledge an anti-Indian policy in the colonial mission movements. It may be true when analysis of cultural crisis among Indian Christians tradition is a concern. Oddie agreed with Said's political theory[510] that says a policy to de-culture Indian people was implemented, not only by colonial power alone but along by mission agencies.[511] Fear and hope is another dimension for Indian converts, but Stephen Neill observed that conversion neither created the worst fear (cultural identity crisis) nor fulfilled the highest hope (equality in Jesus) among Indian

---

506 J. Jayakiran Sebastian, "*...Baptism Unum in Sancta Ecclesia...*" *A Theological Appraisal of the Baptism Controversy in the Work and Writings of Cyprian of Carthage* (Delhi: ISPCK, 1997), 24-25.

507 Julian Saldanha is from the Society of Jesus, formerly the provincial Superior of the Mumbai province, an expert on missiology and author of several books.

508 B.N. Banerjee, "A Hindu Attitude to Conversions" in *International Review of Missions*, No. 287 (1983): 393-397.

509 Geoffrey. A. Oddie, ed., *The Religion in South Asia* (New Delhi: Manohar Book Service, 1977), 43.

510 Edward W. Said, *Orientalism: Western Conceptions of the Orient* (London: Penguin Books, 1995 [1978]), 3.

511 Geoffrey A. Oddie, *Missionaries, Rebellion and Proto-nationalism James Long of Bengal 1814-1887* (Surrey: Curzon, 1999), 184-185.

Christians.[512] Taking his argument, one can argue that fear of losing cultural identity and religion (*svadharma* as Manu mentioned) is much bigger than the hope of equality in Jesus because India having the highest number deprived people (40%), only 1% (Dalits) responded to Christian faith for their social justice and equality. From the beginning of 20th century with the rise of national identity awareness infused in the freedom struggle and seeing how strongly the colonial Church stood with the colonial power, it might be difficult to establish the anti-Indian cultural crusade was part of EWM. The dilemma regarding identity among the native Christians is apprehensive.

6.4.3.1. Conversion and Cultural Issue among High Caste

Caste is an Indian social system. It is not altogether a system of injustice as viewed by many European and Indian scholars. Taking out of caste is taking one social mobility and system. It disintegrates someone from the rest of society.[513] For the case of the high caste convert, there is an attempt to keep a balance between *Samaj Dharma* and Christian spiritual life. Brahmabandhav Upadhyaya, Sadhu Sunder Singh, Narayan Varma Tilak, Pandita Ramabai are some few examples among many. The colonial mission and Indian caste demography are valuable to some extent. High caste (Christian converts and Hindus) being the main voice of society and not lived in receiving end, has always stood against the colonial policy. They questioned mission policy and its negative impact on larger Indian society. Christian converts in some way used many Indian models to incorporate the Indian ethos to actualized Jesus and attempted to avoid the EW cultural mode of communicating Jesus, by using Indian ways, both in theology and practices. Ashram model is one such successful attempt to re-culture.

Another approach undertaken is separating Jesus from Christianity. Among all high caste Indians, this approach is basic. Brahmabandhab Upadhyaya, R.C. Das, Sundar S. Singh, K. Subba Rao are some prominent Christian figures. Vivekananda among who also established this precedent among Hindu. The main reason for such a methodological approach is the Indian tradition of *Istha deva* concept (personal deity). Rituals are not taken as heights obligatory practices. Its understanding of personal deity is projected as a fundamental goal in spiritual life.

High caste enjoyed greater freedom in any given political system in India, so in this religious field, such tradition has been reflected. High caste Hindu, being close to the colonial political and mission agencies and also influenced

---

[512] Stephen Neill, *The Story of the Christian Church in India and Pakistan* (Madras: Diocesan Press, 1972), 119.

[513] Joseph Mattam, "Indian Attempts Towards a Solution of the Problem of Conversion" in *Mission and Conversion: A Reappraisal*, edited by Joseph Mattam & Sebastian C. H. Kim (Mumbai: St. Paul's Press, 1996): 106.

by European education (rationality and secularism), has the advantage to analyze Christianity through European methodology. India, being plural in religious ideas and practices, has taken over the subject of Jesus and Colonial Christian mission as the matter concern for India. Jesus, therefore, appeared to an interesting subject for them. High caste Christian converts in some way continued the traditional Indian (Hindu) way of looking, Jesus. Too many of them, salvation in Jesus and baptism are two separate issues.

The third trend is the use of Indian philosophical aspect to interpret Jesus. Since Indian tradition does not propagate only 'single' system of salvation, so baptism as an obligatory rite that assures salvation was questioned. K. Subba Rao rejected baptism and Manila Parekh said as not necessary.

One of the reasons for cultural alienation is the interpretation in II Corinthians 5.17. It promised to have a 'new life', setting apart the 'old life'. This 'old-new' can be explained with sociologically, not spiritually alone. David C. Scott understood baptism sociologically and looked at it as the means for social salvation from caste injustice. A. P. Nirmal, Nirmal Minz, Samson Prabhakar, James Messey are agreed with Scott's position.[514] Social liberty aspect of baptism-conversion failed to answer the cultural question. S. C. song raised this issue in the book *Tell Us Our Names*. He lucidly explained the importance of identity and culture that has lost after accepting Christianity. Sattam Pillai in 1850s revolted against EWM on the cultural issue and established the first Hindu Church of Christ.

In the context of 'old- vs new' life after baptism, we can apply Jerusalem Council in Acts chapter 15 and Galatians 2.14, where conversion was dealt spiritually, not culturally. Gentiles accepted along with Jewish Christian within a mature cultural plurality and spiritual oneness. Unfortunately, in the later period (after 313 CE) Christian entered and adopted the Roman monarchical monoculturalism attitude which disqualifies any expression outside European root, be it faith, theology, rituals, doctrine, art, symbol, liturgy, administration, etc. The proclamation of colonial Christianity, therefore, drastically failed to acknowledge anything good in other religion or culture.[515]

Baptism as NIC inherited in its form and content in the present day is subject to question and scrutiny. The Church is a perfect society was developed in the third century during St. Cyprian, and this very idea was further strengthened by Robert Bellarmine in the seventeenth century. This idea naturally instigated to have a segregated utopian fallacy that separated

[514] David C, Scott, "Baptism in the Indian Context: An Event of Separation or Human Solidarity" in *The Christian Century*, January 31 (1990): 103-108.

[515] P. Suess, "A Confused Mission Scenario" & F. Castillo, "Christianity and Inculturation in Latin America" in *Concilium* (1994): 2.

the Christian community from the remaining world.[516] By the time, Church didn't take any sincere effort to allow the Gospel to be reincarnated from a local cultural hermeneutics; on the contrary, has developed various artificial approaches like adaptation, inculturation, etc. to communicate Gospel to local people. Our argument is that monoculturalism is a doctrinal problem which Church must overcome and allow people to experience Jesus from their particular context.

6.4.3.2. Conversion and Tribal Culture Issue

Baptism and cultural awareness have two demographical divisions: firstly, the Dalits and tribal Christians who started realizing cultural loss since the 1960s and secondly, high caste coverts opposed mission policy almost from the beginning. The reason for the late awakening of Dalits and tribal Christians on their cultural issue is because of their subaltern status during the colonial era. It is true that they enjoyed a relatively better standard of living after being converted. Christianity appealed differently to these two groups: for the first group, the conversion was is a social reason, and for the latter group was/is a spiritual reason. These general trends are still continuing in India. With the rise of cultural nationalism led by RSS groups and a counter-narrative is getting strong convincing logic among various peoples' groups. A reply to a question asked to a Malto tribal Christian student (of Jharkhand) on culture; she replied with a sigh and said, "Our culture has already lost."[517] Even in North-Eastern Indian tribes like Kukis, Nagas, Mizos have seen that conversion to colonial Christianity has cost heavy on their culture.[518] Revisiting to lost cultural aspects is on the rise among tribes in India.

Looking into the history of tribal converts in the context of European mission, it is evident that religio-political policy has turned down the traditional social system, their world view, their economic, cultural life completely.[519] Eminent Mizo scholar Dr. Lal Dena stated that even though the conversion was a religious issue, eventually, it grasped the whole community and brought a new change in individual and community life. Therefore, it is not wrong to say that the conversion of the EWM was ultimately a theory of total social change.[520] His observation is largely the reality of other tribal communities. Interestingly,

---

[516] N. Greinacher, "Catholic Identity in the Third Epoch of Church History" in *Concilium* 5 (1994): 6-8.

[517] Interview with Mrs. Sangeta Malto on 1st March 2016. Malto is a tribal group generally living in North-Eastern part of Jharkhand State, India.

[518] Frederick S. Downs, *History of Christianity in India*, Vol. V, part 5 (Bangalore: CHAI, 1992), 142.

[519] Ibid., 143.

[520] Ibid.

European cultural and religion are actively involved in proselytization (massive socio-cultural change) only among Christian converts. Non-Christian tribes from such reality uphold their traditional faiths and cultural system. In another way, they are in a state of hybrid tradition, infused with Hindu or Buddhist tradition. Since Hinduism has no obligatory ritualistic rite (like baptism) to include someone into Hindu religious fold, neither has any membership criteria, the cultural issue does get in a serious consideration here. Therefore, conversion and baptism as executed by the EWM are appeared to be the main reason for de-culturation among NICs. It was more a social change under religious clothing.

6.4.3.3. Challenges of Obligatory Baptism Rite in Indian Context

From the inception of EWM in India, the baptism rite which leads to conversion is a controversial issue. It was understood as a tool against Indian culture and social plural ethos. Fundamentally Indian debate acknowledges this socio-cultural issue attach to baptism rite. It does not necessarily argue upon the need of a rite i.e., baptism.[521]

Sociologically conversion reconstructs three aspects in the life of an individual: i. A personal life that keeps faith on Christ and incorporates the tradition of the Church through the deduction process; ii. Family life that demands restructuring religio-ritualistic function (for single convert or one family to deal with other members/relative) in the context of the existence of dual religion within the larger family settings; iii. The social life that demands reconstruction of an individual or family to keep the social relations within society, being a member of the same society.

These above three vital cultural aspects face a serious challenge, not only to an individual or a family who accepts Christianity through baptism in present form but also for society to accommodate New cultural system of a Christian. Based on these contexts, M.M. Thomas argued that Pure Spiritual meaning of baptism might have lost in the Indian context and appeared to be a tool for proselytization that demands de-affiliation from parental religion in totality.[522]

Another two issues to be addressed here is legal and religious. On the legal ground, a conversion from one religion to Christianity is a double trap for a converted. Firstly, one will lose parental inheritance since each religious community is ruled by personal law which was adopted by the colonial ruler and by same law Indian Christian now is deprived. And secondly, one must go through a legal process to seek permission to accept Christianity. The

---

[521] Julian Saldanha, *Hindu Sensibilities towards Conversion* (Bombay: ATC, n.d.), 5.

[522] M.M. Thomas, "Baptism, the Church, and Koinonia: Three Letters and a Comment" in *Religion and Society* No. 19/1 (1972): 73.

consequence of legal conversion deprives one from governmental facilities like reservation in the job, admission in the study, political candidature, etc. Since the majority of Indian Christians are from Dalit, SC, and OBC, this legal status quo is heavy for them. The mental compensation of being saved for heaven and social loss for those who are already lower strata in society has possed a debate on the Indian appropriate utility of obligatory baptism-conversion rite.

As a response to avoid this legal issue along with various cultural issues and social segregation, many opt for alternative baptism rite or deny baptism. Baptism followed by conversion, i.e., end of a previous life is questioned. The rise of unbaptized followers of Christ and Christian converts who used to write 'Hindu' on Govt. documents is the reason in Indian reality.

The most contemporary issue regarding conversion is *ghar wapsi* (homecoming) and *suddhikarana* (purification) that is carried out by Hindu right-wing groups. It is often violent in nature, politically backed, part of the revival of Hindu nationalism and a bigger threat to Christian mission. Since 2014, bringing back Dalits Christian into Hindu fold is on run. Perception is being built that Dalits are lured by Christian mission and converted to Christianity. Majority Hindus to great extent believe that Christian mission used material aspects to tempt poor and converts. It is not yet a national issue but national sentiment, even though such 'homecoming' is locally practiced and a warning is sent nationally.

6.4.4. Baptism-Conversion in Contemporary Mission Movements

6.4.4.1. Yeshu Darbar[523] (Royal Court of Jesus)

Yeshu Darbar can be called the first Jesus movement In North India that is purely non-conventional, developed purely on local cultural settings. It is really a revolution to attract even 20-25 thousand people to worship on Sunday and 98% were from people of other faiths (mainly Hindu). How does it happen? It so happens because not doctrinal rite is ever imposed on anyone who comes

---

[523] Yeshu Darbar: It is a new form of movement in North India that presents Jesus and his saving grace within a cultural reality of people. It was started by Dr. Prof. R. B. Lal, presently Vice-Chancellor, SHIATS University, Naini, Allahabad, Uttar Pradesh, India and also Bishop of Yeshu Darbar. It does not impose any western forms of practices, allow every person to be in his/her own cultural reality, change of religion is completely absence even after baptism (who wishes), they remain socially Hindu, Muslim etc. and come to Darbar to worship Jesus. Mainly it is attracting people from other faiths and having wider Christ-centered fellowship. This mass movement is getting its cultural relevance in North India and many of the social issue is avoided with the dharmic order of India. Someone can call it as extension of Churchless Christianity like of R. C. Das of Beneras, but I differ since it has its ecclesiastical order with being traditional. There is no fixed date of its inscription, but somewhere in 1990-91, a small fellowship began by Dr. Lal and thereafter, it started growing and appeared as Yeshu Darbar in present form.

here to worship. According to Rev. Dr. David A. Phillips (Additional General Secretary, Yeshu Darbar), it is a 'cultural method' that is applied. No visible change, except the change of mind, is the success of Darbar. The baptism is obligatory to attend Holy Communion, even it was asked to do so. The grace of Jesus is open for all who wish to receive so.[524] Traditional Church (In India and surely in Europe) will enter into debate to justify such practices. Within the spirit of Protestant freedom and people-centered spiritual movement, *Darbar* is actually a cultural response to Indian people who need Jesus.

The rite of baptism in *Darbar* is optional and it is left to an individual whether she/he wishes to take baptism. After baptism one is not called as Christian (religion), he/she is still known in society by previous socio-cultural identity. *Darbar* emphasizes on the Book of Acts chapter 10:43, 'Whoever believes in him (Jesus Christ) will receive remission of sins', therefore, baptized (saved) and unbaptized (unsaved) is not considered as an issue to address. The change of mind is the central focus, not a rite. Rites are optional within the cultural traditions of India and cultural is used as an available context to communicate the gospel. According to Bishop R. B. Lal of Yeshu Darbar, Christ is not Christian as traditionally believed and his primary task is to preach the gospel of Jesus, not Christianity. Therefore, *Darbar* is still not Church, but an open fellowship of believers of Jesus, but the gathering of baptized people within a closed building.[525]

6.4.4.2. Unbaptized Christian: The Challenge before Indian Church?

Taking the research of Dr. Herbert E. Hoefer on *Churchless Christianity* (2001) as to pose a serious question before the visible Church what socially represents Jesus under the banner of Christianity and to take up the challenge of growing numbers of the unbaptized believer of Jesus in India. His research suggested that Church, till day, has not taken any step to face this reality, when a growing number of followers of Jesus outside traditional Church is found.[526] Many traditional Christians and pastors, instead of accepting such new social phenomena, are tagging them as remotely living community or cultic. Refuse or taking baptism as optional prevents. The traditional Churches are refusing to acknowledge them as a full believer of Christ. It is unfortunate to notice that Church in Indian fails to face the spiritual and cultural reality of India.
Rev. Paul Sigamony expressed his middle path view, to him, for salvation, for-

[524] An Interviewed with Rev. Dr. David A. Phillips on 25th March, 2016.

[525] Information shared with me by Rev. David A. Phillips and available entitled as, 'Gospel According to Babaji: An Ordinary Man of Yeshu Darbar That You Cannot Ignore', 2-4.

[526] Herbert E. Hoefer, *Churchless Christianity* (California: William Carey Library, 2001), 147.

giveness of sin and spiritual life, baptism is not necessary and they can be part of Church fellowship, then he said that on the issue of Church administration, due to different socio-religious rules, it would be rather difficult to accept them as Christian. The church is not in a position to practice two different systems for two groups. He was very much in the opinion that separating from parent family and society due to baptism-conversion is to be avoided and it is not practical.[527]

The concept of personal God (*Ishtadevta*) is the centrality of such reality, and in this spiritual possibility, the change of religion is not obligatory.[528] It may be true that the Indian Church must deal with this issue culturally and spiritually, not only doctrinally. If the Church does not face this challenge and ignores it, Indian ecumenism would lose its social relevance. Referring to the rigidity of Church, it seems difficult to create a 'space' for a new form of baptism in NICs. There heuristic attitude and struggle are to be taken seriously.

6.4.5. Secular Thinking on Conversion in India

Secular thinkers in India are essentially part of Indian mission discourse since the time of Raja Rammohan Roy. Even if they have a different position in interpreting Gospel and mission policy, they are also taken as a valid voice. In Christian theological writings, those contributors are preferentially used. In this context, Indian discourse might have different tradition than many of world Christian traditions. Since society is religiously plural, therefore, such discourse has got validity. On the issue of conversion, it is seen as an exterior commitment to doctrine and attached to proselytization and an expression of religious intolerance since Christianity holds ultimate truth only in Jesus. Many people think, even being soft to Christianity, that conversion has no 'spiritual dimensions' and it is 'destabilizing' the Indian religious and Society fabric. They view conversion as something alien, a symbol of oppression and enslaving power of imposing upon the people of India against their will and Christian institutions like School, hospital and other social bodies are meant to convert. They identified conversion as violence against humanity and therefore contradicts fundamental socio-cultural ethos of India.

To Gandhi, conversion is the deadliest poison against the flow of truth[529] and emphasized on biblical meaning of individual response to God,

---

[527] Rev. Paul Sigamony, an Assistant Professor and Dean of Practical Work Department of Allahabad Bible Seminary. He is also a pioneer ECI (Evangelical Church of India) Church planting missionary in North India since 1981. Interviewed on 7th April, 2016 at Allahabad.

[528] K. M. George, *Christianity in India through the Centuries* (Hyderabad: Authentic Books, 2009), 265.

[529] P. L. John Panicker, *Gandhi on Pluralism and Communalism* (Delhi: ISPCK, 2006), 100.

not proselytization and strategic.[530] He also opposed the 'truth' claim, since no religion is perfect.[531] He advocated conversion as self-purification which should eventually lead towards a friendly co-existence of all faiths by giving respect to other religion and study them.[532] His kind of dialogue is not based on religion or culture but on common humanity of the participations keeping pure faith in 'Truth' which is God and to live in non-violence.[533] His close associate C. F. Andrews viewed conversion as a personal inward experience and conscience but condemned proselytization which, to him, is a deliberate attempt to persuade someone to change faith.[534] He said that conversion is not a denial of faith, but the discovery of a new faith for which one would sacrifice his/her whole life,[535] and Christian may easily pay respect to other faiths and at the same time believed in the freedom of proclaiming.[536] It is true that Andrews favored conversion without any external force involved in it. Another central figure during Gandhi was B.R. Ambedkar who advocated human equality and viewed conversion over-toned with a notion of denationalization.[537] He objected life-style of Christian, not Christian faith but the national identity was his main concern, for what, he thought any foreign religion might degrade patriotism.

The secular thinkers have rejected ecclesiastical structure of Church which is Western in nature and colonial in affiliation. Therefore, to them, the church is not necessary to understand Christ and attempted to separate Christ from Christianity.[538] This precedent is also found many Christian followers who eventually left Church but not Christ. The emerging Churchless Christianity movement is an extension of this Indian tradition.

---

[530] K.L. Seshagiri, *Mahatma and Comparative Religion* (Delhi: Motilal Banarasidass Pub., 1978), 127.

[531] Ibid., 128.

[532] R.K. Prabhu, ed., *What Jesus Means to Me* (Ahmadabad: Jivaniji D. Desai, 1959), 23.

[533] Nirmal Minz, *Mahatma Gandhi and Hindu-Christian Dialogue* (Bangalore: CLS, n.d.), 148-149.

[534] Marjirie Sykes, *C. F. Andrews: Representative Writings* (Delhi: National Book Trust, 1973), 226.

[535] Daniel O'Connor, *The Testimony of C. F. Andrews* (Madras: CLS, 1974), ix.

[536] Ibid., 121.

[537] Babasaheb B.R. Ambedkar, *Why Go For Conversion*? (Bangalore: Dalit Sahitya Akademy, 1987), 5.

[538] J. Poul Rajashekar, "The Question of Unbaptized Believers in the History of the Mission of India" in *A Call to Discipleship: Baptism and Conversion*, edited by Godwin R. Singh (Delhi: ISPCK, 1985): 325-326.

6.4.6. Legal View of Conversion

There was opposition to Christian conversion even before independence from a section Hindus and some Rajas, in 1936 the 'Raighar State Conversion Act' was passed which banned preaching and followed by 'Surguja State Apostasy Act' in 1945, 'Udaypur State Conversion Act' in 1946, and after independence Orissa Act in 1967, Madhya Pradesh Act in 1969, Arunachal Pradesh Act 2006. Indian Constitutional interpretation never directly opposes the Christian propagation and upholds the freedom to express as per Article 25 (1). Some cases, the court has come out with a certain restriction not on expression but on conversion. It has ordered to take prior permission or acknowledge beforehand to the legal authority to accept Christianity. In some cases, it was banned to protect the homogeneous culture and ethos like Arunachal Pradesh. But, though it seems that before Law all are same, yet it expressed its concerns on this issue and it has restricted to the Christian Mission.

6.5. Baptism-Conversion: Case Study

We shall try to keep this argument in two segments: firstly, to analyze the impact of baptism from a cultural perspective and secondly, analyze this issue from First Generation Christian (FGC[539]) in compare to Born Christian (BC[540]).

6.5.1. Case Study No. I of Researcher Himself

Being FGC, single convert in the family and being the first son, I have some cultural, customary and social duties. Conversion, as I was taught by Church, faced the real situation after my father's death. Being the first son, the obligatory funeral rite falls on me. Church strictly ordered me not to be part of any such rite since they (even father) are Hindus and advised me to pray and keep the testimony of Christ among other faiths. This is a colonial trend that separates a new believer from own family and then from society. Traditionally, my younger brother can't do since I am alive. There comes a serious challenge before a new convert to encounter the new reality of life.

The missionary solution for such a situation is to separate the 'son' from family to keep a Christ identity among other faiths, minimizing and subverting the family relation. The missionary solution results the family breaks up; gradually social break up and this 'break up' has always glorified by mission agencies. In our research we are looking for the consideration of the 'People's Voice' is an attempt to stop this breakup. It requires cultural re-interpretation, doctrinal re-orientation and religious freedom of the individual.

---

[539] FGC: First Generation Christian- a person joining in Christian fold from the other faith tradition for first time.

[540] BC: Born Christian – born in a Christian family or either of his/her parents is Christian.

The researcher was confused to take a decision between father's funeral and Christian obligation. It gave his family social-shame, personal pain, and social segregation. Therefore, the baptism-conversion cannot be taken as a simple rite to confess publicly Jesus as savior. A baptism in India is obviously a conversion of religion, not just the repentance of sin.

6.5.2. Case No. II of an Old Woman

It was at the end of 1993 and the event took place in the then mission office in Kolkata where I was working. I was an eye-witness. A 70 years old woman accepted Jesus and took baptism along with her husband. Back in the office after baptism, she was taken inside the office room where her white and red bangles were broken without her permission as a sudden action. It was done with prayer and loud praise. She begged with tears not to do this, but this poor old woman held fast and her cry has no impact on such religious purification. She was fainted unconscious and later felt home with the saddest experience she could ever experience. This breaking could be only done when a married woman's husband died and his funeral is over. It is a very emotive painful process for women in a particular culture. It speaks a lot why this baptism and conversion are a contentious issue in India.

6.5.3. Key Concerns

1. Since baptism-conversion for the life of a new convert is not just a sacramental rite but on the contrary, it is shifting life from one socio-religious context to another socio-religious context. In case of research's own conversion experience shows the rift within the family
2. The Baptism-Conversion has been encountering social challenges, even though it doctrinally speaks about 'salvation of sin'. This 'saved soul' rite de-roots and then someone enters into an identity crisis. Indian church is nothing less than a systematic expansion of Western church which stands opposite to the plurality of India.
3. The missiological interpretation of the sufferings and challenges of a new convert is often glorified as a hallmark of accepting Jesus (cross bearing). Such glorification hinders re constructing and creating a new 'space' for Indian Christians.

6.6. Baptism a Must for Discipleship? An Indian Open Question

To reflect on this issue, we should look beyond the traditional doctrinal stand of the Church (European originated) and look into the history of the Church. The Sacramental position of Church may not agree to unlock (release) 'Jesus' and allow him to be a public spiritual icon. Jesus and his relationship with people are doctrinalized to the extent that this rite has become obligatory, except the Salvation Army. Our Indian context (especially the Northern part) may provide some alternative as a response to this issue.

As we have discussed that a stream of thought is already advocating the possible alternative for Indian people, not only for Christians. In dharma of India, an individual is free from doctrinal correctness to encounter God, and no 'rite' is obligatory ontologically for 'salvation'.

I would like to bring two examples to deal with this issue: my personal experience, the most powerful North Indian movement 'Yeshu Darbar' and of a *Kristabhakta*

6.6.1. Researcher's Personal Experience

Being born in a Hindu family, I accepted Jesus on 17th November 1990. St Paul directly encountered Jesus (Act 9:1-9) and later he was taken for the ceremonial baptism (Acts 9:18). It was an experiential level and transformation of the heart. I too encountered Jesus without anyone's intervention. Later when I met a pastor (denomination withheld), and he sent me to a small village Church to work for. I was allowed to do all works, except to receive Holy Communion since I was not baptized. On quarry to it, he said that I was not baptized. On 15th August 1991, I was baptized and became a full member of the Church. Over nine-month, my status was 'half-believer'. Since Church has no plurality, so she fails to accommodate people or to offer alternative means for me.

My personal experience is the reality and struggle of millions of people living in India or largely in Asia. Asia needs a different norm for them since they have a different religious culture and tradition. Culture plays a vital role in many Asian countries, including Muslim states like Bangladesh, Indonesia, Malaysia, India, China, etc. I am here the voice of many who wish plurality to follow Jesus. My initial experience has partially separated me from the Church since 1990. Since then, I have developed the 'Space and Place' model to invite and include diverse kind of people who wish to come to Christ.

6.6.2. Yeshu Darbar

Yeshu Darbar is non-conventional Christian movement initiated by Dr. R. B. Lal since 1990 in Allahabad. It has few basic features that stand opposite to the conventional stand of Church on the issue and rite of Baptism. The Yeshu (Urdu) means Jesus and Darbar (Urdu) means royal court. It invited all people regardless of faith to worship Jesus without applying any doctrine to separate 'saved' from 'unsaved' (Christian from other faiths), Christian or Hindu or Muslim. Everyone is free to worship together. No baptism is needed to receive Holy Communion. Baptism is optional and it is left with the decision of an individual. During the first decade of the 21st century, nearly 20000-25000 people used to worship on Sunday and 99% were non-baptized people who never became official Christian. They have no membership system (in the sense the traditional Church practices), no tithes, no cultural change, no separation from home or religion or society. In North Indian, it is still the biggest Christ-centered fellowship outside the Church. Traditional Church is struggling to negotiate with them, but this is possibly the best alternative form of a Church in India, where people are not converted and no baptism rite is imposed yet follow Jesus as savior.

6.6.3. A Response of a *Kristabhakta*: I Follow Christ outside Church-A Testimony

Here I wish to present the most contemporary example that may provide ample evidence to establish the necessity of reconstruction of baptism rite to accommodate Indian people and the cultural way of celebrating life with Christ. Mr. Bikash Sharma, a Kristabhakta, explained this issue.[541]

About Church: Till 2009 I was a Baptist member, but after that, I came back to my own Hindu community. Ever since then I along with many others in Assam are trying to live out an alternative form of Christianity or the faith life in the Lord as per our family context.

Our understanding of the word "Hindu" is the style of life that exists in our country for ages and had welcomed any belief system and happily let each people pursue whatever faith system they believe that would give satisfaction to their souls' quest, but without disturbing the outward style and core values. It is more related to core values such as respecting the elders, submission to the authorities, duties of a husband/wife/children, etc. Therefore, we see in this huge umbrella of Hindu, many schools of belief systems such as atheism of Charback to pluralism or singular devotion to one own beloved god or guru or goddesses, exist together for centuries.

The biblical basis with the type of existence style as a devotee of the Lord Jesus Christ within our own family context within the larger Hindu community that we are born is clearly found in the truth declared in the Bible.

- The God to be the God of all nations.
- That is the new age to come when believers from every nation, tribes, and language would worship Him. (Rev. 7:9) We are therefore not to copy the Western form of extraction as of the existing community the believer belongs to and the expression of faith would be as per their respective community style and values. (1Cor. 7:19-24)
- Believers are converted in heart and not extracted from their existing family/community and its values.

---

[541] Bikash Sharma, Noormati, Guwhati, Assam, India, answered questionnaire by mail.

- Acts 15, the conversion of Cornelius (Acts 10) and Titus (Gal 2:3) all points towards the change of heart rather than a complete change of the entire social identity.
- Timothy's circumcision (Acts 16:1-3), Titus' not to be circumcised (Gal 2), Paul's submission to his Jewish purification rituals though he knew that he is cleaned by the blood of Christ (Acts 21:17-27) shows how the NT believers valued their community's values. Faith in Christ has shown through their submission to their community with values and basic lifestyle patterns.

Q. I. - What should be the best form of baptism/initiation ritual for the new believer in North India?

As we are not grasped by any of the denominational bindings, we believe that baptism is a command of the Lord and anybody who recognizes oneself to be a devotee of the Lord should undertake baptism. As we are Hindu (culturally) and for the centuries dipping in the water before any sacred duties are practiced, taking a dip in the water to signify one's devotion to Christ is beautiful rather than a threat to our family and community values.

Therefore, immersion is one way of receiving baptism, but keeping in mind of the physically disabled and elderly people, we happily sprinkle too. What we keep in mind is the sacredness of this initiation. We, therefore, express through our community style of singing *bhajans* or *kirtans* (devotional songs) with the setting of flowers, garlands, *diya* (oil lamp), incense sticks that are the basic requirements in our culture for expressions of devotion to God. By the lighting of *diya* and *agarbatti* (incense stick), we explain the newness of our life, who is Christ in us. The fire in our cultural heritage is regarded sacred and we too explain the fire in the earthen lamp and incense stick to be symbolically seen as Christ in us who is the Light and also the Sanctifier. As the fire on the lamp and incense stick burn, we remind new *bhaktas* the cost of devotion to the Lord and also the constant burning down of self, carrying one's own death on the cross and following Him in life.

After such explanation, the devotee is then asked to take deep in the water (ponds, rivers) or sprinkle from the *kalash* (mad pot) that every family would have kept aside for sacred purposes.

Q. II. Baptism follows the conversion of faith. How to restore the actual meaning of baptism?

Hans Staffner in his book '*Jesus Christ and the Hindu Community...*' deals with "Obstacles which have to be removed in order to make a genuine synthesis possible between Hindu as a community and Christianity as faith." He writes " ...there is, however, one point which separates Christians from the Hindu community, one relic from the colonial era, which has to be removed before a real synthesis of Hindu culture and the Christian faith becomes feasible, which is that Christian have their own personal law which is different from that of the Hindu community. As long as Christians are ruled by a different personal law, baptism will continue to involve changing over from one social community to another. It will remain impossible to be a Christian Hindu."[542] Therefore, we the followers of the Lord of India need to understand this problem and deal it as soon as possible. Staffner rightly said that Baptism in India not per Biblical tradition but rather it excommunicates the devotee from his/her birth community and this is completely opposite to what the N.T teaches and upholds. It is the ordained ministers who are authorized by the law to give a verdict of someone's faith in Jesus. Therefore, to answer the question frankly, as an Indian devotee of Jesus, it can be taken purely as a sacred spiritual act and a matter of faith alone. I hereby give my views along with the views of many Hindu devotees of the Lord to see an alternative form of Christianity.

Q. III. Is it possible for the existing Church to accept a non-baptized person (who has faith in Jesus) equivalent to baptize one?

If baptism would not have been an entry to a new community, entry to a completely different set of the system but only a matter of the act of obedience to the Lord, there would not be any challenges, but in India, it is a radical paradigm shift. The Indian church demands that a new devotee accepts baptism in present form. Refraining from baptism is not welcomed by the Church because it interprets as the only way to confess faith in Jesus. Therefore, when baptism becomes simple as a matter of obedience to the Lord without unbiblical requirements with the burden, there would be more joyful acceptance.

Q. IV. How to deal with a growing number of unbaptized believers in India?

There is no un-baptized believer since once one accepts Jesus is a full believer. We encourage baptism as a command of the Lord, but not to seclude others on the issue of baptism. It is because a believer is known by faith, not by baptism rite.

The root of the problem of the increasing number of unbaptized believers in India has two reasons:

i. The threat to their birth identity and all that are mark with it.
ii. Dependant on few ordained priests

Possible solutions would be:

i. Repeal the Law of 1865 and not to shift believer from their Hindu community to the Christian community.

---

[542] Hans Staffner, *Jesus Christ and the Hindu Community: Is a Synthesis of Hinduism and Christianity Possible?* (Anand: Gujarat Sahitya Prakash, 1988), 238.

ii. To stop using the word 'Baptism' itself.
iii. To practice baptism in the community context and natural surroundings, preserving the cultural values of the family and community.
iv. Dependant on a priest is reduced and made optional because they give baptism instead one should take baptism. It should be in the presence of other devotees, family members, friends or well-wishers as their blessings important and we encourage to *tilak* (mark on forehead) or garland to be cultural.

6.7. Baptism and Role of Faith

6.7.1. Critic to Baptism

Indian history does not stand to be an antagonist to Jesus Christ, but it has always expressed stiff opposition to Christian mission especially conversion (change of religion) through a baptism rite. Since Indian approach is preferably non-dogmatic, so Jesus must be presented as a symbol of Truth and source of new life (salvation) in experiential level, and church control direction would be reformed to accept the theological plurality within the Indian context.[543] As K. V. Paul Pillai said that India has a deep reservation of (Western Christ) since it does not fit within the culture of the religious plurality of India. No Indian originated religion propagates their faith as absolute Truth and minimizes others. In India, a sense of accommodative spirit is prevailing throughout the centuries. Mission contradicts with it, below the belt.[544]

6.7.2. Re-construction of NIC Culture

India as it has survived ages, cannot accept of dogmatic concept and practice of baptism and conversion. The spiritual growth of 'bad to divine' is very subjective, and repentance (*metanoia*) is beyond a particular religion, hence baptism must be realized within the spiritual culture of India. The Church should reinvent its relevance in the society not because of its imperial contributions in India, but replace her as a source of grace and love in Jesus through a rigorous re-construction within Indian reality. Indian Christianity needs re-culturation within the ambit of the spirit of Gospels. Baptism still stands as a dogmatic monument of European culture and conversion is the extension of such process. Why Christianity in Asia has failed to penetrate in the hearts and minds of people is the serious question. The simplistic answer is that EWM grossly either arrogant to be a sole savior of the whole world or ignored the existing world with a sense of unenthusiastic and unqualified

---

[543] K. V. Paul Pillai, *India's Search for the Unknown Christ* (New Delhi: Fazl Publishers, 1978), 245-254.

[544] Ibid., 236-237.

status. The re-looking for an appropriate future for NIC is the postcolonial quest for new Christian identity.[545]

I would like to use Brahmabandhab Upadhyaya's model of '*Samaj* (social) *Dharma* and *Sadhana* (personal) *Dharma*' within Indian religio-cultural context. It will help us to reflect a new light on this very doctrine and rite of baptism-conversion that often de-cultured Indian Christians who accepted Jesus. This analysis will explain why our attempt of re-culturation has once again taken the central focus of NICs since the late 20th century and rapidly finds its relevance among the mass. Upadhyaya speaks about two important aspects of life: one is the socio-cultural identity, customs, culture, etc. and another one is the freedom of spiritual quest of an individual. He was culturally Hindu and Christian by faith.[546] Very recent movements in North Indian like Goutam Baba of Farukabad, Uttar Pradesh, Bikash Sharma in Assam or Yeshu Darbar of Allahabad are culturally Indian and by faith the follower of Jesus. People find Jesus from their life situation, rather imposed on them. They focus on the conversion of mind. Upadhyaya said, "Our *dharma* has two branches: *Samaj dharma* and *Sadhan dharma*. The former treats of life and living manners, customs, eating and dressing......we are Hindus....While the *Sadhana* is of the individual, its object is *sadhana* and *mukti* (salvation). His Hinduism is not destroyed by embracing an anti-Vedic religion, provided he keeps intact his *Samaj dharma* by submitting to the Social Code."[547] Vivekananda who was contemporary and friend of Upadhyaya, also pointed out such division for better social harmony which Christianity does not permit.[548] Manilal C. Parekh also advocated the same idea and advised Christians not to confuse salvation in Jesus and *samaj dharma*, and remain intact to his/her parental society.[549] When we study carefully, it is evident that for Upadhyaya, his *samaj dharma* has influenced and shaped his *sadhana dharma* as it is reflected in developing an Advaitic framework to interpret Christology.[550] This process allows accepting Jesus without being socially Christian and remaining in culture. Manu's idea

---

[545] Subrahmanyan P. T., "Christ in Indian Thought" in *Indian Theological Journal*, Vol. 8, No. 1&2 (2014): 44.

[546] K. P. Aleaz, *The Gospel of Indian Culture* (Calcutta: Punthi Pustak, 1994), 229-230.

[547] B. Animananda, *The Blade, Life and Work of Brahmabandhab Upadhyaya* (Calcutta: Roy & Son, 1947), 200-201.

[548] Swami Vivekananda, *The Complete Works of Swami Vivekananda*, Vol. V, Mayavati Memorial Edition, (Kolkata: Advaita Ashrama, 2006), 70-71.

[549] R. H. S. Byod, ed., *Manilal C. Parech (1885-1967). Dhanjibhai Fakirbhai (1895-1967): A Selection* (Madras: CLS. 1974), 14.

[550] K. P. Aleaz, *The Gospel of Indian Culture* (Calcutta: Punthi Pustak, 1994), 234.

of *svadharma*[551] (one's own social-religious position) can give us deeper sociological meaning in this regard.

Baptism sharply divided Indian social harmony because of Church places 'baptism' as the gateway to have access to Jesus. This obligatory rite is contradictory to the religious culture of India. Plurality and spiritual freedom are basic tenets of India, but the Church is more concerned with a section of people who accepted baptism and others are counted as an opponent or unsaved. It does not suit to India, where plurality is accepted and dealt as the progress-path in the spiritual life.

The concept of baptism and conversion is inseparable, and in the Indian context, it results in a change of religious affiliation. In postcolonial ear, some movements (like *Yeshu Darbar*) are questioning the very purpose of 'baptism-conversion' from scripture and culture. The traditional practice and interpretation of baptism have given a separate communal identity to Indian Christians since baptism has become the sole symbol to enter into a visible church. It is hard to regard baptism as purely a religious rite.[552] The conversion has become a controversial issue in India, both in society and individual life. In this connection, S. Michael says, "Conversion may bring the individual into conflict with his family, neighbor, society, and culture."[553] Many think it is just like a numerical scoring against Indian religions.

6.8. Reconstruction of Baptism Rite: Encounter to *Manusmṛti* and Torah

The equivalent words for harmony and peace in Sanskrit are *sadbhāvanā* and *śānti*. Every individual is an integral part of society. Thus, his every action may have its impact n whole society.[554] Harmony and peace cannot be expected in a society where people do not get speedy and proper justice. The laws of punishment and justice take their own time to pronounce the verdict. Manusmṛti and other *Smṛti granthas* have brought in the concept of *prāyaścitta* (atonement) as an alternative and reformative method for averting crime.[555] Manusmṛti defines *prāyaścitta* as a "determined resolve undertaken by the offender to observe to penance for being free of his offensive attitude"

---

[551] *Svadharma,* MS 8.41.

[552] J. R. Chandran, "Baptism- A Scandal or a Challenge" in *Religion and Society* 19/1 (March, 1972): 51.

[553] S. Michael, "Sociological Perspective of Conversion in India" in *Indian Missiological Review*, Vol. V, 1983: 43.

[554] Asha Rani Tripathi, *Manu-Smrti: A Critical Study and its Relevance in Modern Times* (New Delhi: D.K. Printworld. Pvt. Ltd., 2015), 267.

[555] Asha Rani Tripathi, *Manu-Smrti: A Critical Study and its Relevance in Modern Times* (New Delhi: D.K. Printworld. Pvt. Ltd., 2015), 268.

(MS XI.46). It is a combination of severe austerity and strong determination for not committing the evil deed again (MS XI.48).[556]

Manu presents a systematic account of the contradiction of human being's original purity of nature and the negative attitude of getting indulged in sin. Every person is born with purity but fails to continue those inborn virtues because of temptation and evil influenced. The perpetual state of mental crisis is commonly existing phenomena among human being. Sensory temptations are powerful enough to deviate a person of weak will power from the part of rectitude. *Prāyaścitta* is a means to reach to the very root of the sinful leaning. It makes a person aware of (realization) sin and then it generates in him/her a sense of repentance. This self-realization makes to decide not to repeat that sin. But, to control the passions is not an easy task. In the process of *prāyaścitta,* the offender is required to torment him/herself voluntarily or sometimes with the command of the public (MS XI.45).[557] On the other hand, the long process of atonement arouses the inner goodness in the person and helps to restrain his/her senses.[558]

6.8.1. Mode of *Prāyaścitta* and Its Relation with Theory of Karma

The mode of *prāyaścitta* depends on the veracity of sin (MS XI 47). Since Karma theory is imperative therefore it is linked to *prāyaścitta.* It talks about the sin of a previous birth (MS XI 48), equivalent to the concept of original sin in Christianity. A quantum of pre-existence of sin is what is important to debate upon. It is not the question here to define whether *samsara* can be equated to the concept of original sin, but one thing is sure that confirms the possibility of continuity of pre-existing sin in the present life of a person. On this particular point, both traditions can converge.[559]

Coming to the subject of repentance, Manu defines inward realization of sin and mental and physical status to confirm the possibility of self-realization. Manu identified some of the physical and mental disorders as systems of past wrongdoing and denied categorically the possibility of self-realization (MS XI 49-53). Manu actually does not denying the possibility of salvation for physically challenge people but placing the role of knowledge to realize him/herself, therefore, taking physical and mental limitation to enter into a state of confessing sin. Considering this logic the baptism/ *prāyaścitta* is not a word of the mouth but the repentance of sin. If somebody is not truly repent the baptism rite reduced to have an only ceremonial observation. Someone born in Christian parents is privy to undergo baptism rite to take part in Holy

[556] Asha Rani, op. cit., 268-269.

[557] Asha Rani, op. cit, 269.

[558] Asha Rani, op. cit., 270.

[559] Asha Rani, op. cit., 270.

Communion and be the member of the church but *prāyaścitta* is simply an oral confession not necessarily honest repentance. On those circumstances, Manu debars those people to take part in the ceremonial baptism rite (MS III.153). If we carefully observe the fundamental logic of Manu and also in the New Testament, it is repentance that takes a person into the ceremonial baptism/ *prāyaścitta* rite.[560]

Atonement is the gateway to cleanse negative fruit of action caused by Adam and Eve and by a person in the present life (MS XI 54). The assurance of eternal life in Christian tradition and rebirth (*samsara*) are actually advocating a futuristic hope and assurance by taking repentance in present life with apt seriousness. The baptism rite is therefore not getting the center state by itself that can assure salvation; rather it is repentance that acquires centrality for next course of life. Remission of *Dosha* (sin) and atonement from deficiencies that would purify the body and mind with good are intentions of *Saṁskāras*.[561]

Proceeding from this argument, the position of the Church on the issue of baptism rite is subjective to face the question. K. Subba Rao argued on this point and rejected the infallible status of baptism rite to enter into the fellowship with Christ and the Church community. Taking Indian situation and the socio-political dimension around conversion administrated by baptism rite one can propose that inner repentance can be expressed any other mode (rite) rather than the present form of baptism rite or like Subba Rao no need to have baptism rite at all.

The cultural conflict and its relation to conversion through baptism is the dialectic notion of Christian argument that divides 'Old vs New' life as advocated by St. Paul (II Cor. 5.17). The development of Church logic on 'Old' has encroached the entire previous life of a person and then replaced that life entirely by the tradition of European Christianity as it happened during the colonial period. If old means entire past life, then the resolution in Acts chapter 15 that permits culture to remain in the life of new believes of Christ is under question. The Old, is we place in the context of 'wrongdoings' of past, St. Paul's writing is meaningful. Not even Jesus after baptism left Jewish cultural life and looked for something new to begin a new life. To me, the colonial Christian tradition lost the spiritual value of Gospel and shifted its focus on rite and doctrine.

Prāyaścitta assures sin (social crime) to be removed in personal life. In the law of Manu and Moses, sin is taken not only on the individual level but also it was understood within a broader social perspective. To create a just society, removing 'sin' is a must. Since society is a composition of individuals,

---

[560] Asha Rani, op.cit., 270.

[561] R.B. Pandey, *The Hindu Sacraments (Samskara)*, Vol. II, 1st Edition (Kolkata: The Ramakrishna Mission Institute of Culture, 2003), 392.

therefore, personal *prāyaścitta* is actually a starting point to achieve the kingdom of God on earth (Mark 1.15). Moses and Manu advocated a social culture in which remission of sin was seriously considered. The colonial mission in India did not carry forward baptism rite to reform Indian society. It was used more on the ground to a Christian community at the expense of eradicating all other existing social-cultural religious traditions.

The concept of *Samaj Dharma* in Moses and Manu would be taken as a model on which present north Indian Christians may find to reconstruct their cultural identity, overcoming subaltern status that was imposed through baptism rite and conversion during the colonial ear. The security of life and property, preservation of the ethical values, social justice, equal right and opportunity, freedom of expression, conducive religious atmosphere are the prerequisites for attending peace and harmony.

6.8.2. Practical Approach to *Prāyaścitta*

A person needs the company of good people for developing good habits. It is very easy to lean on bad things but it is difficult to accumulate virtues. The intrusion of a single desirable person may spoil the whole society. Therefore, it is a must to avoid the company of evil-doers. According to Manu, the people who have committed four major crimes (killing, eating the wrong food, stealing and having sex with forbidden women) are the evil-doers and one should avoid their company.

> No one should sit with bad people and even they should not get the share of the father's property (MS XI.185-86).
>
> One should not live with the people who have killed children, women or the people who have come to them for refuge (MS XI.191).[562]

A man who keeps company with these people should observe *taptakṛccha* or *cāndrāyana vratas* (MS XI.181-82). The social boycott may teach a good lesson to the evil-doers. The *vratas* may make them realize their guilt and purify them.

Stealing of other's property is also a crime as it causes mental agony to the concerned person. Manu-Smṛti prescribes *cāndrāyana vratas* for stealing other's grain, raw or cooked food, carriage, bed, or stealing the articles of the less value from someone's house (MS XI.1165-66).

> Keeping fast for three nights is the atonement for stealing grass, wood, dry food, tree, sugar, clothing and leather (MS XI.167).

[562] Asha Rani, op.cit., 282.

> For lifting valuable articles like gems, pearls, coral, copper, silver, brass, iron and stone, one has to go without food for twelve days (MS XI.168).

> For staling cotton, silk, wool, an animal with cloven hooves, a bird, perfume, medicinal herbs, or a rope, one should live only on milk for three days (MS XI.169).

The rule for *prāyaścitta* connected with different crimes aims to root out the crime from the criminal's mind forever. These methods were based on the principle of self-control. The differently prescribed *vratas* provide the strength to restrain the senses. Yoga is a powerful method of controlling the impulses and inducing spirituality in a person. It may also increase the efficiency of a person for performing good deeds. The recitation of Vedic *mantras* helps a criminal by generation in him the inner heat, which is needed for developing self-confidence. One may have a sacrificial attitude by donating personal belongings to someone else.

> An evil-doers from his guilt by declaring the act, by deep regret for wrongdoing, by inner heat and by donating gifts to others (MS XI.228).[563]

The suppression of evil passions may be possible by taking a particular type of diet and by transformative rituals. These methods may generate inner heat is pure consciousness, which will show a person the right path.

> The intelligent men whose vision is based on Vedas have said that all the happiness of gods and humans has inner heat at its root; inner heat as its middle and inner heat as its end (MS XI.235).

The inner heat reminds a man about his own duties and keeps him away from sins. It broadens his outlook and he will be able to see the vastness of the creation of God. The self-acceptance of the crime reveals the inner goodness of a person.

> The more a man, on his own accord, declares the wrong that he has done, the more he is free from his guilt, like a snake from its skin (MS XI.230).[564]

After being purified by atonement a person decides that he is not going to commit the same crime again and he stays firm on that. After that, he will constantly engage himself the auspicious actions through his mind, body, and speech.

---

[563] Asha Rani, op. cit., 283.

[564] Ibid. 284.

In the present-day scenario where intolerance, selfishness, and immorality have reached the climax, the concept of *prāyaścitta*, as enunciated by Manu, may prove effective in curtailing the crimes, thus bringing harmony and peace in the society.[565]

6.8.3. Purification Rite in Torah

Like any other ancient society Hebrew community during the pentateuchal period initiated to construct a society in which every individual is collectively interdependent to contribute and participate in *Samaj Dharma*. In this process of formulating a just society like of Manu, Torah also emphasized the individual purity as essential criteria both for a social and spiritual reason. The difference between Manu and Moses at this point is when Manu advocated purity through social ethics which leads a person to advance in spiritual life, regulated those ethics within a broader ethical embed namely *Manavadharma*, whereas the ethical codes in Torah are an exclusively divine revelation (ex. Exodus 20).

The concept of purity in the Law of Moses has also regulated and performed through various purificatory rites (Lev. 11-16) and the ultimate example of purity that could be achieved is the Holiness of Yahweh (Lev. 17-26). It is true that since the purification for the Jewish is exclusively Yahweh centered, it separated Israelites from other faith community. The concept of *Sudra* in Manu is not a separate community whereas non-Jewish is outside of Mosaic providence of purity. The purificatory rites in Torah are actually *saṁskāras* in Manusmṛti and in both traditions; rites are attached to the daily life of a person up to the highest spiritual goal: like purificatory daily bathing, selection of food, childbirth, menstruation, funeral, etc.[566]

6.9. Postcolonial Response

From the above exposition and argument, a picture emerges that depicts a conflicting state that church offers something in contrary to how people wish to receive it. Church in India and her mission much emerge from within the insights of people's culture. The Post-colonial India Church cannot effort to see, either church has become an isolated communal identity or Jesus has become irrelevant to meet the spiritual quest of the people. Therefore, the conclusive suggestion much takes the risk to suggest a radical process to make Church and Jesus relevant, considering the urgency of the situation.

1. The proclamation of Jesus and His Gospel must be free from the strategy of the mission. It is to be a spontaneous expression of the

[565] Asha Rani, op. cit., 284.

[566] Roland de Vaux, *Ancient Israel: Its Life and Institutions* (London: Darton, Longman & Todd, 1961, reprint 1991), 460.

followers of Jesus. The salary based mission proclaimer must be replaced by volunteers as a vocation.

2. The end goal of proclamation should not be a numerical growth statistics which is contradictory to the Dharmic culture of India and instruction of Jesus.
3. Proclamation should allow the truth of the Gospel to be emerged by using the cultural hermeneutics of recipients.
4. The conversion that in Indian context understood as a change of religion, is advice to take a new dimension.

Culturally, *Upanayana*[567] or *Diksha* or anointment in Torah as a model is very similar to what Luther prescribed.

God-parents in Hindu originated community, Kukis or tribals, etc. are a viable model available to us.

i. Many of the post-colonial mission in North India have adopted similar to the Calvinistic model which allows a believer to baptize others. Even researcher himself in 2008 baptized many people even though traditional (old) believers objected my decision.[568] Church in multi-religious context fears so falls back into a narrow idea of Church. Sadhu Sundar Singh returned his preacher's license since he wanted to preach the universal Church.[569] Dr. Gir, head of NITA in North India has adopted such an idea, in which the oldest member (mainly man) is permitted to baptize other members of the family. It can be seen a very radical step but solve a lot of social problems that FGC face. It is considered to be a contextual priority to re-construct a new form rite which is theologically acceptable.

Therefore, re-structuring of baptism rite cannot be taken as a contrary to the church tradition, rather it should be taken as a positive heuristic and futuristic hope giving the model, creating a new 'place' for people.

In North India, some Mission movements (Charismatic, Pentecostal or para-church organizations) have passionately (Win India for Christ) adopted a policy for the quick numerical increase. Many of them do it because they believe that end time is near and saving soul is the final command. These

---

[567] MS. II

[568] Research during his M.Th study in Kolkata, baptized many people in Belda, West Midnapore, West Bengal, India. A new Church was established hereafter. I was opposed by some of my priests and teachers on the ground of traditional conflict. I placed my argument that since I was not a member of a church, so none will give me ordination, therefore, I have to take my own decision and in Protestant tradition is am privy to do so. I am not monitored by Vatican like body. The opposition appeared to me just like in Hindu tradition Brahmin wish to control so the priest.

[569] Sunand Sumithra, *Christian Theologies from an Indian Perspective* (Bangalore: Theological Book Trust, 1995), 97-98.

groups almost put psychological pressure to take baptism and be separated from parental society. Such uncontrolled passion is infusing socio-religious tension in India. It is not the argument to justify the spiritual essence of 'baptism-conversion', but it is almost beyond denial that the consequence of this act is perceived in India as negative. And Indian Christian has right to question, scrutiny, alter and re-interpret the existing practice in the post-colonial ear.

These above three areas would be fascinating to Indian culture. Firstly, the idea of 'on demand' or 'in need', is an important spiritual freedom that should be the regular position of Church and mission agencies including CNI. Rev. Praveen Massey[570] in his interview said that CNI is actually heading towards such a system. For many people (mainly for FGC and Churchless Christians), Luther's privacy would be a practical option, socially and spiritually. The idea of accepting new godparents is similar to an old Indian practice which has larger socio-religious dimension.[571] It can be easy to reconstruct only if we revive it. So far as 'water' is a concern, even in Hebrew or Indian culture, purification by water or holy deep is highly symbolic.[572] Jesus' baptism in water (running water is what Luther said) of Jordon river is very similar to what is the purification ceremony in running river water like the Ganges. Water is an undisputed cultural element that is found and used by all three religious traditions. Even though existing Roman Catholic Church viewed that newness in Luther's thoughts as unaccepted and anti-church, yet it was the inception of a new tradition. Then, the same can be repeated now in India too.

The new social context (industrialization, urban-rural division, human nature) of his time is very important hermeneutical tool that was used Taking the social aspiration and gradual change in Europe and in America during Wesley, a possibility of new interpretation was in need to address issues, in the same fashion, newness in baptism-conversion rite in India is to be considered as a need of the time to offer a viable alternative meaning and practice in Church (before FGC) and to bring tradition Christian closer to their lost culture.

---

[570] Rev. Praveen Massey is a new generation pastor of CNI of last 16 yeras, presently ministering at Muirabad St. Peter's Church, Allahabad. Interviewed on 4th September, 2015.

[571] God-parents: in Bengal, it is known by various names. Name is being fixed according to the occasion of spiritual journey. If two men or women go to a holy particular place and take a dip in water holding their hand together, then they share a same spiritual bond which will be accepted by both family and also known by society. It was highly valuable spiritual patenting. Their children and other family members will call him/her by social term: Ma (mother) or Kaka (uncle) etc. It has a very deep social significance and creates social harmony among various caste people. In initiation ceremony, a boy must have a spiritual mother for whole life, hence her husband is father. She will play a role to bring back him in to family life from Brahmacarya (renunciation and celibacy) life during initiation and for life long.

[572] Sister Vandana, "Water Symbolism in the Gospel of St. John in the Light of Indian Spirituality", *Readings in Indian Christian Theology*, ed., R. S. Sugirtharajah & Cecil Hargreaves (Delhi: ISPCK, [1993], 2004), 200.

This movement generally emphasizes on the baptism of an adult, not an infant, outward change due to inward transformation, public testimony, new life, and fellowship, etc. In India, this group along with the Roman Catholic are viciously involved in numerical conversion with a limited reason to use baptism as saving the act of 'lost soul'.

If we look one particular aspect of the baptism of the Holy Spirit, minimizing the role of water, then, we must rely on the interpretation of baptism on metaphysically; hence, unbaptized Christians in India can also be put in this category, since they accept Jesus as an act of Spirit. The ontological probability is to be considered as the possible model of baptism, mainly those who follow Jesus outside of the tradition of the Church in India.

i. When WCC or in India apex theological University (the Senate of Serampore College) accepted the validity of other faiths as means of salvation, then, our cultural re-construction is valid within the later and spirit of Protestantism.

6.9.1. Theological Dimensions

1. Talking about 'baptism' whether it is a mere 'rite' or has a real spiritual essence, the group is widely divided.
2. In the discussion, some emphasis traditional concept to uphold, whereas others think to bring some changes as a given-situation demand.
3. The majority have a view that baptism should not be taken as the dogmatic necessity.
4. Baptism may not be the only criteria to be a Christian.
5. Even, the group is in favor that if needed Lord's Table might be opened before unbaptized people. Such opinion shows that awareness to re-culture is very much in the Christian mind.
6. The authority of Church, in many cases, is still rigid and failed to accept and re-shape herself within the Indian Plurality culture.
7. Due to the Churches over emphasis on rituals and less spiritual freedom of an individual, the Christian community looks like an isolated community in India.
8. The Self-criticism among Christian community is lacking, due to the sustaining spiritual superiority stand over other religious traditions and somehow, wish to reject others as false.
9. It is said that EWM failed to understand Indian cultural ethos and as a result, many communities (mainly tribes) have lost cultural values and group in favor of systematic re-culturation adoption to recover lost identity.
10. Many of us felt that there needs a change but we failed to find any suitable acceptable alternative.

Conclusion

This unlocking 'Christ' is an emerging challenge that established Church must face. Cultural conversion through baptism has encountered by the spiritual interpretation of the Gospel. Baptism doctrine and rite are interpreted in India, using culture and philosophy as new hermeneutics. Baptism is facing such a challenge because the Church demands people to fall in her line without addressing the socio-cultural implication of this rite. Unlocking Christ in the context of baptism has two possibilities: Church must be flexible to develop different forms of baptism to accommodate differently aspired people and secondly, he needs to separate salvation from baptism within a spiritual realm, not doctrinal. This contextual reconstruction of baptism is a growing demand. Accepting Jesus is not the conversion from others faith and culture, but it is a spiritual journey and therefore, the Church must treat baptism as an option rite which would not discriminate one from others. This risk-taking reconstruction is contextually Indian to address the diverse socio-cultural-religious-spiritual-political challenge, one encounter to follow Christ.

In the Indian context, baptism should not be taken as a dogmatic necessity. The whole issue of conversion-baptism creates an impression that without baptism, Jesus Christ is out of reach. It raises the pertinent question of whether Jesus Christ is the monopoly of baptized people? The thought of Subba Rao is very relevant in this religious pluralistic Indian society where baptism is reduced into the level of counting the numerical calculation. In the context of proselyte image of baptism, should we continue symbols which were not meaningful in a particular context? It is such a situation that we should think about the possibilities of allowing Christ-centered fellowship outside the visible church and giving up insistence on external religious rites. This is the right time to rethink on the issues of baptism and act according to the given context.

Since there are many people who are unbaptized believers and are outside the visible church, we need to think about the boundaries of the church. It can also be seen as a suggestive step to forsake the rite of baptism and conversion if it is necessary. T.M. Philip said:

> Baptism as a religious rite is influenced by socio-cultural factors. It came into existence in the church in what has been described a baptismal age...there is no divine virtue in simply continuing symbolisms and imageries that had been meaningful in a particular socio-cultural milieu. That will only help to perpetuate a magic notion of the rite. What we need is a sort of demythologizing of

the baptismal practice so as to meet the socio-cultural challenge presented by the church's environment in India today.[573]

Most of the people like Manilal Parekh, K. Subba Rao, M. M. Thomas or J. R. Chandran think that conversion does not require a change of religious affiliation and membership of the Christian Church. It is true that it denies the socio-cultural crisis of a person being converted since the remaining member of family and society are now categorized as 'other'. The Little Movements have denounced the 'present' form of baptism rite and its meaning and allowing to Jesus without cultural and social conversion and separation. The possibility of use rites of 'purification' that are available in MS and Torah that has the same inner meaning of what baptism has also taught, can provide an alternative *saṁskāra* as Indian way of baptism. The Churchless Christian or rural movements are practicing many alternative rites. This protest against the act and meaning of the EWM has challenged almost from the beginning of the colonial mission. The challenges before these two groups are to be seen how they negotiate and find wider ecumenism in India.

Open Question for Further Debate

1. Whether or not conversion to Christianity should mean ceasing to be a number of one social community and joining another?
2. What aspects of his/her culture and social life should the convert be encouraged to preserve and who decides that?
3. A distinction is to be made between proselytizing (an attempt to change outward sign) and conversion (inward change due to experience).
4. What would be the future form and meaning of baptism would possibly be for NIC and how to visualize the model of M. M. Thomas that invites all kinds of people before the Lord's Table setting aside the ambiguity of the meaning of baptism[574] as a *Koinonia.*

---

[573] T. M. Philip, "A Historical Survey of Baptismal Practices and Theologies" in *Debate on Mission*, edited by Herbert E. Hoefer (Madras: Gurukul LTCRI, 1979): 321.

[574] M. M. Thomas, *The Church's Mission and Post-Modern Humanism: Collection of Essays and Talks 1992-1996* (Tiruvalla/Delhi: Christava Samithi/ISPCK, 1996), 159.

Chapter 7

Visible Relation, Social Dimension of Re-cultured Christianity in Northern India and Post-colonialism Subaltern Quest

Introduction

We draw our concluding argument on the postcolonial challenges before NIC [also IC] by stating the opinion of Dayanand Bharti, the leader of the Kristabhakta Movement, Tamilnadu, "Don't think or talk much about the culture. God is above culture and you cannot limit God's hand in the name of culture.' is another of the comments that I usually receive. After saying this they generally start to list out all the shortcomings in our country–caste, untouchability, bribery, corrupt politics, laziness, etc. We Indians are like this and we will never grow, See the western countries. What kind of progress they have made', etc., are their arguments, they will naturally forget that they too are part of such a system. But, the real tragedy in it is that while glorifying the western countries and their concept of 'work orientedness' that are still glorifying the past rule of the British both directly and indirectly. This hurts the true son of this soil."[575] His observation is simple that talks about 'self-pride' and 'determination'. The colonized people are always going through this cultural uncertainty since **mimicry** has become a reality of psychology. NICs and rest of Indian Christians are generally living in a deep dilemma of culture which would have been easily addressed through a cultural orientation of the Gospel/Christianity. The reconstruction of *saṁskāras*, the cultural expressional mode of India that is available in every cultural group. Bhabha argued in his book *The Location of Culture* (1994) this issue. And because

[575] Dayanand Bharti, *Living Water and Indian Bowl* (Delhi: ISPCK, 2004), 176.

such nature, the colonized people after achieving the political freedom, remain colonized invisibly and this is also true to NIC. Re-locating Christianity within Indian culture is largely an unsettled issue of NIC. Bhabha's idea of mimicry is the colonial ambivalence.[576] This uncertainty and a psychological dilemma (Ambivalence of Bhabha) to settle the pertinent question of harmony between the 'being Christian and being culturally Indian' is the biggest challenge before NIC [also IC] for the reconstruction of Christian *saṁskāras* on the light of Indian *saṁskāras*.

Saṁskāra is multi-dimensional, so far its expression is concerned in Indian culture. NICs have to engage in exploring the cultural values as a responsible religious community in India. The larger social mobility (within SD) goes beyond religious fencing. In SD, NIC is duty-bound to exercise certain principles to integrate culturally. The main rift between Christianity and other Indian originited religions [mainly Hindu] is not that they oppose Christianity due to its projection of 'Jesus' as the 'savior', but it aggravates when the Church projects 'Jesus' as the only Truth above all other religion in the expense of existing religions. India's unity is actually a cultural unity which the colonial mission and colonized Christians did not accept and therefore, implemented their agenda on converts [NIC]. Subalternity is as an artificiality created situation to separate them from Indian culture (SD). It is a sustaining teaching even present time. There are some Christians [mainly NICs in Northern Indian] who are known as 'Little Movements' opposed by the colonial Churches who hold the colonial culture as the ultimate Christian identity in India.[577] This new challenge has deeply divided Indian Christian community and factually the Little Movements are growing silently because they are not directly evangelized by the mainline Churches and they deny accepting the binary colonial argument that Indian culture is Hindu-culture and so, remain within the culture. Subaltern NIC now has headed towards reconstructing the colonial tradition. The path-breaking process is the challenge that the IC must encounter. In this chapter, we will try to analyze some of the very important socio-cultural aspects to actualize how a new re-culturation journey should take off from here.

7.1. Public Festival and the Postcolonial Reconstruction

7.1.1. Social Dimension of Indian Festival

Festivals of Indian originated religions have identical sociological matrix and the celebration has been evolving on social condition, not by the religious

---

[576] Homi K. Bhabha, *The Location of Culture* (London & New York: Routledge, 1994), 122.

[577] P. Victor Premasagar, 'The Gods of Our Fathers-Towards a Theology of Indian Religious and Cultural Heritage' in *Asian Expressions of Christian Commitment* (1992): 137-146.

authorities but by the common people. From such people's autonomy to celebrate in society rather within walls of temple stands in contrast to the Christianity and Islam in India. Festival has three segments: firstly, rituals related to the temple; secondly, function in the family that is very crucial for Christian reconstruction, since it is a family that teaches the social importance of festival which actually begins in family reaching to temple and ends in family. Every family wishes and expects people to visit their house, not as an invitee, but it is a festive mobility and greetings. Neighbors are socially duty bound to visit maximum houses that transmits to kids to do the same. It makes the festival a social event and thirdly, its social significance. This social engagement is religiously oriented but excecuted through *samskaras*.

The Christian teaching still reflects the colonial rejection of festival of other faiths and Church or people stay away for the plural culture of India. The reason lies in the teaching that equates other faiths with 'Satan or Devil' or something may possible dilute Christian value or protecting the purity of celebration or in some extent reflects the symptom of social segregration. The festival like Christmas even through popular in India, but ICs [also NICs] wish to celebrate within denomination or in Church in isolation. It is surprising to know in North Indian that the numbers other faith people [mainly Hindu] visit churches during Christmas are mote than the total population of Christians. In contrast to the traditional Christians, the Little Movements have socialized festivals, keeping *saṁskāras* as means to communicate faith.

7.1.2. Festival and Public Hospitality Food

This is another area which is a fascinating model for Christian re-culturation. Public festival and feast are interconnected. Publicly serving food (not Prasad) for passer-by on roadside freely is a part of religious Dharma. Giving *Anna* (strict sense rice but loosely food) is valued as the best gift. It connects each other and meets the need of pilgrimage. Christian festival also celebrates food but within Church boundary among the members of Church that is exclusive in nature and does not reach out to common people, being part of society. The exception is in some places like Ajmeer Methodist Church has such social food festival but it must be explored as general norms of celebration. In Torah, in various occasions, we notice that food and festival are socialized but during the colonial period, Indian Christians are oriented within the European system which not only excludes the common public from other faiths but also other denominations. Indian festival is a center of mass gathering[578] beyond denominations, sects or religions, hence it gets social acceptance. There would

[578] Kumbha Mela-2013 in Allahabad, on a single day little over 3 million people gathered and overall around 120 million people came to this particular religious festival. One can't take this mass gathering as reason of India's over population, but as a tradition of festival. Same is the true for elsewhere if there is really a public festival: secular or religious.

be spontaneous free food stalls organized by many groups, individual, family, temple, and even Govt. It is the part of the festival, a kind of blessed act to get some good karma. For example, many Sikh *Gurudwaras* have 24x7 food canteen free for any people, known as *langar*. This is not social welfare, but the part of religious practice. In contrast, my 27 years of Christian experience, even inside Church after Sunday service, tea and snacks are sold. The commercial use or fundraising policy has rationalized those practices. Indian Christian is still following a colonial 'cake' making at home to welcome guests. Cake in Indian is not traditional or religious food that would make a social communicative religious meaning. It actually affirms the grip of colonial culture over native Christians. Even in religious food-sharing, IC [NIC] does represent the colonial culture.

7.1.3. Partaking in Festival

Socially, the festival of Indian originated religions has mass appealing capacity since it believes in human harmony rather religious purity or purity is where human gathers. Christianity has imposed the doctrine of 'othering' that prevents or discourages to be part of the social celebration of festivals. Social unity is a pluralistic demand of dharmic *saṁskāra* in India and religious festival plays a positive role to create a better social harmony. India as a nation needs the plurality as the reality of life, not the conflict. It is noticed that the Church does not initiate to convert the Christmas or Good Friday as the festival of Indians, boarding it within Christians. In dharmic tradition, public place festival is important and any contradiction to it is the segregation from the mass. It is the social inter-religious dialogue that Indian has been practicing down the centuries. The Christians are in dilemma to decide the social role even in the postcolonial period. This colonial ambivalence must be socially dealt to find the Indian identity for NIC because NIC [IC] feels to be part of Indian culture but at the same time, hesitate to give up or re-construct the colonial culture. This is a postcolonial challenge before the NIC [IC].

7.2.1. Denominational Observation and Religious Superiority: Obstacle

The dharmic notion unlocks the exclusive idea and places someone and something on the social platform and in contrast, NIC suffers from two ambivalence colonial aspects: firstly, the denominational mobility of believers and secondly, doctrinalization of 'only true religion'. To reconstruct this stand, the 'Space and Place' model provides a new platform to re-look both aspects to socialize the Christian faith in India. The socializing is not compromise or syncretism, but it is an openness to explore the inner strength of faith, compassionately accept the plurality as the Indian reality of religious coexistence. In the context of festival utility, the Christian community has failed to attract the common people's imagination. What does it mean? Since the colonial period, the mood of Church was only on 'conversion' and its function was restricted among 'baptized' people. And baptized people were further divided by the denomination. This EW tradition has separated the Christian festivals from the rest. The 'saved and unsaved' diachotomy and dilemma among the Christian mind have deeply isolated and socially ostracized. Therefore, the 'Space and Place' model may change this static situation. Numerical sociological phenomenon established that more Hindu celebrates Christmas than Christians in India, and this spontaneous social acceptance of Christmas in India can be utilized as the start-up to reconstruct the colonial status qua. Jesus said: The harvest is plentiful but the workers are few (Mt. 9.37 NIV) might get a sociological interpretation here.

7.2.1.1. Harvest No 1: Christmas Cake

It may appear to be a very non-academic aspect. *Saṁskāras* are the mode of socio-religious life. From cities to rural villages in India during December, one can find Christmas cake in shops and at temporary stalls. People want to buy at least one 'Cake' for their family. Whom do they celebrate and why? This is an astonishing social reality in India. NIC must enter into this social 'space'. Christmas can easily be celebrated within social plurality. The 'Cake' symbolizes the possibility of re-culturation and the public mood towards Christians. Yet, the Christians in general still wish to exchange 'cake' as a personal level not used as a social tool of engagement. If people of other faith can bring Jesus as social 'icon' for celebration, then this model for re-culturation can be used as a duty of 'Samaj Dharma'. A festival is *samajic*, not exclusive.

7.2.1.2. Harvest No. 2: Public Merry-Making

Christmas is also the time of public feast/picnic and merry-making. The common people decorate with Christmas symbol, red Santa cap, etc. For example, one can find huge sell of 'Santa Claus' cap during this time, but there are no Christians. At my home town where I am a single Christian among 80,000 people, yet many shops are selling Star, Cake, Santa Claus, and Cap, etc during Christmas. The social celebration does not rest upon the doctrinal position of faith, mainly here in India and NIC must harvest this opportunity for re-culturation. Socializing faith is the human expression of joy.

7.2.1.3. Harvest No 4: Good Friday Tears

As a door to door evangelist (1990-2001), I used to go for film ministry and we generally show a movie on 'Jesus' life' among Hindus. In my long 12 years, it is noticed that the common people are crying when crucifixion episode comes. The moment people of other faiths cry for Jesus, that very moment 'Jesus' was not a Christian deity, but God for humanity. The tears can't be doctrinally justified. Christian compassion is expressed mainly through mission projects, it is sad. Are NICs in position to actualize the plurality of India as an opportunity to reconstruct the colonial exclusive projection of 'Jesus' and made Him as social reality? If other faith people are only the object for 'conversion', then the 'crying for Jesus' would be explored to expand Christianity. For re-culturation, 'social tears' is a positive context available before NIC.

7.2.2. International Missionary Conference

Edinburgh 1910	Edinburgh 2010
1. Emphasis on the mission of Church 2. West to Non-West, for conversion and Church planting 3. Other faiths as invalid, similar to the Old Testament, Christ is the only way 4. Assimilation of native within Western culture as superior 5. Praxis on 'foreign and home' mission, old and new church, western controlled.	1. Emphasis on the mission of God 2. Accepting plurality, complexity and contextual, inter-faith dialogue part of the mission 3. The uniqueness of all faiths 4. Accepting the diversity of culture as a gift of God 5. Multi-culturalism, globalization, church-center to people-center.

The Edinburgh 2010 has changed its previous position on its view on other faiths and people. It also reflects the global contextual demand of our present multi-dimensional social system and wider co-operation which is not only driven by the religious motif. This is a postcolonial and modern world. This new praxis is to be implemented by the Churches in India and other Asian countries. The colonized Asian Christian community has been going through a new kind of dilemma that rests upon a duality: i. Christianity is a growing religion in Asia and in most places they are numerically minority and bound to live in the midst of other faiths, so a growing sense of competitiveness is motivating mission and personal life; ii. the rapid change of the worldview of the Western world which demands and advocates human liberty, individual freedom of religion and self-defining spirit that is minimizing the global gap of communication. The Asian Christians have been struggling to define what would be the best way to live as a Christian or how to harmonize between these two realities. But, the Edinburgh 2010 has clearly posed the biggest challenge before to accept the 'uniqueness of all faith' and Church-centered to people-centered' fellowship, because mostly, the Asian Church wish to negate the existing local/nation-culture as something to be used as the tool to communicate Gospel. This is a colonial dilemma and challenge of the colonized Christian, either religious or political.

7.2.3. Inter-denominational Official Approach in Postcolonial India

The involvement of the Church and her engagement for socio-religious harmony is to be reviewed. Taking Edinburgh 2010 or Vatican II, it seems Christianity has constructed itself to make it relevant in a particular given context. In some extent, it may have a positive effect. The church is a part of social forums like inter-religious dialogue, but the question is when a Christian approach appears to an artificial position on paper and discussion, Indian dharmic and saṁskāric social is spontaneous engagement. Previously inculturation, adaptation, dialogue, ecumenism, etc. are actually a policy matter because they are not the subject of common people, neither communicates 'People's Voice'. Therefore, re-culturation in this research has been attempting to address 'local life', their struggle, aspiration, etc.

Dharmic saṁskāras are not the official position of Indian or Hindu culture, it is a process and evolution and it is open for further changes. Therefore, faith can be static, but faith expression can't be static or through alien mood. If Christianity in North India can actualize Non-European Christian traditions then a new may easily be found.

7.2.4. Artificial Unity: A Dharmic Hypocrisy

The ecumenism or joint worship contradicts to the dharmic *saṁskāras* in India. These efforts have a very limited impact on people's life. The social re-culturation can't be achieved through the ecumenism until common people naturally engage among themselves at the human level as a human being, not as a representative of the faith. Christian Ashram movement, Subba Rao movement, Sadhu Sundar Singh are few attempts that are capable of organic change and Yeshu Darbar is one such major movement with great success since it has adopted the Samaj Dharma to unlock Jesus for common people. This 'unlocking' is not doctrinal and human expression.

7.3. Space and Place Model and Some Examples

In the beginning, it has to be made clear that all the suggestions which are brought forth are not just the suggestion but there is an attempt to work a theological framework for the given context of Eastern Uttar Pradesh context in North India. In doing so it may sound little extreme or radical, but for some concrete change, there has to be radicalism in order to bring change and to liberate people. The general response what has been found in the given context that those who belong to the regular churches become very negative towards those in para-churches, or who do not belong to any church. They view them as syncretistic or weak and label them as compromising Christians. On the other hand, those who belong to Para-churches view that the regular churches (traditional) as not being Indian and being a part of the western culture that is rigid in their theology and practice.

Due to this kind of understanding, people are also confused and even to some extent go through different kinds of opposition. The first step for any positive solution or suggestion is that the regular churches and the Para-churches should get together and realize the need of the hour and understand the context in which we are. In practice, the empirical studies and case studies show that people have to undergo many problems due to the rite of baptism, and so church needs to understand the issue first instead of being rigid and losing people forever. As it had been stated before, faith commitment is not the issue in the given context. There is an effort at this juncture to try and bring some suggestions and as well as few models which might help people to be the Disciples of Christ with minimum oppositions in the given context. The criminal at the cross who was hung along with Jesus when he believed in Christ and affirmed his faith in him and he assured him of the salvation. There was no discussion on the ritual that without baptism he could not have salvation. This affirms one thing clearly that faith in Christ and becoming his disciples is must for an individual to have eternal life, not any rituals. Ralph winter opines that the real challenge is no longer to extend the boundaries of Christianity but to acknowledge that Biblical, Christian faith which has already extensively flowed beyond Christianity as a cultural movement, just as it has historically flowed beyond Judaism and Roman Catholicism. He also suggests that the task of the mission now is to allow and encourage people of other faith to follow Christ without identifying themselves with a foreign religion.[579]

7.3.1. Christ-Centered Fellowship: A Possibility?

In the Indian context, this issue had been discussed by many theologians and some suggestions have been given. NIC can explore the Christ-centered fellowship to harmonize social life with the common people in daily life. This Christ-centered fellowship does not deny the role of the Church, but it advocates finding a new 'space' for formal and informal human engagement. This is not be used to preach Gospel to convert others. It is a humanizing process. M.M. Thomas said, "...in the perspective of the Bible, conversion is turning from idols to serve a living and a true God and not moving from one culture to another and from one community to another as it is understood in the communal sense in India today.[580] The present church has a 'fellowship-

[579] Ralph. Winter, "Eleven Frontiers of Perspectives" in *International Journal of Frontier Mission*, Vol. 20, No. 4, (Oct-Dec, 2003): 135-141.

[580] M.M. Thomas, *The Church's Mission and Post-Modernism: Collection of Essays and Talks*, 1992-1996 (Tiruvalla/Delhi: Christava Sahitya Samithi/ISPCK, 1996), 156.

in-Christ', not Christ-centered fellowship. To him, the church must be a wider community with the capability to realize the full humanity.

Thus, the church is the community given by God to humankind to achieve full humanity-affirming true personhood to all.[581] It is true that the church should be people-oriented and to be very true as Thomas views it, the church is essentially people and not any institution or clergy.[582] The basic task for us is to see that people are not alienated because of some rite. It is Christ who is the center of all fellowship and it is faith in Christ which is the foremost point of entry in the fellowship, not baptism. Thomas wanted to see the church beyond the communal identity, especially in the Indian situation where there is a lot of opposition to the preaching of Gospel. Therefore, *saṁskāras* like Baptism or Lord's Supper must not be the barrier but the possibility to welcome people: both baptized and non-baptized believers into the fellowship of Christ. This is the vision of the Christ-centered fellowship.

7.3.2. Yeshu Darbar Movement

The Yeshu Darbar is the most successful space-creating Jesus-centered movement in North India. The movement has been initiated by Dr. R.B Lal with a vision to present Jesus Christ from Indian way. He has, in fact, redefined the mission of the church in a new that there is no barrier of any ritual or rite which would serve as a priori to meet Jesus and believe in him. As a whole R.B. Lal has opened a new way to rethink the function of the church. He was very clearly demonstrated that church is not just the mainline church but it is the gathering of people who worship Jesus. The traditional Christian usually doesn't visit Yeshu Darbar, but it has attracted the common people (not official Christian). Yeshu Darbar uses many words from Indian vocabulary such as *Yeshu Mandir* (Jesus Temple), *Babaji* (for Bishop), *Rein Basera* (guest house), *Mataji* (for madam), *Bhajan* (songs), *Jai Yeshu* (praise the Jesus as greetings), *Mukti Marg* (path of salvation), *Manav Mukti Diwas* (Christmas) etc. belong to Indian culture and context. Gospel-oriented *bhajans* have been written by *Babaji* (approximately 266) in the local dialect (*dehaiti*, Bhojpuri, Hindi and Urdu). Through these songs, devotees of Yeshu Darbar are able to identify with the culture and people don't have fear of conversion.[583] Around 5000 people (99% are non-Christian) gather for Sunday worship. There is no baptism-conversion issue to follow or worship or receive the Lord's Supper. This is also a new kind of Christ-centered-fellowship in North India.

---

581 M.M. Thomas, *New Creation in Christ* (Delhi: ISPCK1976), 41-42.

582 M.M. Thomas, *Church and Human Community* (Delhi: 1885), 39-41.

583 Dr. Samuel Richmond Saxena, "The water of life in Indian Cup: Towards an Indian Eschatology with reference to the Ministry of Yeshu Darbar" in *Journal of Mission and Intercultural Studies* 2/1 (April, 2015): 67.

7.4. Postcolonial Subaltern Christian Quest and Indian-ness: Final Assessment

The subalternity is a given state of life not self-created, but the subaltern quest is the postcolonial quest for identity-research, overcoming the deep-rooted internal conflict and dilemma among the colonized people's psychology. Homi Bhabha pointed out is as mimicry and ambivalence, but subaltern can speak out as Spivak argued. The subaltern quest goes through mimicry dilemma and holds fast the colonizer's idea as superior that is the intellectual surrender. NIC has the same dilemma and so identity struggle is an unsettled issue. Let will now analyze the survey data to highlight the direction of NIC towards the re-culturation.

7.4.1. Cultural Reconstruction and Subaltern Quest: Answer of NIC (Survey)

Q. I - Do you think that Indian Christian culture is different from Indian culture?

The answer of two Study Groups and the general interview is this, 'Indian Christian should be Indian first and they must uphold the Indian culture and Christian faith together. Then, they also express the socio-religious problem that poses challenges before them when they face persecution from the Hindus. It holds them back even though there is always a sense of alienation that can't be denied due to the right-wing uprising in India. In order to define the NIC culture, they reflect the 'concept of hybrid' of Bhabha, i.e., NIC has a mixed culture. In the end, they even said that the Christian culture and Indian culture must hand-in-hand.

Q. II - Do you like to include Indian culture in Christian life? How & where?

The existing Christian culture is not fully fitting with Indian culture like using shoe inside the Church, hand-shake (report divided into 45% each and 10% no answer) and chick-kiss as greetings, etc. Among the general interview report, the culture of eating 'beef' is fully divided 42% in favor and against and only 16% expressed either one. It shows that 'beef' eating among NIC is there to stay.

Q. III - What are the difficulties adopt Indian culture into Christian life and Church?

There are three areas that have come up in the report: i. there is a sense of fear of 'idolatry' of Hinduism and it is felt that some influence may come into the Christian life and habit which the Bible completely prohibits; ii. The majority think that there are many superstitious practices in the Indian culture (among Hindus) that stand against the Christian value; iii. the doctrine of salvation only in Jesus has also prevented many to be close with other faiths, fearing of compromise.

Q. IV - Do you feel a change of religion is a cultural loss?

The Study group's opinion has reflected the result of the colonial policy that has disassociated them from the cultural root. They also said that due to the crisis of culture after conversion, many converts (FGC) have thrown out of parental family or from society. The caste mobility issue is also addressed by them and a feeling is expressed that having no caste identity, they face difficulty to have social integration, even though they think that caste is not good. They also raised the question of caste with Church. Being Christian is a pride-factor for NIC and it separates them from others because Christian does not accept other religion similar to them. It is said that Christians socially face strong opposition from the right-wing groups in the North.

Q. V – Do you feel the Western impact on the Indian Christian tradition and thinking?

The Study Groups feel that the Indian Church largely follow the Western system and because of this tradition there is a negative feeling against the Indian traditions since there is a confusion to separate Indian culture from Hindu culture. They do think this a bad notion yet most Christians struggle to own Indian culture whole-heartedly as they accepted the Western culture.

Q.VI – What kind of Church you want to see in the future?

The best thing what the Study group thinks positive is the congregational worship (*Satsang*), the mainline Church leaders in this group said that the emphasis on liturgy has made the Sunday service because it is the same repetition. Most pastors are thinking to induct more indigenous elements in worship like Indian music, instruments, oil-lamp, language, etc. Interestingly, the general interview opines that worship even can be named as *Satsang* or *Aradhana Sabha*. 52% said in favor and 32% was against any such change 16% has no clear answer. 71% wants Hindi as a preference over Urdu in the Northern region.

7.4.2. *Nāmakaraṇa Saṁskāra* and Postcolonial Reconstruction

Q. I – What kind of name Indian Christian should have?

The Study Groups have said in favor of changing the naming system of Indian Christian. They also express that the social problem like people can't pronounce correctly, sometimes make fun/mock, on official paper it comes incorrect, etc. They also have no complete solution for them, since a tradition is continuing and Christian identity also matters. In the general interview, 84% thinks that NIC must have more Indian name in place of the Western name and only 10% favor the colonial name as social identity with 13% didn't express their view.

Personal interview of the mainline Churches (CNI and Methodist) said that they have already started some changes, not as a policy, but developing a tradition towards such change. They mostly wish to follow mixed naming system which has social and Christian communicating meaning. Researcher's own naming experience can enlighten this logic. We have a mixed marriage: wife from Mongolian tribe (North-Eastern region of India) with a typical clan name (Ms. Hoikhonem Lunkim) and I have a Bengali (refused to change after conversion) name, Tapas Ghosh and we named our daughter as Naomi (from the Bible) Neijakim (from mother's side) and Ghosh (as family name from father's side). Among NIC the mixed is an emerging trend in postcolonial India. This change is not so radical among the Roman Catholic.

The rural converts (FGC) from the recent indigenous mission movement (also in past) has not changed the name even many names are taken from Hindu god/goddess and they refuse to accept any external change but only internal change to follow Jesus. Among FGC, many are using a biblical name (single word) for their children with two reasons: i. Christian identity ii. love to the Bible.

7.4.2.1. Reply of *Kristabhakta* (Believer outside the Institutional Church)

Q. I - Name change after baptism was common colonial practice, what is the main purpose of doing so?

The reply of this group is more straight-forward since they are accountable to the institutional Church. It says that the name change is a complete wrong tradition of the Church. The traditional Church argues that the name of 'Saul' was changed into 'Paul' but is not correct and according to Acts 13.9, Saul was also known as Paul. They also advocate a larger picture of the Eastern culture in contrast to the Western culture, so the narrative is not only local but also global. They strongly advocate the preservation of the local culture including the name.

Q. II - Many people are given a typical western name like Mr. Vinison Dixon or Lorance Matthew, etc., do you think by doing it, we are de-rooting a person from his/her culture?

There is a very vicious answer that condemned the British religious law and identity (the Civil Law of 1865 for each religious community) which has played a significant role in the naming system of Indian Christian and it has separated Christian not only from the culture but also from people. It has extracted all birthright and identity and hence de-rooted Christians. It has also deprived the family, parents, and grandparents of the joy of giving the name to their child. It is, to them, a direct insult/neglect of the social system and family traditions. This is also unbiblical.

Q. III - Do you believe that cultural name helps a person to be in culture with new faith?

They argue with the biblical text from 1Cor. 7 in which St. Paul says, "Be at the same place when the Lord called you" then how much more our names that our parents and dear ones gave us! Indeed it helps a person with his/her ethnic identity. A name defines a person's community, tribe and lot more in our country. How can western perspectives ever understand this? But again, there are people who would not like to be called by their original name for that reminds them of the caste system- the Dalits, S.C, S.T or O.B.C. I would say these are more political issues and issues of the heart rather than of the Kingdom of God. I believe our names bind us closely to our culture, people, and community. Keeping our original names help us to be rooted within our community and therefore be a better witness of the Lord's love in this journey of life.

7.4.3. Conversion-Baptism Issue: What next for NIC?

The outcome of group-discussion on the 'Conversion and Baptism' has given some insights to re-look the existing practice. From the pre-Christian era to present India's situation, our discussion suggests a few things:

1. The majority among us have expressed their view in favor of propagation of what we believe, the Lordship of Jesus and His saving Gospel to the world be continued.
2. The majority are in the opinion that India has no unified homogeneous cultural ethos. It is diverse and ethically located.
3. To many of us, Indian Cultural diversity is mistakenly taken as Hindu culture.
4. The tribals (minor groups) are in the borderline of losing or have lost their culture due to such reclusive rite and doctrine of Church. Therefore, Nagaland, Manipur, and Mizoram are now struggling for re-culturation by acknowledging the negative impact of mission policy.
5. The Constitutional religious freedom is to be properly interpreted within the spirit of religious plurality and safeguard of all, so Church should not take as a tool of propagation Christianity among other faiths.
6. The general survey shows that only 26% people are agreed to change the word baptism with a native word '*Diksha*' (initiation) and 58% has opposed to such change and 17% will have no view on

this matter. It is noticeable that more and people are looking for a change and 42% is open for any change. It is a huge contextual shift among NIC.

7.4.3.1. The response of *Kristabhakta* on Conversion-Baptism Issue: An Assessment

On the issue of the conversion-baptism, the responses are as follows:

Q. I - What should be the best form of baptism ritual for a new believer in North India?

The Christians are under control of the denomination and they believed that the biblical practice of Jesus' baptism can be regulated only by the organization. One's faith is a personal matter. They believe that Hindu by culture, so religious use of water (river or pond) is very common and every sacred work, be it religious or secular, taking a dip in water is *saṁskāra*, so in Indian context, it has an advantage but the threat to family or society, fearing he/she will leave everything after this rite.

The immersion is one way of receiving baptism but except the disabled and elderly people on whom they sprinkle, focusing mainly on the sacredness of this initiation. It was conducted in public place with local tuned songs (*Bhajans* or *Kirtans*) with flowers, garlands, oil lamp (D*iya*), incense sticks to express the meaning through the culture. The symbolism of the lighting of an oil lamp (*Diya*) and incense sticks (*Agarbatti*) is the newness of our life in Christ, and the use of fire (*Agni*) has culturally reflected Christ as the Light and the Sanctifier. As the fire on the oil lamp, incense stick burn down, it shows that the life of a *bhakta* is dead on the cross and decision to follow Jesus is the life. A pot (*Kalash*) that is used for water during baptism is to be kept at home forever as the remembrance of baptism. *Kalash* is highly symbolic in Indian sacred culture.

Q. II - Baptism follows the conversion of faith. How to restore the actual meaning of baptism?

Hans Staffner in his book 'JESUS CHRIST AND THE HINDU COMMUNITY' holds accountable the British law of 1865 as the Indian Succession Act which separated a convert from the parental right and identity. He writes:

> There is however one point which separates Christians from the Hindu community, one relic from the colonial era, which has to be removed before a real synthesis of Hindu culture and the Christian faith becomes feasible, which is that Christian have their own personal law which is different from that of the Hindu community. As long as Christians are ruled by a different personal law, baptism

> will continue to involve changing over from one social community to another. It will remain impossible to be a Christian Hindu."[584]

Therefore, Indian Christians need to understand this problem and deal it as soon as possible, because this law 'relic from the colonial era' as Staffner rightly puts it, makes Baptism in India not per Biblical tradition but rather without the knowledge of the devotee that it excommunicates the devotee from his/her birth community and this is completely opposite to what the N.T teaches and upholds. It is in our country only that baptism is not a statement of faith but rather a change of community identity. The agent to this is the ordained ministers who are authorized by the law to do this task and his/her verdict becomes final and is respected by the law. Therefore, as an Indian devotee of the Lord, of a certain birth origin of any given community, we pray that the churches would ask the Government to repeal this colonial law and practice baptism without making any legal document like the certificate, without any authority behind ordained person, without any denomination tag but in the natural surroundings of pond and river, by any lay devotee of the Lord, as purely a sacred spiritual act and a matter of faith alone. Whereas, we as Hindu (cultural) devotee of the Lord would continue to discourage a devotee of the Lord in our country to take Baptism in any given denominational churches as they still all fall under the civil law of 1865 and encourage him or her to take baptism as obedience to the command of the Lord in his/her own natural surroundings that the Lord has put him/her in.

Q. III - Is it possible for the existing Church to accept a non-baptized person (who has faith in Jesus) equal to a baptize one?

They believed the argument of Hans Staffner that puts an example of the baptism of Narayan Vaman Tilak (from High Caste Hindu) to follow Christ in public in Maharashtra through the Editorial Notes, *Dnyanodaya,* on November 22, 1894. Staffner writes,

> Here we notice again a remarkable fact. Nobody seriously objected to Tilak's public confession of faith in Jesus Christ. The question of his being excluded from his family and caste, at this stage, did not arise at all. There was no blame attached to a Hindu believing in Christ. But, receiving baptism was regarded as an unspeakable disgrace and disaster. The reason was that baptism in the eyes of Hindus was not so much a spiritual, as a social and civil act. It signified the change over from one social community to another.[585]

---

[584] Hans Staffner, *Jesus Christ and the Hindu Community* (Anand; Gujarat Sahitya Prakask, 1988), 238.

[585] Hnas Staffner, *Jesus Christ and the Hindu Community* (Anand: Gujarat Sahitya Prakash, 1998), 63.

If baptism would not have been an entry to a new community, entry to a completely different set of systems but only a matter of act of obedience by the devotee of the Lord, then there would not be any challenge for the devotee and whatever challenges there would remain he/she would happily endure with the Lord's strength within their family and community environment.

But, that to happen in India would take a radical paradigm shift and great sacrifice on the part of the Church. The current settings of the Indian church and the demands she puts before a new devotee who comes forward for baptism overwhelm him/her. The settings where baptism takes place and the manner it is done are the same pattern that many countries in the world practiced in the past or even today. But, it is not beneficial for the devotee of this soil or for the Kingdom of God.

The demands the church puts are unbiblical. Acts 15 deals with such a problem and the basis of their solution was based on this principle "not to burden those who are turning towards God" (v19) but the church puts things in front of the new devotee that are related to his family/community life and identity and very dear to him/her, such as *sindur* (red dot on forehead of a married woman) to be wiped off, name to be changed, *tilak* (religious mark on forehead) to be forbidden, family worships/festivals/events to be avoided/forsaken, sacred thread of a Brahmin devotee to be removed , tuft of hair to be cut off, caste to be mingled (the evil of caste system is hidden in being pride of your high birth or inferiority feelings for being a low caste-in Christ both the pride and inferiority is removed and not the birth identity of the devotee itself. Jewish and Gentile Christians both existed happily in the first couple of centuries), bangles, *mangalsutras* (marriage chain like marriage ring) to be removed and foolishness such as these are so much presented as required by the Lord Himself.

The church also wrongly links and stresses the forsaking of family values and their identity as Hindu as bearing the cross and following the Lord. The cost of following the Lord for a new devotee is presented as the wiping off the *sindur*, removing the thread, marrying a person that the church decides, forsaking family values, etc. The cross kills the self inside and not the person he/she is. He/she lives for God in his/her given situation and shining brightly for the Lord there in a given situation. We believe that we are not called to change society but rather to make disciples of every nations, tribes, and language. We are called to shine for our families/communities and that is only possible by shining through our family values and context and not devoid of it.

Therefore, when baptism becomes simple as a matter of obedience to the Lord without the unbiblical requirements to burden them, there would be more joyful acceptance.

Q. IV - How to deal with a growing number of unbaptized believers in India?

To them, baptism is a command of Jesus Christ as He commanded other laws like 'love your enemies', 'don't tell lies' and all commands are equal. It is also not true if one commandment is not obeyed, the entire life in Jesus is failed. By faith, people are saved, not by works alone. Prior to works, faith leads. Since by faith one is a full believer, therefore one who declares to have faith in the Lord is a full believer.

Q. V - What would be a possible new paradigm of a conversion-baptism issue in India?

In repose of searching a new model to address this issue, they said:

i. The Christians in India must appeal to the Government of India to repeal the Succession Act of 1865 which accepted the separation from the parental community after conversion and it must be assured that the conversion-baptism has nothing to do with the social system of his/her culture. It should be kept and dealt with a spiritual journey, not shifting from one religion to another or culture.

ii. It would be better to stop using the word 'baptism' and find any local linguistic suitable word from the culture that would express the same meaning. In this regards, the traditional Christian of NIC has differed and 58% does not agree to change this word, but 26% are favoring a change.

iii. To emphasize on the necessity to obey the Lord's command of receiving baptism without tagging any unbiblical and the Western requirements (as mentioned above) but with the blessings of the body of devotees of the Lord, the family and community elders and in their presence (wherever is possible). This answer also reflects the postcolonial or anti-colonial notion that India has been dealing on this issue.

iv. This rite must be celebrated within the local context of a person and the natural surroundings, not inside the church or in hiding. The presence of family members (with other faiths), parents, friends, community elders, etc and with the cultural use of *diya, agarbatti*, flowers, *bhajans*, etc., is essential for this rite. It should be observed as the beginning of a sacred life not the departure from the family and culture so that others will participate with joy. Then it would not be a social issue.

v. The dependant on the few legal ordained is a self-made burden by the church on herself. The church should come out from this. In Indian settings as a devotee of the Lord or as a Hindu, one should 'take' baptism, not that someone 'gives' baptism. It should be an act of joy not fear of social consequences. The presences of other devotees are to bless the devotee. After the devotee takes the dip or sprinkle, baptism is thus completed.

7.5. Reconstruction of Culture as New Model of Subaltern NIC in the context of postcolonial India: Final Words of Researcher

The research has incorporated three segments of NIC, namely: I the tradition Christian, ii. the new converts (FGC) mainly in rural North India and the Churchless followers of Jesus to search for an answer whether NIC is really 'subaltern' and if yes, how the subalternity has been a prevailing reality life in postcolonial India, then it has proceeded to know how the prevailing 'subalternity can be overcome through the re-culturation of *saṁskāras* with the use of MS and Torah. Here are the findings of our argument:

i. The opinion of field research has clearly shown the 'cultural subalternity' of the colonized NIC. The variation in expression and the realization of being culturally subaltern differs one segment from other, because of the context of life and faith of a given social situation and the role of Church teachings they are nurtured. The subalternity among NIC is to be discovered by analyzing the prevailing culture. It is felt that NICs are often unaware of their subalternity, even when they acknowledge the colonial culture among them. It is a natural phenomenon of the colonized community. The state of subalternity is realized only when the reconstruction of the colonial culture is talked and they used to feel the challenge of accepting it. The psychological resistance is the product of inner conflict of the colonized people. This inner conflict is the colonial ambivalence (of Bhabha) which is a state of mind that governs with a duality.

ii. Spivak talked about the possibility of subaltern resistance to the colonial culture but she then, argued that the context of the social system (elitism) does not allow the subaltern to speak of their own. The voice of subaltern is subverted and further oppressed by the powerful section of the society. Spivak can be supported with the contemporary narrative of Indian culture by the RSS wings that propagate a particular cultural narrative on every Indian, diluting the diversity of India. The voice of Dalits (after 2014) has further suppressed by this elite-narrative. This is the challenge before the NIC to make the colonized Indian Church listen to them and take steps for 'self-reliance' being an Indian Christian.

iii. From such an argument, it is factual that the voice of the early converts was unheard to the colonial Church authority and native culture was replaced (elite-behavior) by the colonial culture. The postcolonial theory of Edward Said argued that the ideological disguises of imperialism as a hegemonic epistemological project must be unmasked, According to Said, the Orientalism' unveils the Western style of dominating, restructuring and having authority over the non-European cultures and people.[586] The NIC was put into the category of 'worlding and othering' of Spivak to impose the colonial

[586] Y.T. Vinayaraj, "Representation of the Subaltern: Spivak and Historiography" in *Mar Thoma Seminary Journal of Theology*, Vol. II, No. 2, December (2013): 24.

culture on the native converts, lowering the status of NIC as 'object' of the experiment.[587]

iv. The present cultural question is argued through the concept of 'hybrid' (of Bhabha) culture of the subaltern NIC. The hybridity is the end cultural result of the colonized people. The argument to revive the 'pure' culture is practically impossible but hybrid culture is the natural outcome of the colonized community. It seems that the hybridity is there to stay among NIC but the new Christian movement in rural India and *Kristabhaktas* who follow Christ outside of the colonial ear and in postcolonial India, have a native cultural orientation of Jesus. This critical satiation is not harmonized yet in India and the gap between these two is widening because of two realities.

v. The issue of the name has also reflected the ambivalence and mimicry when the challenge of re-culturation is concerned. The colonized NIC seems moving towards a cultural reconstruction of the name, even if it is slow in progress. Any radical change for the colonized NIC is taken as the fear of losing the identity, even if it is colonial. NIC is re-looking this matter and unofficially has accepted a changed system which hybrid in name but close to the Indian culture. FGC and Kristabhaktas are away from such challenge since they do not wish to change the name. The colonized name-giving was the part of establishing the hegemony which had a motive to alter the 'others' within their plan. The colonized name was a social policy of the Church and natives lost their socio-cultural mobility.

vi. The conversion-baptism issue which is more sensitive but not free from the debate in Indian since the inception of the colonial Church. There two main arguments: inner part of this rite that none opposed but the outer-path and after baptism socio-cultural life is argued time and again. Many objected even to alter this rite all together and others have started their own movement etc. Overall research finds that India needs an alternative rite to follow Jesus. India is emerging towards more indigenous Christian movement of different kinds, so the rejection of the colonial meaning and rite of baptism and conversion is already a reality in India. What is very valid to notice that even the colonized Christian (CNI and Methodist) has been staying away from the colonial teachings like separation from culture, family, society, etc, even though, the rite is there to stay.

vii. I personally believe that plurality in baptism rite is essential in India and individual freedom to decide the *saṁskāra* of this rite can be accepted. The decision to follow Jesus can be taken as a final seal to call someone Christian. Baptism can be celebrated in any simple form when one wishes. The cultural separation and 'super-holy' notion must be pluralized contextually.

---

[587] Y.T. Vinayaraj, "Representation of the Subaltern: Spivak and Historiography" in *Mar Thoma Seminary Journal of Theology*, Vol. II, No. 2, December (2013): 24.

The membership of the Church is to be repealed completely. It does not have any sense in Indian ethos. In another way, it is this act which has taken to separate and divide people as 'saved and unsaved'.

viii. The introduction of 'Space and Place' model to integrate NIC within the Samaj Dharma is heuristically futuristic because this model is capable to improvise two major aspects for the colonized subaltern NICs: i. by creating a new space means NIC will be heading towards the cultural plurality and diversity of India as the ultimate future of Christian faith with harmony and peace. It is surrender to the major culture of India (or Hindu culture) but each tiny ethnic group will use their cultural aspects for re-culturation. It will also help to re-interpret the colonial dogmatic position of Christianity as the second to none and find a new way to express the meanings of Gospels of Jesus to the local people through the local symbolism and tools. This model is potential enough to harmonize with Indian diversities and yet remain unique within plurality.

Conclusion

The finding of this chapter is as follows:

1. NIC can look into the social aspect of the festivals and may take the opportunity by socializing the Christian festivals to integrate with the mass and this can be a move to 'unlock Christ' for common Indians. NIC can also take the festival of other faith that has a social celebration and cherish as a social event to bring better harmony.
2. There are some pertinent challenges before NIC to overcome like an attempt to dilute the denominational mobility and rigidity, accepting good-will gift during the festival, not to the confused with idolatry but a neighbor next door.
3. The need of the hour as the postcolonial quest if to build a grass-root level integration to the culture and it will help to re-define the conversion related issue that demands that cultural disintegration as well after baptism.
   a. The colonial mimicry and ambivalence are the biggest challenges for the re-culturation of NIC but at the same time, the new culture will be a hybrid culture, mixed with both native and the colonial. This new cultural will be resulted from the quest and will be free from the colonial imposition. Whether the 'Idea of Ambivalence' of Bhabha will persist among NICs between hybrid culture as their own and the colonial culture since it is seen that the colonized people neither able neither to revive the past nor to accept the colonial culture completely as their own but it continues to be the reality of life.

4. The baptism rite which separates one from the rest can be altered, ingrained in culture without diluting the inner meaning of it. It is not social change, but a change of inner aspect towards a spiritual life. The Yeshu Darbar, Kristabhaktas and the contemporary rural converts may show the new direction to the mainline church for the construction of the present *saṁskāras*.

Final Conclusion

This research, titled "**Re-culturation: An Attempt to Reconstruct Northern Indian Christian Saṁskāras in the Light of Manusmṛti and the Law of Moses: A Postcolonial Subaltern Response**" has found the followings:

1. The Indian ethnocultural heterogeneity was interpreted by the EWM as a homogeneous culture which was identified only with **Hinduism**, negating the multi-dimensional plurality of religion, ethnolinguistic traditions, regional rigidity and mobility and also the invisible social structure of Dharma which is responsible to integrate diversity without diluting the difference.
2. Thus, NIC [also IC] was separated from the Indian [Hindu] culture and eventually disintegrated from India culture and came under direct control of the colonial culture and the authority of Church, and the 'freedom of choice' of religious life [not religion] being Indian Christian was determined by the EWM; hence, they became culturally subaltern to the colonial culture.
3. The postcolonial subaltern methodology is to question the colonialism that is prevailing religiously among NICs and for the reconstruction of new Indian Christian cultural identity as the quest for selfhood. The binary of being colonized and the colonizer is the prevailing challenge to define the future of NICs because the psychological status of NICs [also IC] often accepts the colonizer as superior. A hybrid culture (View of H. K. Bhabha) is the most natural the outcome of the subaltern quest for the reconstruction of culture and identity.
4. MS and Torah are selectively used to find a model for NICs since MS provides the basis *saṁskāras* to India and the Torah gives the Laws [Dharma and *saṁskāra*] to the biblical traditions. It is proved to be possible that if the location of culture is to be taken as the important context for re-culturation, then, the tradition, customs and *saṁskāra* of these books, it has the capacity to provide a new model because

they have laid down the basic cultural norms for Indian and Hebrew people, therefore, re-culturation minus MS in India is abstract.

5. The concept of Dharma (cultural framework and doctrine that envisage the plural expression of One Truth) can harmonize Christian faith and Indian culture because Dharma is the axis of Indian culture which goes beyond the religious limitation. The SD of India rests and works only on the dharmic foundation that integrates diversity as the reality.
6. *Saṁskāra* is not used with the same meaning of sacrament (of Christian tradition) because *saṁskāra* has a wide function in Indian society and culture. It is religious and also cultural that includes the conduct of life, religious duty, family duty, customs, manners, food habit, etc. *Saṁskāra* is actually the expressional mode of Indian culture, not only religious rituals.
7. De-constructing Indian culture after conversion to Christianity during the colonial period, the policy of name change of natives with European or the biblical names has completely halted the social mobility of NIC. It has uprooted them from the genealogical lineage and family tradition as well as the ethnographical location of an individual. When Matthew chapter 1 has reaffirmed the genealogy of Jesus [accepting various other interpretations], the colonial mission did just opposite to the native converts with the European system, diluting the importance of the family genealogy. This has created a deep-rooted family and social problem to identify and mobility with others.
8. An Indian name is religiously, linguistically, regionally, caste-wise, ethnically structured and by imposing the EWB names, converts have lost social relevance because it has no communicative meaning and identification index with 'others'. Names were not chosen or made optional before converts, it was just put on them and this process has de-humanized native as 'object' of the colonial Church property. It has disempowered them socially and subjugated them to be under the Church. So, name-subalternity is a serious issue that is found here.
9. There is a postcolonial trend among new converts mainly in rural Indian indigenous mission movements outside of the mainline Churches that upholds the Indian names with the biblical meaning or typical Indian names or keeping same names after accepting Jesus or sometimes avoid the typical religious names of god and goddess or in the most cases, the name change does not take place at all. Yet, a dilemma of identity being Indian and being Indian Christian is prevailing (Mimicry of Bhabha). A balancing naming system

is yet to develop among NIC [IC]. The hybrid (of Bhabha) name that is composed with one biblical word and one Indian word is an emerging trend among many traditional Christians.

10. Conversion and baptism are the most controversial issue in India since this rite demands a complete cultural separation because Indian culture was identified to the Hindu culture. The formation of a Christian life (seen as the fruit of conversion) has not considered the socio-cultural reality of a person or the society. This process has not only caused a cultural disintegration but also separated from family (in case single convert), relatives, friends, and so on, since they now belong to 'other' faith. Many Christians and Indians have objected to this 'rite' and developed the 'alternative rite' like no-baptism, the baptism of heart, un-baptized follower of Jesus, etc. The Little Movements have denounced the 'present' form of baptism rite and its meaning and accepting Jesus without cultural and social conversion and separation.
11. The possibility of use the 'purification' rites that are available in MS and Torah that has the same inner meaning of what baptism has also taught can provide an alternative *saṁskāra* as an Indian form of baptism. The Churchless Christians or rural movements are practicing many alternative rites. This protest against the act and meaning of the EWM has challenged almost from the beginning of the colonial mission. The challenges before these two groups are to be seen how they negotiate and find wider ecumenism in India.
12. There are many challenges before NICs before they actualize the process of the re-culturation as the practical reality. The psychological dilemma has widened the challenge to define 'how much Indian-ness' is to be incorporated within the present Christian tradition so that the Christian identity would not be in danger? This dilemma is a natural phenomenon among the colonized converts. In one hand, the postcolonial quest for new independent identity and on the other, to overcome the mimicry and ambivalence of their colonial past and find the new identity for NICs [ICs] has the right to re-define culture.

It is true that NIC [also IC] in contemporary India is going through a transition phase and a cultural reconstruction has appeared to be a serious issue since the mainline Church and the independent movement has failed to come together and on the other, narrow cultural narrative of right wings that have appeared to be an obstacle to visualize a dharmic plural India as a practical reality into which even the smallest may cherish the diversity.

Bibliography

Books

Aleaz, K. P. *The Gospel of Indian Culture.* Calcutta: Punthi Pustak, 1994.

Ali, S. M. *The Geography of the Puranas.* New Delhi, 1966.

Ambedkar, Babasaheb B.R. *Why Go For Conversion*? Bangalore: Dalit Sahitya Akademy, 1987.

Animananda, B. *The Blade, Life and Work of Brahmabandhab Upadhyaya.* Calcutta: Roy & Son, 1947.

Ashcroft, Bill, Gareth Griffiths and Helen Tiffin, eds., *Post-Colonial Studies: The Key Concepts,* 2nd ed. London; New York: Routledge, [2000] 2007, reprint 2009.

Asirvatham, Eddy. *Christianity in the Indian Crucible.* Calcutta: YMCA Publishing House, 1955.

Athyal, Jesudas M. and John J. Thatamanil, eds. *Metropolitan Chrysostom on Mission in the Market Place.* Tiruvalla: Christava Sahitya Samithy, 2002.

Augustine of Hippo, *Treatise on the Gospel of John LXXX. 3.* (ca. 416). Cf. Jeffrey A. Truscott, *The Sacraments: A Practical Guide.* New Delhi: Christian World Imprints, 2016.

Baago, Kaj. *Pioneers of Indigenous Christianity.* Madres/Bangalore: CIS/CISRS, 1969.

Baago, Kaj. *The Movement Around Subba Rao: A Study of the Hindu-Christian Movement around Kl. Subba Rao in Andhra Pradesh.* Madras: CLS, 1968.

Baillie, D.M. *The Theology of the Sacraments.* London: Faber & Faber Ltd. n.d.

Banerjee, Brojendra Nath. *Religious Conversion in India.* New Delhi: Harnam Publications, 1982.

Banerjee, NikunjaVihari. *Studies in the Dharmasastra of Manu.* Delhi: Munshiram Manoharlal Publishers Pvt. Ltd. 1980.

Barral, M. Merleau-Ponty. *Phenomenology of Perception*, Trans. By C. Smith. New York: The Humanities Press, 1962.

Barral, M. Merleau-Ponty. *The Prose of the World*, ed., C. Lefort, Trans by J. O'Neill. Evanston: Northwestern University Press, 1973.

Barral, M. Merleau-Ponty. *The Role of the Body-Subject in Interpersonal Relations*. Pittsburgh: Duquense University Press, 1965.

Barua, Ankur. *Debating 'Conversion' in Hinduism and Christianity*, ed., Govin Flood, *Routledge Hindu Studies Series*. New York: Routledge, 2015.

Basham, A. L. *The Wonder that was India*. Calcutta: Rupa/Pontana Books, 1971.

Bayly, Susan. *Caste, Society and Politics in India from the Eighteenth Century to the Modern Age*. N.p.,: Cambridge University Press, 1999.

Bhabha, Homi K. *The Location of Culture*; Bart Moore-Gilbert, *Postcolonial Theory: Contexts, Practices, Politics*. London: Verso, 1997.

Bhabha, Homi K. *The Location of Culture*. London/New York: Routledge, [1994] reprint 2010.

Bhadra, Gautam. "The Mentality of Subalternity: Kantanama or Rajdharma," in *Subaltern Studies VI: Writings on South Asian History and Society*, edited by Ranajit Guha. New Delhi: Oxford University Press, [1989] 4th Impression 1999.

Bhagavandas, *The Science of Social organization*, vol. I, 2nd ed., Madras: Theological Publishing House, 1932.

Bharti, Dayanand. *Living Water and Indian Bowl*. New Delhi: ISPCK, 2004.

Birla, Ritu. "Postcolonial Studies," in *Can the Subaltern Speak? Reflections on the History of an Idea*, edited by Rosalind C. Morris. New York: Columbia University Press, 2010.

Bliss, Kathleen. *The Future of Religion*. N.p.,: Penguin Books, 1972.

Bowker, John. *The Message and the Book: Sacred Texts of the World's Religions*. New Haven: Yale Uni. Press, 2012.

Bratton, F. G. *The History of the Bible*. London: n.p., 1961.

Brett, M.G. "*The Political Ethics of Postmodern Allegory*," in M. Daniel Carroll R., D.J.A. Clines and P.R. Davies, eds., *The Bible in Human Society: Essays in Honour of John Rogerson*, JSOT Sup, 200. Sheffield: Sheffield Academic Press, 1995.

Brett, Mark G. "Nationalism and Hebrew Bible," in *The Bible in Ethics: The second Sheffield Colloquium*, edited by John W. Rogerson, Margaret Davies & M. Denial Carroll R. Sheffield. England: Sheffield Academic Press, 1995.

Briggs, Richard S. & Joel N. Lohr, eds., *A Theological Introduction to the Torah: Interpreting the Torah as Christian Scripture.* Michigan: Baker Academic, 2012.

Brown, L.W. *The Indian Christians of St. Thomas*. Cambridge: Cambridge University Press, 1956.

Byod, R. H. S., ed., *Manilal C. Parech (1885-1967), Dhanjibhai Fakirbhai (1895-1967): A Selection.* Madras: CLS. 1974.

C. D. Aairan, *Kalagora Subba Rao: The Mystic of Munipalle.* Vijayawada: N. Kutumba Rao and Co., n.d.

Calvin, John. *Institutes of the Christian Religion*... 513, and in *The Catholicity of Protestantism*, 110.

Calvin, John. *Institutes of the Christian Religion* IV 15.22 (1559), ed., John T. McNeill, Trans., Ford Lewis Battles in LCC XXI. Philadelphia: Westminster Press, 1960.

Calvin, John. *Institutes of the Christian Religion* IV 14.1 (1559), ed., John T. McNeill, trans., Ford Lewis Battles, in LCC, 21.21. Philadelphia: Westminster Press, 1960.

Calvin, John. *Institutes of the Christian Religion* IV 16.2 (1559), ed., John T. McNeill, Trans., Ford Lewis Battles in LCC XXI. Philadelphia: Westminster Press, 1960.

Calvin, John. *Institutes of the Christian Religion*, vol. II. London, James Clarke & Co. Ltd., 1949.

Chakrabarty, D. and Homi K. Bhabha, *Habitations of Modernity: Essays in the Wake of Subaltern Studies.* Chicago; Illinois: University of Chicago Press, 2002. Ranajit Guha, ed., *A Subaltern Studies Reader, 1986-1995.* Minneapolis: University of Minnesota Press, 1997.

Chandran, J. R. *"I Believe..." Christian Faith Re-articulation*, 2nd ed. Bangalore: SCMI, 1998.

Chapman, Graham P. *The Geopolitics of South Asia, From Early Empires to India, Pakistan and Bangladesh.* Ashgate: Aldershot, 2000.

Chatterjee, Partha. "Caste and Subaltern Consciousness," in *Subaltern Studies VI: Writings on South Asian History and Society*, edited by Ranajit Guha. New Delhi: Oxford University Press, 1989.

Chaturvedi, Badrinath. *Finding Jesus in Dharma.* Delhi: ISPCK, 2004.

Chaudhuri, Nirad C. *Hinduism: A Religion to Live By.* New Delhi: OUP, 8th Impr., 2003; 1979.

Chenchiah, P. "The Church and Indian Christian," in *Rethinking Christianity in India*, edited by V.G. Job. Madras: A. N. Sundarisanam, 1938.

Cherian, M. T. *Hindutva Agenda and Minority Rights: A Christian Response.* Bangalore: Centre for Contemporary Christianity, 2007.

Cheriyan, C.V. *A History of Christianity in Kerala.* Kottayam: Kerala Historical Society, 1973.

Chowdhry, N. K. *Indian Constitution and Education.* Delhi: Shipra Publications, 2009.

Clarence, McMullen. *Rituals and Sacraments in Indian Religions.* Delhi: n.p., 1979.

Clarke, Sundar. *Let the Indian Church Be Indian,* 2nd Print. Madras: The Christian Literature Society, 1985.

Cohen, Stephen. *India Emerging Power.* Washington D.C.: Brookings Institution Press, 2001.

Collins, Paul M. & Paul Pulikkan. *The Church and Culture in India, Re-culturation: Theory and Praxis.* Delhi: Cambridge press, 2010.

Constantine and Licinius, "*The Edict of Milan,*" in documents of the Christian Church, trans. & ed. Henry Bettenson. London: Oxford University, 1963.

Coward, Harold G. *Pluralism: Challenge to World Religions.* Delhi: Sri Satguru Publications, 1996.

Daniel J.T.K. and R.E. Hedlund. *Carey's Obligation and India's Renaissance.* Serampore: Council of Serampore College, 1993.

Derrett, J.D.M. *Religion, Law and the State in India.* London: Faber & Faber, 1968; and *A Critic of Modern Hindu Law.* Bombay: N.M. Tripathi, 1970; and also see, Marc Galanter, *Law and Society in Modern India.* Delhi: Oxford University Press, 1989.

Derrett, J.D.M. *Religion, Law and the State in India.* London: Faber & Faber, 1968.

Derrida, J. *The Other Heading: Reflections on Today's Europe.* Bloomington: Indiana University Press, 1992.

Desai, Satyajeet A. *Mulla Principles of Hindu Law*, 17th edition, vols. I-II. New Delhi: Butterworths, 1998.

Dharmaraj, Jacob S. *Colonialism and Christian Mission: Post Colonial Reflection.* New Delhi: ISPCK, 1993.

Diwan, Paras & Peeyushi Diwan. *Modern Hindu Law*, 9th edition. Allahabad: Allahabad Law Agency, 1993.

Doniger, Wendy and Brain K. Smith. *The Laws of Manu.* Penguin, 1991; Hoerschelmann Werner, *Christliche Gurus: Darstellung von Selbstverständnis und Funktionindigenen Christseinsdurch.*

Dosick, Wayne. *Living Judaism: The Complete Guide to Jewish Belief, Tradition, and Practice.* San Francisco: Harper, 1995.

Downs, Frederick S. *History of Christianity in India*, vol. 5, part 5. Bangalore: CHAI, 1992.

Fadia, B.L. *Indian Government and Politics.* Agra: Sahitya Bhawan Publications, 2008.

Finkenzeller, Josef. *Handbuch der Dogmengeschichte.* Basel & Wien: Herder Freiburg, 1981.

Firth, C.B. *An Introduction to India Church History.* New Delhi: ISCPK, 1998.

Gaikwad, Roger. "Rethinking Theology in India for the Twenty-first century: Ecclesiastical Perspectives," in *Rethinking Theology in India: Christianity in the Twenty-first Century*, eds., James Massey & T. K. John SJ. New Delhi: Manohar, 2013.

Gandhi, Leela. *Postcolonial Theory: A Critical Introduction.* Delhi: Oxford University Press, 1999.

George, K. M. *Christianity in India through the Centuries.* Hyderabad: Authentic Books, 2009.

Gernet, Jacques. *China and the Christian Impact.* Cambridge: Cambridge University Press, 1987; Cf. Flex Wilfred, *Asian Dreams and Christian Hope: At the Dawn of the Millennium.* Delhi: ISPCK, 2000.

Gopalachari, C. Raja. *Our Culture,* 5th Edition. Bombay: Bharatiya Vidya Bhavan, 1981.

Grafé, Hugald. *The History of Christianity in Tamilnadu, History of Christianity in India,* vol. 4, Part. 2. Bangalore: Church History Association of India, 1982.

Gramsci, Antonio. *Selections from the Prison Notebooks*, trans. by Quintin Hoare and Geoffrey Nowell Smith. New York: Lawrence and Wishart, 1971.

Gregorious, Paulos Mar. *The Indian Orthodox Church: An Overview.* Kottayam: Sophia Publications, 1982.

Gross, David C. *The People's Almanac.* New York: Hippocrene Books, 1988

Guha, Ranajit. "On Some Aspects of the Historiography of Colonial India," in *Subaltern Studies I: Writings on South Asian History and Society*, edited by Ranajit Guha. New Delhi: Oxford University Press, [1982] 4th impression 1999.

Guha, Ranajit. "Preface," in *Subaltern Studies I: Writings on South Asian History and Society*, edited by Ranajit Guha. New Delhi: Oxford University Press, [1982], 4th impression 1999.

Hedlund, Roger E. *Quest for Identity: Indian Churches of Indigenous Origin: The "Little Tradition" in Indian Christianity.* Chennai/N. Delhi: MIIS/ ISPCK, 2000.

Heidegger, Martin. "The Age of the World Picture," *The Question Concerning Technology and Other Essays*, trans. & introduced by William Lovitt. New York: Harper and Row Publishing Inc., 1977.

Hick, John. *God has Many Names.* Philadelphia: The Westminster Press, 1982.

Hoefer, Herbert E. *Churchless Christianity.* Pasadena & California: William Carey Library, 1991.

Hugh of St. Victor, *On the Sacraments of the Christian Faith* I.9 (1140). Cf. Jeffrey A. Truscott, *The Sacraments: A Practical Guide.* New Delhi: Christian World Imprints, 2016.

Husain, S. Abid. *The National Culture of India.* New Delhi: National Book Trust, 1978.

Jaitly, Ajay Kumar & Madhu Rani, eds., *Cultural India.* Delhi, Chennai, Patna: Globus Press, 2012.

Jaminisutras III.1.3, 8.3, IX 2.9 also R. Pandey, *Hindu Saṁskāras.* Delhi: Motilal Banarsidass, 1969.

Jones, E. Stanley. *The Christ of the Indian Road.* New York: The Abingdon Press, 1925.

Joseph, M.P. "Rethinking the Edinburgh Conference in the Context of Globalization," in *Witness in Context: Essays in Honor of Eardley Mendis*, ed., Monica J. Melanchthon and George Zachariah. Tiruvalla: Christave Shitya Samith, 2007.

Kadankavil, Thomas. "Preface," in *Religion and Politics from Subaltern Perspective*, edited by Thomas Kadankavil. Bangalore: Dharmaram Publication, 1999.

Kangle, R. P. Trans., *The Kautilya Arthasastra.* Bombay: University of Bombay, 1972.

Kant, Immanuel. *Religion within the Limits of Reason Alone* (1793), trans., Theodore M. Green and Hoyt H. Hudson. New York: Harper and Row, 1960.

Karokaran, Anto. "Cultural Alienation of Converts and radical Inculturation of Faith", in *Mission and Conversion: A Reappraisal*, Joseph Mattam, ed., Mumbai: St. Pauls, 1996.

Keay, John. *India: A History.* London: HarperCollins, 2000, Chapter 1; Cf. Paul M. Collins, *Context, Culture and Worship: The Quest for Indianness.* New Delhi: ISPCK, 2006.

Keer, Dhananjay. *Dr. Ambedkar: Life and Mission.* Mumbai: Popular Prakashan, 1952, reprint 2005.

Khan, Rasheeduddin ed., *Composite Culture of Indian and National Integration.* Allahabad: Indian Institute of Advance Study, 1987.

Kim, Sebastian C.H. *In Search of Identity: Debate on Religious conversion in India.* New Delhi: Oxford University Press, 2003.

Knitter, Paul F. *No Other Name: A Critical Survey of Christian Attitudes towards the World Religions.* London: SCM Press Ltd., 1985.

Kohler, Ludwig. *Lexicon in Veteris Testamente Libros*. Leiden: E. J. Brill, 1953; Cf. J. Barton Payne, *The Theology of the Old Testament*, 5th print. Michigan: Zondervan, 1973.

Koodapuzha, Xavier. *Faith and Communion of the Indian Church of the Saint Thomas*. Vadavathur: Institute of Religious Studies, 1982.

Kooiman, Dick. *Conversion and Social Equality in India*. New Delhi: Manohar, 1989.

Kunnunkal, T. V. "Our Glorious Heritage and Challenges of the Future," in *Composite Culture of India and National Integration*. Allahabad: Indian Institute of Advance Study, 1987.

Landry, Donna and Gerald Maclean, eds., *The Spivak Reader*. London: Routledge, 1996.

Leeming, Bernard. *Principles of Sacramental Theology*. London, 1956.

Lieber, David. ed., *Etz Hayim*. Philadelphia: Jewish Pub. Society, 2001.

Longchar, Wati. *Returning to Mother Earth: An Indigenous Perspective*. Kway Jen: PTCA, 2012.

Longhurst, Brain. et. al. *Introducing Cultural Studies*. London: Pearson Longman, 2008.

Lunkim, Tongkhojang. *Multiplying Pure Meitei Churches in Manipur Valley*. Imphal: The Upper Room Press, 1986.

Mahadevan, T.M.P. *Outlines of* Hinduism, 3rd ed. Bombay: Chetana, 1999.

Majundar, R. C. *Indian Religion*. Calcutta: Calcutta University Press, 1969.

Malhotra, Rajiv. *Being Different: An Indian Challenge to Western Universalism*. Noida: Harper Collins, 2013.

Manu Smṛti, edited and translated by Pushpendra Kumar, as *Hindū Dharmaśāstra*, 1st edition, vol. II. Delhi: Nag Publishers, 2011.

Marak, Krickwin C. and Plamthodathil S. Jacob, eds., *Conversion in a Pluralistic Context: Perspectives and Perceptions*. Delhi: CMS/ISPCK, 2000.

Massey, James. *Dalits in India*. New Delhi: Manohar, 1995.

Mathew C.P. & M. M. Thomas, *The Indian Churches of Saint Thomas*. New Delhi: ISPCK, 1967.

Mattam, Joseph. "Indian Attempts Towards a Solution of the Problem of Conversion," in *Mission and Conversion: A Reappraisal*, edited by Joseph Mattam & Sebastian C. H. Kim. Mumbai: St. Paul's Press, 1996.

Mayhew, Arthur. *Christianity and the Government of India*. Delhi: Gian Publishing House, 1988.

McMullen, Clarence O. ed., *Rituals and Sacraments in Indian Religions*. New Delhi: ISPCK, 1979.

Menon, K. P. P. *History of Kerala written in the form of notes,* vol.1. New Delhi: Asian Educational Services, 1982.

Menon, K. P. P. *History of Kerala written in the form of notes*, vol. 2. New Delhi: Asian Educational Services, 1983.

Menon, Narayana. "The Foundations of Composite Culture in India," in *Composite Culture of India and National Integration.* Allahabad: Indian Institute of Advance Study, 1987.

Michael, S.M. ed., *Dalits in Modern India: Vision and Values*. New Delhi: Vistaar Publications, 1999.

Minz, Nirmal. *Mahatma Gandhi and Hindu-Christian Dialogue.* Bangalore: CLS, n.d.

Moberly, R.W. L. *Old Testament of the Old Testament: Patriarchal Narratives and Mosaic Yahwism. Overturesto Biblical Theology.* Minneapolis: Fortress, 1992, repr. Eugene, OR: wipf & Stock, 2002.

Morgan, Kenneth W. ed., *The Religion of Hindus.* New York: The Ronald Press Company, 1953.

Mundadan, A. M. *Indian Christians Search for Identity and Struggle for Autonomy.* Bangalore: Theological Publishing in India, 1982.

Mundadan, A. Mathias. "From the Beginning up to the Middle of the Sixteenth Century (up to 1542)," *History of Christianity in India,* vol. I. Bangalore: Church History Association of India, 1989.

Mundadan, A.M. *History of Christianity in India,* vol. 1. Bangalore: Theological Publications in India, 1982.

Neill, Stephen. *A History of Christianity in India.* Cambridge: Cambridge University Press, 1985.

Neill, Stephen. *The Story of the Christian Church in India and Pakistan.* Madras: Diocesan Press, 1972.

Newbigin, Lesslie. *The Gospel in a Pluralist Society.* Eerdmans: Grand Rapids, 1989.

O'Connor, Daniel. *The Testimony of C. F. Andrews.* Madras: CLS, 1974.

Oddie, Geoffrey A. *Missionaries, Rebellion and Proto-nationalism James Long of* Bengal (1814-1887). Surrey: Curzon, 1999.

Oddie, Geoffrey. A. ed., *The Religion in South Asia.* New Delhi: Manohar Book Service, 1977.

Omvedt, Gail. *Seeking Begumpura: The Social Vision of Anticaste Intellectuals.* New Delhi: Navayana Publication, 2008. Sathianathan Clarke, *Dalits and Christianity: Subaltern Religion and Liberation Theology in India.* New Delhi: Oxford University Press, [1998] 2nd Impression 2002.

Pandey, R. B. "The Hindu Sacraments (Samskaras)," in *The Cultural Heritage of India,* vol. II. Calcutta: Ramakrishna Mission, [1937], reprint 1969.

Pandey, R. *Hindu Saṁskāras.* Delhi: Motilal Banarsidass, 1969.

Pandey, R.B. *The Hindu Sacraments (Samskaras)*, vol. II, 1st Edition. Kolkata: The Ramakrishna Mission Institute of Culture, 2003.

Panicker, P. L. John. *Gandhi on Pluralism and Communalism.* Delhi: ISPCK, 2006.

Panikkar, K. M. *Asia and Western Dominance.* London: George Allen & Unwin Ltd. [1953], reprint 1993.

Panikkar, K. M. *Asia and Western Dominance.* London: George Allen & Unwin Ltd., 1974.

Panikkar, K.M. India Through Ages. New Delhi: Discovery Publishing House, 1988.

Panikkar, R. "Indian Christian Theology of Religious Pluralism from the Perspective of Interculturation," in *Religious Pluralism: An Indian Christian Perspective*, Kuncheria Pathil, ed. Delhi: ISPCK, 1991.

Parekh, Manilal C. "An Autobiographical Sketch," in R. H. S. Boyed, ed., *Manilal C. Parekh – 1885-1967 & Dhanjibhai Fakirbhai – 1895-1967: A Seclection.* Madras: CLS, 1974.

Parekh, Manilal C. *Christian Proselytism in India: A Great and Growing Menace.* Rajkot: Harmony House, 1947.

Pathil, Kuncheria ed., *Religious Pluralism: An Indian Christian Perspective.* New Delhi: ISPCK, 1991.

Philip, T. M. "A Historical Survey of Baptismal Practices and Theologies," in *Debate on Mission*, edited by Herbert E. Hoefer. Madras: Gurukul LTCRI, 1979.

Pillai, K. V. Paul. *India's Search for the Unknown Christ.* New Delhi: Fazl Publishers, 1978.

Podippara, Placid J. *The Thomas Christians.* London: Longman and Todd, 1970.

Possehl, Gregory L. *The Indus Civilization: A Contemporary Perspective.* Rowman Altamira, 2002.

Prabhu, Pandarinath. *Hindu Social Organization.* Bombay: n.p., 1954.

Prabhu, R.K. ed., *What Jesus Means to Me?* Ahmadabad: Jivaniji D. Desai, 1959.

Pratt, M.L. *Imperial Eyes: Travel Writing and Trans-culturation.* London: Routledge, 1992.

Rahula, Walpola. *What the Buddha Taught.* n.p.: Grove Press, 1974.

Rajashekar, J. Poul "The Question of Unbaptized Believers in the History of the Mission of India," in *A Call to Discipleship: Baptism and conversion*, edited by Godwin R. Singh. Delhi: ISPCK, 1985.

Rao, Kalagara Subba. *Three Letters: Become Christ, Don't Pray, Man Created God.* Secundrabad: n.p., 1965.

Rao, Kalagora Subba. *Retreat Padre*, 2nd ed. Machilipatnam: n.p. 1972

Rao, Rao Sahib K. Subba. *The Outpouring of my Heart*, edited and translated by C.D. Airan. Guntur: Srimathy Parripati Sita Mahalakshmi Sayanarayana, 1964.

Richard H. L. & R. C. Das, *Evangelical Prophet for Contextual Christianity.* Delhi: ISPCK, 1995.

Richard, H. L. ed., *R.C. Das: Evangelical Prophet for Contextual Christianity.* Bangalore/Delhi: CISRS/ISPCK, 1999.

Richards, Jeffrey. *The Popes and the Papacy in the Early Ages 476-752.* London: Routledge & Kegan Paul, 1979.

Ridley, Aaron & Judith Norman eds., *Friedrich Nietzsche: Anti-Christ, Ecce Homo, Twilight of the Idols, and Other Writings*, trans. by Judith Norman. Cambridge: Cambridge University Press, 2005.

Ross, Kenneth R. *Edinburgh 2010: New Directors for Church in Mission.* Pasadena: William Carey University Press, 2010.

Said, Edward W. *Culture and Imperialism.* London: Vintage, 1994.

Said, Edward W. *Orientalism.* London: Penguin Books, [1978] 2003.

Said, Edward W. *Orientalism: Western Conceptions of the Orient.* London: Penguin Books, 1995 [1978].

Samartha, S.J. *One Christ-Many Religions: Toward a Revised Christology.* Bangalore: SATHRI, 1992.

Samuel, Simon. *A Postcolonial Reading of Mark's Story of Jesus.* London: T&T Clark, 2007.

Schauss, Hayyim. *The Lifetime of a Jew.* Cincinnati; Ohio: Union of American Hebrew Congregations, 1950.

Schmidt, Robert. *Explanations to the Ninety-Five Theses on Church Control* (1999).

Scott, David C. ed., *Keshub Chunder Sen.* Madres: CLS, 1979.

Sebastian, J. Jayakiran "Baptism and the Unity of the Church in Indian Today," in *Baptism and the Unity of the Church*, eds., Michael Root and Risto Saarinen. Grand Rapids: William B. Eerdmans Publishing Company, 1998.

Sebastian, J. Jayakiran. "...Baptism Unum in Sancta Ecclesia..." *A Theological Appraisal of the Baptism Controversy in the Work and Writings of Cyprian of Carthage.* Delhi: ISPCK, 1997.

Sen, Amartya. *The Argumentative Indian: Writings on Indian History, Culture and Identity.* Penguin Books, 2005.

Sendar, Shailendra. *Ancient Indian Rituals and their Social Impact.* New Delhi: Anmol Pub. Pvt. Ltd., 2007.

Seshagiri, K.L. *Mahatma and Comparative Religion.* Delhi: Motilal Banarasidass Pub., 1978.

Sharma, Arvind. *Hinduism for Our Times.* Delhi: OUP, 1997.

Sharma, J. *Hindutva: Exploring the Idea of Hindu* Nationalism. New Delhi: Viking / Penguin, 2003.

Sharma, R. *Indian Society.* Bombay: n.p., 1981.

Singh, Yogendra. *Modernization of Indian Tradition.* Faridabad: Thomson India Press Ltd, 1977.

Song, C. S. *Tell Us Our Names: Story Theology from an Asian Perspective.* New York: Orbis Books, 1984.

Spivak, Gayatri Chakravorty. *A Critique of Postcolonial Reason: Towards a History of the Vanishing Present.* Harvard: Harvard University Press, 1999.

Ashcroft, Bill. Gareth Griffiths and Helen Tiffin. Eds. "Can the Subaltern Speak," in *The Post-colonial Studies Reader.* London: Routledge, 1995.

Harasym, Sarah.*The Post-Colonial Critic: Interviews, Strategies, Dialogues.* London: Routledge, 1990.

Staffner, Hans. *Jesus Christ and the Hindu community: Is a Synthesis of Hinduism and Christianity possible?*Anand: Gujarat Sahitya Prakash, 1988.

Sugden, E. H. ed., *John Wesley's Fifty-Three Sermons.* Nashville: Abingdon, 1983.

Sugirtharajah, R. S. *The Bible and the Third World: Pre-colonial, Colonial and Postcolonial Encounters.* Cambridge: Cambridge University Press, 2001.

Sugirtharajah, R.S. *Asian Biblical Hermeneutics and Post-colonialism: Contesting the Interpretations.* Sheffield: Sheffield Academic Press, 1998.

Sugirtharajah, R.S. *Postcolonial Criticism and Biblical Interpretation.* Oxford: Oxford University Press, 2002.

Sugirtharajah, R.S. *Postcolonial Reconfigurations: An Alternative Way of Reading the Bible and Doing Theology.* London: SCM Press; St. Louis, Chalice Press, 2003.

Sumithra, Sunand. *Christian Theologies from an Indian Perspective.* Bangalore: Theological Book Trust, 1995.

Sykes, Marjirie. *C. F. Andrews: Representative Writings.* Delhi: National Book Trust, 1973.

Sylvester, Jerome. *Khristabhakta Movement: Hermeneutics of a Religio-cultural Phenomenon.* Delhi: ISPCK, 2013.

Tachikawa, Musashi, Shoun Hino and Lalita Deodhar, *Puja and Samaskar.* Delhi: Motilal Banarsidass Publisher, 2001.

Taylor, C. 'The Politics of Recognition,' in *Multiculturalism and "The Politics of Recognition"* edited by A. Gutman. Princeton: Princeton University Press, 1992.

Thapar, Romila. *Ancient Indian Social History: Some Interpretations.* Hyderabad: Orient Longman, 1984.

Thazhath, A. *The Quest for Identity.* Trichur: TIT publications, 1992.

Theodore, Pereira. *Towards an Indian Christian Funeral Rite.* Bangalore: n.p., n.d.

Thomas, M. M. *Acknowledged Christ in Indian Renaissance.* Madras/Bangalore: CLS/CISRC, 1970.

Thomas, M. M. *Risking Christ for the Sake of Christ.* Delhi: ISPCK, 1999.

Thomas, M. M. *Salvation and Humanization: Some Critical Issues of the Theology of Mission in Contemporary India.* Bangalore/Madras: CISRS/CLS, 1971.

Thomas, M. M. *The Church's Mission and Post-Modern Humanism: Collection of Essays and Talks 1992-1996.* Tiruvalla/Delhi: Christava Samithi/ISPCK, 1996.

Thomas, M. M. *Church and Human Community.* Delhi: n.p., 1885.

Thomas, M. M. *New Creation in Christ.* Delhi: ISPCK, 1976.

Thomas, M. M. *The Church's Mission and Post-Modernism: Collection of Essays and Talks* 1992-1996. Tiruvalla/Delhi: Christava Sahitya Samithi/ISPCK, 1996.

Thomas, V.V. *Understanding Subaltern History: Theoretical Tools.* Bangalore: BTESSC/ SATHRI, 2006.

Tisserant, E. *Eastern Christianity in India.* London: Orient Longman, 1957.

Torrance, Thomas F. *Calvin's Doctrine of Man.* Eugene OR: Wipf & Stock Publishers, 2001.

Toynbee, Arnold Joseph. *Christianity: Among the Religions of the World and One World and India.* New Delhi: Indian Council for Cultural Relations, 1960.

Tripathi, Asha Rani. *Manu-Smrti: A Critical Study and its Relevance in Modern Times.* New Delhi: D.K. Printworld. Pvt. Ltd., 2015.

Truscott, Jeffrey A. 'Luther's Pastoral Approach to baptism,' in *A Living Tradition: On the Intersection of Liturgical History and Pastoral Practice*, eds. David Pitt, Stefanos Alexopoulos and Christian McConnell. College ville: Liturgical Press, 2012.

Truscott, Jeffrey A. *The Sacraments: A Practical Guide.* New Delhi: Christian World Imprints, 2016.

Tylor, E. B. *Primitive Culture: Researches into the Development of Mythology, Philosophy, Language, Art and Customs.* London, 1874.

unabhängige, charismatisch geführte Gruppen in Südindien. Frankfurt: Peter Lang, 1977.

Vandana, Sister. "Water Symbolism in the Gospel of St. John in the Light of Indian Spirituality," in *Readings in Indian Christian Theology*, ed., R. S. Sugirtharajah & Cecil Hargreaves. Delhi: ISPCK, [1993], 2004.

Vaux, Roland de. *Ancient Israel: Its Life and Institutions.* London: Darton, Longman & Todd, [1961] reprint 1991.

Vivekananda, Swami. *The Complete Works of Swami Vivekananda*, vol. III. Calcutta: Advaita Ashrama, 1951 & 1999.

Vivekananda, Swami. *The Complete Works of Swami Vivekananda*, vol. v, Mayavati Memorial Edition. Kolkata: Advaita Ashrama, 2006.

Walter, James J. "Conversion," in *The New Dictionary of Theology*, eds. Joseph A. Komonchak, Mary Collins and Dermot A Lane. Bangalore: Theological Publications in India, 2014.

Wesley, John. "The New Birth" IV .3, *Works of Wesley* 2, 198.

Wesley, John. *Treatise on Baptism* II. 1-5, *Works of Wesley* X, 190-92.

White, James F. *Introduction to Christian Worship*, 3rd rev. exp., ed. Nashville: Abingdon, 2000.

White, James F. *Protestant Worship: Traditions in Transition.* Louisville: Westminster John Knox Press, 1989.

Williams, Blair. *Anglo Indians.* CTR Inc. Pub., 2002.

Wilson, Stephen. *The Means of Naming.* London: 1998.

Zwingli, Ulrich. *Commentary on True and False Religion* (1525), in *The works of Huldreich Zwingli*, ed. Clarence H. Heller, trans., Samuel M. Jackson. Philadelphia: Heidelberg Press, 1929.

Journals

"Editorial," *Religion and Society*, Vol. 19, No. 1 (March, 1972): 4.

Appadurai, Ajun, "Putting Hierarchy in Its Place," *Cultural Anthropology*, Vol. 3, No. 1, (February, 1988): 36-49.

Appadurai, Arjun. "Putting Hierarchy in its Place," *Cultural Anthropology.* Vol. 3, No. 1 (1988): 36-49.

Banerjee, B.N. "A Hindu attitude to Conversions," *International Review of Missions*, No. 287 (1983): 393-397.

Bierbrauer, G. "Toward an Understanding of Legal Culture: Variations in Individualism and Collectivism between Kurds, Lebanese, and Germans," *Law and Society Review*, No. 28(2) (1994): 243-264.

Chandran, J. R. "Baptism – A Scandal or a Challenge," *Religion and Society* 19/1 (March, 1972): 51.

Chandran, J. R. "Christianity and World Religions-The Ecumenical Discussion," *The Indian Journal of Theology*, Vol. 30, No. 3&4, (July-Dec., 1981): 186-203.

Das, A. K. "Scheduled Tribe-A Socio-Economic and Cultural Profile in West Bengal," *Bulletin of C.R.I.*, Kolkata (1991): 2-4.

Dearlove, Des. "On the Verge of Something Extraordinary," *Business Strategy Review*, London Business School (Spring, 2009): 17-20.

Dharmaraj, Jacob S. "A Brief Review of Alexander Duff: English Education and Colonial Connections in 19th Century India," *ICHR*, Vol. XXV. No. 2 (December, 1991): 82-83.

Dien, D. S. "The Evolving Nature of Self-identity across Four Levels of History," *Human Development*, No. 43 (2000): 1-18.

Duraisingh, Christopher. "Indian Hyphenated Christians and Theological Reflection," Part I "A New Expression of Identity," *Religion and Society*, Vol. XXVII, No 2 (June, 1980): 80-101.

George, Poikail John. "Racist Assumptions of 19th Century Missionary Movement," *IRM*, Vol. LIX, No. 235 (July, 1970): 271-283.

George, Samuel. "Conversion with 'In' for Missions with 'Out,'" in *Journal of Mission and Intercultural Studies*, Vol.3, No.1 (January-June, 2016): 39.

Gouveia, V.V. & F.J.B. de Albuquerque, "Human Values and Social Identities: A Study in Two Collectivist Cultures," *International Journal of Psychology*, No. 37(6), (2002): 333-342.

Gregorios, Paul. "Not Gospel and Culture," The Star of the East, Vol. XI, No. 1-2 (March-June, 1989): 24-26.

Greinacher, N. "Catholic Identity in the Third Epoch of Church History," *Concilium* 5 (1994): 6-8.

Grunder, H. "Christian Mission and Colonial Expansion," *Mission Studies* XII/23, (1995): 18-21.

Gupta, Akhil and James Ferguson, "Beyond 'Culture': Space, Identity and the Politics of Difference," *Cultural Anthropology*, vol. 7, No. 1 (Feb. 1992): 6.

Hamsun, T. ed., *Knut Hamsuns Brev Til Marie*. Oslo: Aschehoug, 1988; Cf. B. Helleland, C. E. Ore & S. Wikstrøm, eds., *Names and Identities*, Oslo Studies in Language 4(2), (2012): 273-284.

Hans, Cyril. "The Adivasis of Jharkhand: Contemporary Issues and Responses," *Sevartham*, Vol. 36 (2011): 35.

Hembrom, Timothy. "Ministry and Mission from a Primal Perspective," in *Gurukul Journal of Theological Studies*, Vol. v, No. 172, (January-July, 1994): 41.

Herriot P. & W. Scott-Jackson, "Globalization, Social Identities and Employment," *British journal of Management*, No. 13 (2002): 249-257.

Higgins, Kelvin. "The Key to Insider Movements: The Devoted's of Acts," *International Journal of Foreign Mission*, 21:4 (Winter 2004): 156.

Hudson, D.D. "Hindu and Christian Theological Parallels in the Conversion of H.A. Krishna Pillai 1857-1859," *The Journal of American Academy of Religion*, Vol. 40 (June, 1972): 196-205.

James, Woba. "Methodological Issues and Historiography of Christianity in the 19th and 20th Centuries with Special Reference to Postcolonial Perspective," in *Journal of Tribal Studies*, Vol. XX, No.1&2, (Jan-June & July-Dec, 2015): 135.

Joseph, T. C. "The Myth of the Colonial Connection," *The Sunday Statesman*, (September 20, 1987): 4.

Kattackal, Jacob. "Dharma the Great Goal of Life," *Jeevadhara*, Vol. XII, No. 67, (1982): 29.

Kothari, Rajni. "Integration and Exclusion in Indian Politics," *Economic and Political Weekly*, 22 (October, 1988): 22-23.

Legrand, Pierre. "How to Compare New," *Legal Studies*, Vol. 16, No. 2 (1996): 232-235.

Lott, Eric J. "Religious Faith and the Diversity of Cultural Life in India," *Christian faith and Multiform Culture in India* ed., Somen Das. Bangalore, United Theological College (1987): 48-84.

Majumdar, D. N. "A Study of Religious Practices among the Son Koch of Garo Hills," *Bulletin of the Dept. of Anthropology*, Govt. of India, Calcutta, Vol. XVII, No. 3 (1970): 325-55.

Massey, James. "Christianity and Culture: Their Relationship in 19th and 20th Centuries in Punjab," *Religion and Society*, (December, 1989):18-32.

Michael, S. "Sociological Perspective of Conversion in India," *Indian Missiological Review*, Vol. v, (1983): 43.

Minz, Nirmal. "Religion, Culture and Education in the context of the Tribal Aspirations in India," *Journal of Dharma*, Vol. XII, No. 2 (April-June, 1987): 153.

Moltmann, J. "Covenant or Leviathan: Political Theology for Modern Times," *SJT41* (1994): 19-41 (esp. pp. 38-39), reflecting on the German experience under Hitler; see further Moltmann, *Politische Theologie-Politische Ethik.* Mainz: Griinewald, 1984.

Mundu, S.J. John. "Tribals in Transition: Upward or Downward Movement?" in *Sevartham*, Vol. 36 (2011): 7.

Nirmal, Arvind P. Some Theological Issues connected with Inter-Faith Dialogue and their Implications for Theological Education in India," *Bangalore Theological Forum*, vol. XII, No. 2 (June-Dec, 1980): 107-129.

Opoku, K.A. "Skinny but Imperishable Truth: African Religious Heritage and the Regeneration of Africa," *Studia Historiae Ecclesiaticae*, No. 38 (Suppl. 2012): 151.

P. T., Subrahmanyan. "Christ in Indian Thought," in *Indian Theological Journal*, Vol. 8, No. 1&2 (2014): 44.

Parekh, Manilal C. "The Spiritual Significance and Value of Baptism," *National Council of Churches Review*, 44/9 (September, 1924): 324.

Perusek, Darshan. "Subaltern Consciousness and Historiography of Indian Rebellion 1857," *Economic and Political Weekly* 28 (1993): 19-31.

Philip, T. V. "Christianity in India during Western Colonisation: Conflict, Reconciliation or Adjustment", *ICHR*, Vol. XXI, No. 1 (June, 1987): 20.

Pieris, Aloysius. "Non-Christian Religions and Cultures in Third World Theology," *Vidyajyoti*, vol. 46 (1982): 158-170.

Premasagar, P. Victor. "The Gods of Our Fathers-Towards a Theology of Indian Religious and Cultural Heritage," *Asian Expressions of Christian Commitment* (1992): 137-146.

Rayburman, B. K. "Structure of the Sacred Ritual Terracottas," *Man in India*, Vol. 54, No. 1 (1974): 85-89.

Roller, E. "Reforming the Spanish Senate: Mission Impossible?" *West European Politics*, No. 25(4), (2002): 69-92.

Samuel, Simon. "Review of Postcolonial Biblical Criticism: Interdisciplinary Intersections," *Doon Theological Journal* 3/2 (July, 2006): 197.

Samuel, V. C. "Christianity and Indigenization," *Abba Salama*, Vol. VII (1976): 60-92.

Saxena, Samuel Richmond. "The water of life in Indian Cup: Towards an Indian Eschatology with reference to the Ministry of Yeshu Darbar," *Journal of Mission and Intercultural Studies* 2/1 (April, 2015): 67.

Scott, D.C. "Baptism in Indian Context–An Event of Separation or Human Solidarity?" *The Christian Century*, January (1990): 103-108.

Scott, David C. "Baptism in the Indian Context: An Event of Separation or Human Solidarity," in *The Christian Century* (January 31, 1990): 103-108.

Spivak, Gayatri Chakravorty. "Can the Subaltern Speak? Speculations on Widow Sacrifice," *Wedge* 7/8 (1985): 120-130.

Suess, P. "A Confused Mission Scenario," & F. Castillo, "Christianity and Inculturation in Latin America," *Concilium* (1994): 2.

Thomas, M. M. "Baptism, Church and Koinonia: Three letters and a Comment," *Religion and Society* 19/1 (1972): 73-74.

Thomas, M. M. "Christ-Centred Syncretism," *Religion and Society*, vol. xxvi, No. 1 (March: 1979): 26-35.

Thomas, M.M. "Baptism, the Church, and Koinonia: Three Letters and a Comment," *Religion and Society* No. 19/1 (1972): 73.

Upadhyaya, Brahmabandhav. "The Clothes of Catholic Faith," *Sophia*, Vol. v, No. 8 (9August 1898): n.p.

Vide P.V. Kane's Article in the *Journal of the Bombay Branch*, Asiatic Society, XXVI, (1922): 57-82.

Vigil J. D. & G. Hanley, "Chicano Macrostructural Identities and Macrohistorical Cultural forces," *Journal of Historical Sociology*, No. 15(3) (2002): 395-426.

Wilfred, Felix. "Subaltern Religious Experience," *Journal of Dharma*, 23/1 (January-March, 1998): 67.

Winter, Ralph. "Eleven Frontiers of Perspectives," *International journal of Frontier Mission*, Vol. 20, No. 4 (Oct-Dec, 2003): 136.

Vinayaraj, Y.T. "Representation of the Subaltern: Spivak and Historiography". *Mar Thoma seminary Journal of Theology*, Vol. II, No. 2 December (2013): 24.

Dictionary and Encyclopedia

Chamber's Twentieth Century Dictionary. Allied Publications, 1965.

Channa, S. M. ed., Encyclopeadia of Indian Tribes and Castes, vol. I. New Delhi: Cosmo Publications, 2004.

Frankel, Ellen & Betsy Platkin Teutsch, *The Encyclopedia of Jewish Symbols.* Northvale: N. J. Aronson, 1992.

Kapoor, Subodh ed., *The Hindus: Enclclopaedia of Hinduism*, vol. V. New Delhi: Cosmo Publications, 2000.

Margaret and James Stutley, *A Dictionary of Hinduism.* London & Henley: Routledge and Kegan Paul, 1977.

The Oxford Dictionary of the Christian Church. Oxford University Press: London, 1957.

Unpublished Source

Church of England, *Articles of Religion* (1563), Art. XXV, in *Book of Common Prayer.* Oxford: 1784), SW, 20.

George, K. M. "Mission and Its Discontents: Towards a New Humanity," a paper presented during BTESSC Seminar on 3rd Feb., 2010 at United Theological College, Bangaluru, 4.

Katju, Markandey. Judge the Supreme Court of India, speech deliver on "Ancient Indian Jurisprudence" at Banaras Hindu University on 27th Nov, 2010, 14.

Luther, Martin. *Babylonian Captivity*, LW, 36.92.

Luther, Martin. *Small Catechism* (1529), BC, 360.12 and *Large Catechism*, BC 465.74.

Luther, Martin. *The Holy and Blessed Sacrament of Baptism* (1519), LW 35. 29.

The Westminster Confession of Faith. Edinburgh: T & T Clark, n.d.

Westminster Assembly of Divines (1643-49): The Westminster Confession with Shorter and larger Catechisms 28:8 London. Question No. 95.

Official Documentation

Judgment of the Supreme Court of India, 12th September, 2002, against the writ petition Civil No. 98 of 2002.

Newspapers

'Do Christians also practice caste system? Asked by the Supreme Court,' Chief Justice of the Supreme Court, K.G. Balakrishnan, Times of India (Delhi Edition) 20th July, 2007.

Times of India (Delhi), 20th July, 2007.

'Who, What, Why?' (26 September, 2007) 'Should it be Burma or Myanmar,' BBC News.

BBC News, 26th September, 2007.

Internet Source

"Scheduled Caste and Schedule Tribes" http://en.wikipedia.org/wiki/ (10/05/2016).

Deivanayagam, M. and D. Devakala, http://www.geocities.com/Athens/ Ithaca/1412.

http://www.edinburgh2010/org/en/resources/html.